Social Media in Legal Practice

There are multiple aspects of electronically-mediated communication that influence and have strong implications for legal practice. This book focuses on three major aspects of mediated communication through social media. Section 1 examines social media and the legal community. It explores how this has influenced professional legal discourse and practice, contributing to the popularity of internet-based legal research, counselling and assistance through online services offering explanations of law, preparing documents, providing evidence, and even encouraging electronically mediated alternative dispute resolution. Section 2 looks at the use of social media for client empowerment. It examines how it has taken legal practice from a formal and distinct business to one that is publicly informative and accessible. Section 3 discusses the way forward, exploring opportunities and challenges. Based on cases from legal practice in diverse jurisdictions, the book highlights key issues as well as implications for legal practitioners on the one hand, and clients on the other.

The book will be a valuable reference for international scholars in law and other socio-legal studies, discourse analysis, and practitioners in legal and alternative dispute resolution contexts.

Vijay K. Bhatia retired as Professor from the City University of Hong Kong and is now a Visiting Professor at the Hellenic American University in Athens, and Adjunct Professor at the Chinese University of Hong Kong.

Girolamo Tessuto is Professor of English Language, Linguistics and Translation, Department of Law, University of Campania 'Luigi Vanvitelli', Italy.

Law, Language and Communication

Series Editors

Anne Wagner

Université du Littoral Côte d'Opale, France

and

Vijay Kumar Bhatia

Formerly of *City University of Hong Kong*

This series encourages innovative and integrated perspectives within and across the boundaries of law, language and communication, with particular emphasis on issues of communication in specialized socio-legal and professional contexts. It seeks to bring together a range of diverse yet cumulative research traditions in order to identify and encourage interdisciplinary research.

The series welcomes proposals – both edited collections as well as single-authored monographs – emphasizing critical approaches to law, language and communication, identifying and discussing issues, proposing solutions to problems, offering analyses in areas such as legal construction, interpretation, translation and de-codification.

For more information about this series, please visit: www.routledge.com/Law-Language-and-Communication/book-series/LAWLANGCOMM

Social Media in Legal Practice

Edited by Vijay K. Bhatia and
Girolamo Tessuto

LONDON AND NEW YORK

First published 2021
by Routledge
2 Park Square, Milton Park, Abingdon, Oxon OX14 4RN

and by Routledge
52 Vanderbilt Avenue, New York, NY 10017

Routledge is an imprint of the Taylor & Francis Group, an informa business

British Library Cataloguing-in-Publication Data
A catalogue record for this book is available from the British Library

Library of Congress Cataloging-in-Publication Data
A catalog record has been requested for this book

ISBN: 978-0-367-34772-7 (hbk)
ISBN: 978-1-000-16635-4 (ebk)

Typeset in Galliard
by MPS Limited, Dehradun

Contents

SECTION 3
CHALLENGES AND WAY FORWARD   197

Figures

Tables

Notes on contributors

Janet Ainsworth is the John D. Eshelman Professor of Law at Seattle University. Her research interests lie at the intersection of law, language, and culture, applying linguistic theory to critical analysis of legal practices and problems. Her scholarship appears both in law journals and in social science publications. She is co-editor of the Oxford University Press Series, Studies in Language and the Law. Currently she serves as the president of the International Association of Forensic Linguists.

Aditi Bhatia's main interest is in political discourse. Her research employs a novel multiperspective theoretical framework, that of 'discursive illusions', on which she has published in a number of international journals, including the *Journal of Pragmatics*, *Journal of Language and Politics*, *World Englishes*, and *Discourse & Society*, and her recently published monograph, *Discursive Illusions in Public Discourse: Theory and Practice* (Routledge, London and New York, 2015). She is now engaged in further extending the concept of discursive illusions by investigating the discourses of public square movements and representation in digital professions.

Vijay K. Bhatia retired as Professor from the City University of Hong Kong and is now a Visiting Professor at the Hellenic American University in Athens, and Adjunct Professor at the Chinese University of Hong Kong. Some of his research initiatives include, *Analyzing Genre-bending in Corporate Disclosure Practices*, and *International Arbitration Practice: A Discourse Analytical Study*, in which he led research teams from more than 20 countries. His research interests include, Genre Analysis of academic and professional discourses in legal, business, newspaper, and promotional contexts; ESP and Professional Communication; simplification of legal and other public documents. Three of his books, *Analysing Genre: Language Use in Professional Settings* and *Worlds of Written Discourse: A Genre-based View*, and *Critical Genre Analysis: Investigating Interdiscursive Performance in Professional Communication* are widely used in genre theory and professional communication studies.

Marco Canepa is the President of the penal section of the Court of Justice of Savona. He has been a lawyer since 1992, a judge/prosecutor since 1996, and first practiced in Sardinia as a prosecutor and then in Sicily as a judge. Later he worked in Savona as a judge and since 2018 has presided over the penal section. Work experience in England has given him a good understanding of that country's criminal procedure. In June 2016, he had the opportunity of shadowing judges at the Crown Courts of Wolverhampton and Birmingham, and he has been invited to deliver many talks on the subject of comparative law.

Roy Carpenter received his doctorate from the University of Versailles and is now Assistant Professor of Cultures and Civilizations of Anglophone Countries at the University of Grenoble. He specializes in political and legal institutions of the United States. His first book, *Jonathan Edwards: La Théologie des lumières* was published by Editions Ampelos in 2015. He co-authored *The Republicans from Eisenhower to George W. Bush, 1953–2008* (Editions Atlande, 2016) and is currently working on a biography of Paul Revere. More recently, he has studied the influence of political institutions on national identities and specifically the case of Poland, undertaken from a comparative perspective.

Gerald Delahunty is Professor of Linguistics at Colorado State University, where he teaches courses on all aspects of linguistics. He has published on Hiberno-English, discourse analysis, phraseology, pragmatics, syntactic theory, sociolinguistics, and Irish landscapes and archaeology. He has published articles and reviews in *English Journal, Journal of Linguistics and Language Teaching, Linguistic Analysis, Linguistics, Pragmatics, The Yearbook of Phraseology,* and *Written Communication*. He is author of *The English Language: From Sound to Sense* (2010) (with J. J. Garvey). His recent research explores the interactions of linguistic form and pragmatic principles, and currently investigates ideological manifestations in human rights discourse.

Roxanne Barbara Doerr is an adjunct professor at the Universities of Brescia, Milan, Padua, and Verona. She holds a PhD in English Studies from the University of Verona, the title of Dr. Phil. from the University of Köln, and the title of Doctor Europaeus for an international co-tutored interdisciplinary doctoral thesis. Her current areas of research and publication include language of and in new and social media, knowledge dissemination and popularization, military discourse, Corpus Assisted Discourse Studies, online discourse communities, workplace communication, distance learning, English for specific purposes.

Kim Grego is Assistant Professor of English Language and Translation at the University of Milan, where she teaches English Language and Linguistics. Her interests include Translation Studies, ESP, Critical Genre Analysis and Critical Discourse Studies. She leads the University of Milan's research unit of the "Age.Vol.A. – Ageing, Volunteers, Assistants – Multilingual tools for assisting the ageing" project, funded by Fondazione Cariplo (2018–2021). Her recent publications include: "Ethical Aspects in Web Marketing for Seniors" (in *Languages Cultures Mediation* 5: 1/2018) and "'Meat gives you cancer': the popularisation of scientific news with public health relevance" (in *Lingue e linguaggi* 26/2018).

André Lazaro Ferreira Augusto is a PhD candidate in Linguistics at the Federal University of Juiz de Fora, Brazil. He holds a master's degree in Law from the same university. Working as a Federal Judge since 2009, his research interest is video evidence and how it is admitted and interpreted in the judicial process.

Rosita Maglie is a Researcher and Lecturer in English Language and Translation at the University of Bari. Her main research interests are in Specialised Discourse, Corpus-based Translation Studies, and Applied Linguistics. Her PhD dissertation, along with other publications, focuses on the use of domain specific parallel and comparable corpora specially collected in order to investigate English and Italian Medical Discourse (2004, 2005, 2007, 2009, 2011 and 2015, 2017). Her publications include three volumes: *Understanding the Language of Medicine* (Aracne, 2009), *English4Fashion* (Wip Edizioni, 2010), and *The New Discourse of Healthcare* (Aracne, 2015).

Carmina Meola is Lecturer in English Language at the University of Sannio, Benevento, Department of Law, Economics, Management and Methods. She was awarded a doctorate in English for Special Purposes by the University of Naples Federico II in 2013. She has published a book which analyses the discourse of patient information medicine leaflets. She has held several seminars on teaching strategies and discourse analysis. She has taught courses of English for Special Purposes (Business, Commerce, Law and English for Pilots) at private and public boards. She is currently working on a project dealing with European Citizens. Her domains of interest are multimodality, functional grammar, popularization and sociolinguistics.

Antonella Napolitano is Researcher in English Language and Translation at the University of Sannio, Benevento, Department of Law, Economics, Management and Quantitative Methods. Her research activity has centred on the field of ESP theory and applications, professional and institutional discourse, the language of advertising, legal English, identity-building and gender studies. Some of her recent works focus on online customer reviews, corporate scandals and the discourse of and about President Trump. She is currently conducting research on Institutional and corporate communication and new media. She is also scientific coordinator of the Language Centre at the University of Sannio.

Jekaterina Nikitina has a PhD degree from the University of Milan. Her academic interests include legal discourse and legal translation studies, with a particular insight into legal phraseology, LSP theories and applications, knowledge dissemination dynamics, discourse of healthcare, medicine and bioethics, applying qualitative and quantitative, specifically corpus linguistics, analytical approaches. Currently, she holds a fixed-term research position at the Saint Camillus International University of Health and Medical Sciences (UniCamillus, Rome). Her published academic work includes publications on legal translation and dissemination of bioethical knowledge, with a focus on medically assisted procreation and gene editing.

Anna Franca Plastina is Associate Professor in English Language and Translation at the University of Calabria. Her research focus is mainly on specialised discourse in computer-mediated, ESP and multilingual contexts. Her most recent publications include the chapters: *Reframing as a Persuasive Method in Public Speech: Beyond Globalized Biodiversity* (John Benjamins, 2018); *Creating Specialised Corpora in English for Medical Purposes: A Study on Learners' Direct Use* (Peter Lang, 2017); the edited volume: *L3 Lexical Construction Processes: Current Issues and New Perspectives*, 2018, *Journal of Applied Psycholinguistics (RiPLA)*; the article: *Hashtagging for Health Promotion: Constructing Meaning as an #AntibioticGuardian*, 2018, *Altre Modernità*.

Douglas Mark Ponton is Associate Professor of English Language and Translation at the Department of Political and Social Sciences, University of Catania. His research interests include political discourse analysis, ecolinguistics, interactive sociolinguistics, applied linguistics, pragmatics, corpus linguistics and critical discourse studies. His main publications are For Arguments Sake: speaker evaluation in modern political discourse, and Meaning Politics: a Manual of Political Discourse Analysis. As well as politics, his research deals with a variety of social topics, including tourism (he has published on the Montalbano effect and cruise tourism), the discourse of mediation; ecology, local dialect and folk traditions, including proverbs and Blues music.

Gianluca Pontrandolfo holds a PhD in Translation and Interpreting Studies. He is currently Senior Lecturer at the University of Trieste (IUSLIT, Department of Legal Language, Interpreting and Translation Studies). His research interests include legal terminology and phraseology, judicial discourse, corpus linguistics, specialised genre studies, text linguistics, translation training. He is a member of CERLIS (Research Centre on Languages for Specific Purposes) of the University of Bergamo, the EDAP group (Studies on Professional Academic Discourse) of the University of Barcelona and CLAVIER (Corpus and Language Variation in English Research Group) of the University of Modena and Reggio Emilia.

Vicente Riccio holds a doctorate in Sociology from *Instituto Universitário de Pesquisas do Rio de Janeiro* and is a professor in the graduate program of Law and Innovation at the Federal University of Juiz de Fora, Brazil. His research interests are police reform, legal systems in developing democracies, media and justice. His recent publications are: Police and Society in Brazil

(Routledge) co-edited with Wesley Skogan, *Crime and Visual Media in Brazil* (Oxford Research Encyclopedia of Criminology), Legal Culture, Video Evidence and Court Decision in Brazil (IN: Frameworks for Discursive Actions and Practices of the Law).

Rajesh Sharma is Senior Lecturer, Legal and Dispute Studies, Criminology and Justice, RMIT University, Melbourne, Australia; Adjunct Professor at Academy of International Dispute Resolution and Professional Negotiation (AIDRN); Honorary Professor at Xiangtan University Law School; Core member (representing Australia) on the Committee for the Establishment of the Centre of Excellence for Dispute Resolution for Indian Ocean Rim Association; Arbitrator at KCAB and IIAM; a Member of the Governing Board of the Indian Institute of Arbitration and Mediation.

Amitza Torres Vieira holds a PhD in Language Studies from *Pontifícia Universidade Católica of Rio de Janeiro*, Brazil, and is an Associate Professor at the Federal University of Juiz de Fora, Brazil, on the Linguistics Graduate Program. Her main research interest is interaction and argumentation in conflict settings. Her work aims to describe and explain social and discursive practices in institutional contexts.

Introduction

Vijay K. Bhatia and Girolamo Tessuto

The present-day rapid invasion of electronic media in all aspects of social and professional life is unprecedented and overwhelming. The explosion of digital media in our lives has been so rapid that it is almost impossible to predict what might happen in the coming years. Although the influence and use of digital media has been slow and relatively more recent, it is fast catching up in all aspects of legal practice. It has now become common practice in the storage and retrieval of information not only for legal research, but equally significantly, in other aspects of the legal profession, including the use of search engines in court. It has encouraged lawyers as well as judges to become increasingly efficient in digital literacy.

In more recent years, other forms of electronically mediated communication, particularly social media, have successfully invaded almost every aspect of legal practice bringing larger sections of the lay population into action, raising awareness about the specific legal issues and challenges facing not simply the legal community but also, perhaps more importantly, the masses, who, until recently, were kept at a safe distance from the complexities of legal perspectives and their implications for the interpretations of current issues in socio-political and economic contexts.

Since the explosion of new media in legal practice is relatively recent, very little research has so far been published in this area, particularly focusing on the role of social media in various aspects of socio-legal communication. The present book is largely based on a careful selection of research papers presented at the 5th international conference on *Legal Discourse: Context, Media and Social Power* in Caserta, Italy. Most of the papers have been thoroughly revised to fit the thematic focus of the proposed book, whereas some have been specially solicited from established scholars.

There are multiple aspects of electronically mediated communication that influence and have strong implications for legal practice; however, it is not possible to cover all of them in a single book without diluting its focus and depth. The 15 chapters in this book are therefore organized into three sections specifically focusing on three major aspects of mediated communication through social media in legal practice.

Section 1 Social media and the legal community

The first section of this volume draws inspiration from the increased presence of social media and the ways it has influenced professional legal discourse and practice, by contributing to the popularity of internet-based legal research, counselling and assistance through online services offering explanations of law, preparing documents, and even encouraging electronically-mediated alternative dispute resolution. These developments have inspired studies in the discursive construction of various aspects of legal practice. In addition, social media is also being used in the adjudication of disputes by counsels, judges, and sometimes jurors, though cautiously without undermining judges' impartiality. The online social networking profiles of the parties in a case that form part of the public domain are increasingly being allowed as evidence in judicial proceedings. It is recognized that publicly available material can be examined by counsels and the police and used as evidence. Sometimes, this overpowering influence of new media can also result in a parallel trial by the media in social contexts.

The first chapter in this section by Roy Carpenter sets the scene of the study by describing the events of November 2009, when armed federal agents raided the iconic Gibson guitar factory in Nashville (Tennessee) in search of illegal wood and related legal documents. The company was accused of violating the Lacey Act. The US Fish and Wildlife Service claimed that Gibson had knowingly imported illegal ebony from Madagascar. In its defense, Gibson said they had documentation from the Madagascar government proving the legitimacy of their purchases and agreed to relinquish their claim on the imported wood and pay a $300,000 fine in return for the Justice Department dropping its charges against them. On the surface, the author argues, it would appear that the federal agencies had scored a significant victory in successfully shaming a major corporation into admitting ecological wrongdoing. However, the rhetorical firestorm that the Gibson factory raid set off among alt-right media outlets dwarfed any meagre propaganda gain to which the federal government may have laid claim. From "government overreach" to "swat teams" armed with "automatic weapons," populist channels and websites quickly gained narrative advantage and eventually dominated the rhetorical landscape entirely. Against this backdrop, the author examines how this contest played out primarily over the Internet and focuses on quantitative measurements of narrative influence to demonstrate the weakness of legal discourse when it runs up against contemporary media outlets.

In Chapter 2, by Douglas Ponton and Marco Canepa, the framework for the study is provided by England and Italy which have, in principle, the same criminal procedure model. One of its central ideas is that a fair trial requires the complete "cognitive virginity" of the person passing judgment on facts relating to the crime – that is, jurors in England and professional judges in Italy. In the digital era, however, new media, social networks and extensive external sources of information pose a fundamental threat to this assumption of cognitive virginity, and "trial by media" may impinge on what goes on in court. In the English system, the authors point out, this is a matter of major concern. At the outset of the trial, jurors are warned by the judge that they must not discuss the case with anybody, read newspapers, check issues or points of law on the internet, post on social media, etc. In the Italian system, however, though the phenomenon of trial by media is extremely frequent, there are no similar provisions to guarantee impartiality. Inspired by the critical discourse analysis framework, the authors compare the two legal systems and explore a recent case from the United States, the Bill Cosby trial. Their study suggests that existing legislation should be extended to cover the dimension of social media, and that Italy would do well to follow the example of Britain and America in this field.

In Chapter 3, Kim Grego is motivated by the state of "cryonic suspension". Apart from what local, national and supranational laws say (or do not say) about it, the cryonics technique enjoys little consideration on the part of the scientific community. Despite a series of ethical concerns being raised as to its objective, promotion and implementation (Grego, 2017[1]), cryonics is regularly practiced throughout the developed world and provides the author with an opportunity to see how (bio)ethical issues are discursively constructed by cryonics service companies and by the media. Using two corpora of texts, one made up of texts from the four known cryonics providers' websites and the other based on articles from English-speaking media dealing with this practice, the author interprets the data through critical discourse analysis approaches (Fairclough, 1992, 2003, 2018; Wodak and Meyer, 2001; Rajah, 2018). Results show the ways in which legal aspects are mentioned by both providers and the media, with providers discussing contracts and agreements and the media being less interested in the legal focus. Both categories, however, insist on the notion of legal death, together with that of clinical death, as opposed to the chance at life after death offered by cryonics. The discourse of death constructed by providers is shown to be questionable from an ethical point of view and flawed in dialectic terms.

In Chapter 4, Gianluca Pontrandolfo draws from the case of a famous dermatologist (Dr Elisa Pinto), who accused a renowned entrepreneur (Mr Javier López Madrid) of harassment and aggression. The businessman, on his part, accused Dr Pinto of having harassed him and his family for many years. Two paradoxically opposite judicial proceedings were held: one in the *Juzgado 39 de Instrucción de Madrid* and the other in the *Juzgado 26 de Instrucción de Madrid*. Against this background, the author explores the multifaceted relationship between law and media through the lens of this media case. In order to study how role, power, identity and ideology interact with the legal environment and the media (Orts Llopis et al. 2017), a monolingual corpus of Spanish newspaper articles dealing with the case are compiled from the traditional press along with magazines and other press sources specialized in gossip. Through a corpus-assisted media discourse analysis, the author's findings confirm the hypothesis guiding his study: the media representation of the case is biased by an ideological manipulation of the details of the story (Bhatia and Bhatia, 2017) used to undermine the readers' sympathy for Mr López Madrid and to take sides with Dr Pinto. His analysis reinforces a binary representation of good ("she") and evil ("he"), an emotional dichotomy that is functional to the "sensationalism" characterising the whole media case and to the intrinsic need to reach the widest audience arousing curiosity and interest in the story.

Chapter 5, by Gerald Delahunty, focuses on the enactment of ideology in discourses that are generally regarded as benevolent and typically taken to be non-ideological. The author examines a set of Amnesty International multi-modal documents in relation to the United Nations Universal Declaration of Human Rights and the Geneva Conventions, and identifies intertextual and re-genreification traces among such documents. The author demonstrates that, despite Amnesty's claim to the contrary, Amnesty documents meet the criteria for ideological discourse – i.e. they are unifying, action-oriented, rationalizing, legitimating, universalizing, naturalizing, and normative. Drawing from Goffman (1981), in particular, his study also demonstrates how the participants in this discourse are ideologically positioned – i.e. producers may be animators, authors, and/or principals; recipients may be addressees, ratified, intended, or in-general recipients. In addition, participants are shown to enact various roles – i.e. they are individuals who are committed to the claims and stances expressed in the documents and thus ideologically positioned, as well as to the criteria of methodological neutrality and fairness.

The final chapter in this section, Chapter 6, by André Augusto Ferreira Lazaro, Vicente Riccio and Amitza Torres Vieira, examines a case brought to a Military Court in Brazil dealing with a physical aggression committed by a corporal against a soldier under his command. The aggression was recorded on a cell phone and then disseminated to an entire battalion through social media. The study discusses how legal professionals working on the case (lawyers, prosecutors and military judges) utilized the video content to sustain their decisions during the case and analyzes the video evidence responsible for starting the judicial procedure. The legal acts discussing the evidence performed by military prosecutors, defence lawyers and military judges in lower and upper levels of jurisdiction are also analyzed. The authors answer the following questions:

1 is the video evidence interpreted in a different manner compared to traditional evidence such as witnesses or documents?
2 what are the linguistic-discursive resources of the argumentation employed by legal professionals in the process?
3 to what degree is the video evidence validated by legal professionals acting in the process?

To answer these questions, the authors adopt a qualitative methodology aimed at grasping the intricacies and particularities of the legal professionals' arguments. Findings demonstrate:

1 legal professionals do not hierarchize the kind of evidence employed in the process;

2 video evidence is not submitted to a formal validation process considering its linguistic-discursive nature;
3 legal professionals interpret the video evidence based on their institutional experience without considering its particularities.

Section 2 Social media for client empowerment

The other important aspect of social media covered in this section is that it has taken legal practice from a formal and distinct business to one that is publicly informative and accessible. It has thus empowered information seekers through online legal advice. An interesting impact of this development is that it has brought into focus the effects of restorative justice, encouraging social rehabilitation of offenders. Public organizations, especially NGOs have been successfully using social media to increase their presence through social networking. The most common feature of online social networking is the ability to post comments or opinions on a user's personal page and even on the page of others. This has made sharing of information and interpretations by legal practitioners not only possible but also very common. While this practice has become commonplace, posting by lawyers, judges, jurors and journalists potentially raises ethical issues.

The opening chapter in this section by Aditi Bhatia supplies the rationale for the study by describing the Hong Kong Central Government Office (colloquially known as the "Civic Square" in the media), which was the site of a number of key protests, including the Hong Kong Umbrella Movement, until the grounds were barricaded in 2014, resulting in much public dissatisfaction. Heated discussion about right of public access and assembly at the Civic Square, the author adds, has recently resurfaced with the arrival of Hong Kong's new Chief Executive. Various discourse clans (Bhatia, 2015a), including democracy activists, local law-makers, and pro-Beijing loyalists, have participated in a much-contested legal debate about the public's right to demonstrate at the Square, generating competing narratives that represent different versions of reality. Drawing on Bhatia's (2015a) framework of the Discourse of Illusion (comprising three interrelated components: historicity, linguistic and semiotic action and the degree of social impact), the author analyzes a corpus of digital media voices reflective of different participants in this legal debate, in order to explore the creation of interdiscursive illusions by different discourse clans that variously conceptualize the Square as a symbol of threat, of concession and of rights.

In Chapter 8 by Antonella Napolitano, the topic of restorative justice is introduced as an alternative path to punitive justice, with the aim of bringing victims and offenders into communication and overcoming the consequences of crime committal. It encourages the production of narratives about the incident, empowering the injured party and allowing offenders to take responsibility and experience forgiveness. In the UK, the Restorative Justice Council (RJC) represents the official membership body in the field. With this in mind, the author's study considers the discourse of popularization and promotion performed over the RJC website in its informative sections, stories and Twitter posts. The website, the author argues, appears to efficiently popularize and advertise the service online using different media and genres and offering resources for both victims and practitioners. In particular, informative pages lay emphasis on the restorative power of the programme, while avoiding legal references and terminology. Narratives of successful experiences endorse the service, generating empathy and showing the positive impact of RJ in people's lives. Tweets provide constant updates about events and results and authoritative testimonies of appreciation.

Chapter 9, by Carmina Meola, is inspired by the new world of the Internet, which poses new challenges for law application. Users deliberately or inadvertently spread their personal information on the web, often under the illusion that a monitor may grant them privacy, anonymity, distance from their interlocutors. Yet, the Internet has actually also created an environment which may encourage inappropriate behaviours. In particular, malevolent subjects may exploit a person's vulnerabilities making use of technology to harass other people, by making unwanted contact, sharing private pictures or videos, accessing private information or online profiles, posting humiliating or intimidating comments on social media, monitoring someone's movements. It is often difficult for law enforcement to act against online abuse, since in many cases legislation in the field has not been introduced yet and incidents often cross multi-jurisdictional boundaries. In Australia, the eSafety Commissioner is a statutory office providing online safety education for children and addressing cyberbullying and illegal Internet contents. The eSafety Women initiative, in particular, offers advice and legal help to women who are abused, controlled or frightened through technological media. Based on this, the author explores the resources offered by the Australian government to support women who are object of online abuse. To this end, textual and audio-visual materials published on the eSafety Women platform are collected with a view to analyzing how legal issues are popularized by the Australian Government through web-mediated communications and how the victims and abusers are constructed through textual and multimodal representations.

In Chapter 10, Jekatarina Nikitina overviews the European Court of Human Rights' judgment *Parrillo v. Italy* and its representation in blogs to analyse the phenomena of discursive alterations in legal blogs covering the controversial issue of embryo donation. Her study applies the popularization framework to the transfer of information from the institutionalized context of the court, represented by its final judgment, to the less regulated web-domain of legal blogs. Inspired by the general methodological framework of critical discourse analysis and, in particular, by van Dijk's triangulation approach to discursive manipulations or illusions, the author aims to identify the complex mechanisms that shape the discursive illusion and lead to readership manipulation in the popularized context of blogs as compared to the institutional settings of judgments. This aim is verified on a small ad hoc created corpus of ten blog posts and the final judgment on the case accompanied by six concurring and dissenting judicial opinions. The author shows that blogs employ a vast array of techniques that could be defined as ideological manipulations or discursive illusions in that bloggers use legitimate information in a selective manner. In addition, blogs provide subjective interpretations, both textual and paratextual, attempting to pass them off as objective, and trigger selective appraisal patterns, including the use of evaluative language.

In Chapter 11, Roxanne Barbara Doerr gets the source for her study from the increased presence of web-based technologies and social media, which have affected professional legal discourse and practice. These emerging online discourse communities facilitate the layperson's access to justice and lighten the load on traditional institutions by providing brief service and advice (Zorza, 1999) on whether or not a potential party should pursue face-to-face legal procedures and how to do so. Online legal advice may be particularly helpful in military law, due to the military community's geographically dislocated and mobile nature (Parcell and Webb, 2015) and its variety in terms of jurisdictions and legal statuses. The author's research thus focuses on the interaction and trust- building strategies employed by military law experts and laypersons in the Q&A forums of the *Justia Ask a Lawyer* and *Just Answer. Military Law* websites. It starts by outlining linguistic trends signalling ongoing changes in legal discourse, and then adopts a methodological framework based on corpus-assisted discourse studies combining qualitative analysis – and more specifically critical discourse analysis and pragmatics – with quantitative analysis. Moreover, the author enquires into the discursive strategies that foster popularizing linguistic accommodation and reduce potential misunderstanding, as well as pragmatic markers such as hedging and certainty evaluation that endow the legal expert's advice and predictions with a flexible degree of accuracy and empower the client while protecting the lawyer should the client not be satisfied.

In concluding this section, Chapter 12 by Anna Franca Plastina and Rosita Belinda Maglie starts from the premise that personal websites may be appropriated as *mediational means* (Jones and Norris, 2005) to construct unique social spaces, where the action of reporting medical matters of public interest can be mediated (Scollon, 2001). The controversy over MMR vaccine-induced autism is a hotly-debated issue triggered by the 1998 Wakefield paper and retracted by the *Lancet* journal in 2010. The conflict was fuelled by Deer's website, where the action of reporting can be "traced to the interplay of larger Discourses and relations of power in the sociocultural environment" (Jones, 2005: 154), and the media texts are positioned within "multiple, overlapping, and even conflicting discourses" (Scollon, 2001: 8) due to the libel suits filed by Wakefield against Deer in the UK and the US. Based on this, the authors explore how mediated discourse is constructed by Deer as social interaction in the light of its interdiscursive and interdisciplinary links with subsequent legal texts produced for UK and US courtrooms. Drawing on Shuy's (2010) parameters of defamatory language, a corpus of media texts from Deer's website is analysed for potentially written defamation (libel). Their study is framed by the method of mediated discourse analysis and centred on the historical body of the social actor (s), the interaction order, and the discourses in place (Scollon and de Saint-Georges, 2012). The authors' findings reveal how mediated action of reporting constructs a complex social, medical and legal *nexus of practice* (Scollon and Scollon, 2004), besides highlighting the role of defamation law in the dichotomy between the rights to reputation and freedom of speech.

Section 3 Challenges and way forward

In addition to the lines of research above, the volume brings into focus some of the main challenges that the socio-legal community faces as a result of this large-scale invasion of social media in their everyday practice. Insight into social media's impact on legal practice, on the one hand, and equally importantly, the evolving nature of social media itself has raised significant challenges for both legal practitioners and clients as well. So far as legal systems are concerned, cyber-crimes, fake news, and other negative aspects of misuse of social media are not yet a top priority for most governments as they are unsure of how real the threats they pose are. However, there are obvious ethical and professional conduct considerations with a practitioner's use of social media. This final section, then, identifies some of these challenges and opportunities that might be significant not only for legal practitioners but also for clients and laypersons.

In Chapter 13, by Janet Ainsworth, social media provides a platform for the propagation of purported news items. Unfortunately, an increasing proportion of news items shared via social media are misleading or even outright lies. False social media items that "go viral," the author points out, can cause harm to those falsely accused of outrageous behaviour, and to the body politic at large by increasing political polarization. Those who agree with the slant of fake news items become more convinced of the viciousness and unworthiness of their adversaries, and those who disagree are outraged by the dishonesty and craziness of those who created and shared the fake news story. False social media items like the "Pizzagate" story are not merely harmless entertainment. Clinton, running for president at the time, was politically damaged, and the innocent restaurant owner lost employees and customers. US libel law is ill-equipped to stem the flow of "fake news" shared via social media or even to provide redress after the fact for those harmed by it. American jurisprudence assumes that the cure for "bad speech" or even "false speech" is to counter it with "good" and "true" speech. Against this backdrop, the author outlines the law's weaknesses in dealing with the challenge of false social media stories and contrasts European and American legal approaches to online defamation along with extra-legal solutions in combatting the harms caused by false news items spread via social media.

In Chapter 14, Vijay K. Bhatia puts his study into the context of conventional media where, he argues, an awareness has long been raised about news as satire or parody (for humorous effect) and propaganda as manipulated or misleading slants on factually original content (for political or commercial advantage). More recently, however, fake news, particularly in the social media, has rapidly acquired notoriety, notably inspired by Donald Trump during and after the last American presidential election. Today, the author points out, it has become established as a form of alternative news, deliberately meant to mislead and misinform readers through fabricated content. In his study, which creates compelling reading for the academic community, the author proposes a theoretically informed multiperspective approach integrating "interdiscursivity" (Bhatia, 2017) and "discursive illusion" (Bhatia, 2015) to account for the complexity of the on-going contentious interpretations of "alternative" and "fake news" in the conventional and not-so-conventional media by sharing a unique perspective and adding value to current field knowledge.

In the concluding chapter of this section, Chapter 15, Rajesh Sharma considers some of the issues raised in Alternative Dispute Resolution (ADR) as a result of the increasing growth of Information and Communication Technology (ICT). Advances in ICT have inspired the concept of the "Court of the Future" helping legal experts in decision making in areas such as indictment, bail applications, sentencing and so on. A similar movement has also begun in ADR. Several technology platforms have been established to provide services for case management, selection of arbitrators/mediators, evaluation of evidence, preparation of negotiation strategies or identifying timing and criteria to enter into negotiation or mediation. Technology can even predict the outcome of a case. However, it is vital to ensure that while using these facilitative technologies, the primary objective of the dispute resolution process i.e. justice and fairness, is adequately maintained. In this context, the author discusses the recent trend in using evidence obtained from social media, WikiLeaks and even illegal hacking and its effect on fairness and justice during court or arbitration processes. He first provides an overview of decisions of court cases and arbitral tribunals dealing with illegally-obtained evidence or unverified information on the internet. He then evaluates whether the current rules relating to evidence are sufficient to deal with such evidence and considers the extent to which the use of ICT is facilitative or disruptive to the administration of justice and whether the use of Artificial Intelligence could be used to decide on these issues. Finally, the author suggests some of the changes needed in existing rules and regulations in order to make ICT effective without compromising the delivery of, or access to, justice for the disputing parties.

The significance of this book

One of most innovative aspects of this book is that it is the first to consider the role of social media in a specific professional context addressing issues, challenges, and constraints targeting both sides of the users: legal specialists and non-specialist clients and laypersons. Second, the book is based on a careful selection of research studies based on specific cases from legal practice from diverse jurisdictions highlighting issues as well as implications for the two broad categories of audiences identified in the first two sections. Moreover, based on specific cases, the present book is an attempt to demonstrate that social media, on the one hand, opens up what was once considered a serious business for the insiders to the ordinary masses, especially clients; on the other hand, it imposes equally serious obligations on both audiences to be cautious and ethically responsible. Finally, this book is unique in another respect, that is, its emphasis on the use of social media in legal communication through discursive construction of legal issues, processes and practices, thus combining three crucial aspects of legal communication – i.e. communication through social media in legal contexts.

Note

1 Full details of all books cited may be found lin the Introduction may be found in the References section of the relevant chapter.

Section 1 - Social media and the legal community

1 Environmental justice or "government overreach"

The rhetorical landscape of the Gibson guitar factory raids

Roy Carpenter

Introduction

In November 2009, armed federal agents raided the iconic Gibson guitar factory in Nashville, Tennessee in search of illegal wood and related legal documents. The company was accused of violating the Lacey Act, a conservation law targeting illegally harvested wood and paper products with a view to preventing American companies from doing business with foreign suppliers whose activities contribute to global deforestation. The US Fish and Wildlife Service, in conjunction with the Department of Justice claimed that Gibson had knowingly imported illegal ebony from Madagascar.

In its defense, Gibson said they had documentation from the Madagascar government proving the legitimacy of their purchases. They pointed out that other instrument companies used the same wood species, thus raising the specter of selective prosecution, perhaps stemming from political bias. And in any case, Gibson asked, why would the American government be involved in enforcing laws of other countries, let alone applying its own laws to foreign jurisdictions? In the end, Gibson agreed to relinquish its claim on the imported wood and pay a $300,000 fine in return for the Justice Department dropping its charges against them. On the surface, therefore, it would appear that the federal agencies had scored a significant victory in successfully shaming a major corporation into admitting ecological wrongdoing.

However, the rhetorical firestorm that the Gibson factory raid set off among alt-right media outlets dwarfed any meager propaganda gain to which the federal government may have laid claim. From "government overreach" to "swat teams" armed with "automatic weapons," populist channels and websites quickly gained narrative advantage and eventually dominated the rhetorical landscape entirely.

How we got here: background on the political context of the Gibson Case

To understand the appropriation of the narrative of the Gibson factory raid by right wing media outlets, it is first necessary to be familiar with the historical context in which the actors emerged and thrived and without which the present story could not have happened. A brief recap of the major milestones in the evolution of institutional dissemination of American political information is thus in order.

With the dawn of "fake news," a radical shift in the way political issues are debated has come: whereas previously pundits of different political leanings clashed over the interpretation of commonly accepted facts, the same people today dispute the very veracity of the facts in question. As Kellyann Conway, one of Donald Trump's closest advisers famously said in response to a journalist's pointing out the inaccuracy of one of the president's comments,

> Don't be so overly dramatic about it, Chuck. [...] You're saying it's a falsehood. And [...] Sean Spicer, our press secretary, gave alternative facts to that.
>
> (Sinderbrand, 2017)

Gone are the days when the whole of America watched Walter Cronkite's "Evening News" live at 7pm and argued about what it meant; today, Fox News now provides the opportunity for conservatives to remain safely within the confines of their ideological homeland and to eschew other news sources by virtue of their having been tainted by the "mainstream liberal media bias." And while most observers will readily recognize the phenomenon, it's perhaps worth pointing out that it is actually a novelty in the American context: whereas Europeans have been used to newspapers having a specific slant, Americans – until recently – were not. Indeed, the idea that an Englishman's reading *The Guardian* or *The Telegraph* on the London tube, or a Frenchman's reading *Libération* or *Le Figaro* on the Paris metro signaled the reader's political bent was no more than an amusing fact for the American observer. In the United States, let us say up through the end of the 20th century, newspapers were above all regional, a category that could subsequently be divided into specialties or degrees of analysis: *The Wall Street Journal* focused on economic questions, for instance, while *The New York Times* was global in focus and in-depth and *The New York Post* had no pretension of delving deeply into issues. The novelty of purely partisan news sources goes a long way to explaining the political establishment's inability to respond adequately to the challenge posed by this new situation.

This all began to change some time during the Clinton years. And while the specific moment of change would be difficult to pinpoint, two points of reference are helpful to understand the shift. First, the arrival of Newt Gingrich in Congress marked a deliberate change in the Republican Party's approach to governance.[1] Having been excluded from control of the House of Representatives for decades, the newly-arrived representative from Georgia made a conscious decision to apply a strategy of obstructionism, which included portraying the president and his policies in the worst possible light, regardless of their actual merits. Bi-partisan cooperation was to be shunned and a scorched earth tactic became the default position. To accompany the new diabolization of political adversaries, the rise of alternative media sources was intended to radicalize the voting base, spearheaded by such pundits as Rush Limbaugh's EIB (Excellence In Broadcasting) radio network. It was at this time that Limbaugh and others began referring to the inherent untrustworthiness of the "mainstream media" – meaning the big three television networks (ABC, CBS and NBC) along with the largest, nationally distributed newspapers, above all *The New York Times* and *The Washington Post*, all of whom were designated as having a "liberal media bias."

The proponents of this idea found strong support in Bernard Goldberg's 2001 book, *Bias: A CBS Insider Exposes How the Media Distort the News*, in which he depicted the reigning atmosphere within the television news media as overtly left-leaning. According to Goldberg, the producers and reporters at CBS regarded all things Republican at best with a sort of condescending toleration and at worst with undisguised scorn. His argument went something like this: the biggest media outlets are located in New York City and recruit journalists from the most prestigious journalism schools in the country, most of which are part of America's most elitist universities in large East-coast or West-coast cities like Boston or San Francisco; moreover, it is no secret that the students of Harvard, Columbia and Berkeley are often from well-to-do families and that the general political orientation of these universities is toward the left with a strong penchant for political correctness; as a result, a sort of group-think phenomenon occurs in the major media companies with everyone basically sharing the same perspective and having little contact with those parts of the country – the South or the Mid-West – where their perspective would be challenged. Clearly, Goldberg's critique is not without merit and ironically it closely resembles that of Noam Chomsky,[2] who also denounces the media for their social isolationism: according to Chomsky, those running the major media companies, the highest levels of government and the most elite educational institutions are all part of the same social class, seeking to protect their vested interests; as a result, there is no serious attempt at calling into question the government's underlying motives because in the final analysis, the critic and the object of criticism share the same socio-political goals and values. Be that as it may, the makings of a new political alignment were in place.

The arrival of Australian media mogul Rupert Murdoch was the final piece in the puzzle. In 1996, Murdoch recruited former NBC political analyst Roger Ailes and together they created the Fox News network. Importing techniques he had honed in previous international ventures, especially in the UK, where his newspapers overtly sought to strengthen the positions of politicians with whom the owner agreed, most notably Margaret Thatcher and later Tony Blair, Murdoch thus began his ambitious conquest of America. By the time George W. Bush was elected and began accusing Iraq of possessing weapons of mass destruction, the stage had been set for a major media campaign in support of the president's ill-fated policies: for the first time in recent American political history, voters were beginning to reject information out of hand because it came from so-called "liberal" sources that were of necessity biased against conservative policies and perspectives. With the arrival of Barrack Obama on the scene, the political divide was such that objectively provable falsehoods were being peddled on prime time. On Fox News, the "debate" raged about whether Obama's birth certificate was a forgery and if he was in fact an American. One frequent guest was Donald Trump, the patron of the "birther" movement, dedicated to promoting the idea that Obama was not actually born in the United States. There was no longer any attempt to persuade opponents to change their minds; it was now sufficient to seek to reinforce the support of one's own constituency and increase the fervor of their dedication – even if it meant knowingly trafficking in lies.

The internet naturally increased the breadth of the partisan divide exponentially, providing so much content purporting to be news that it became easy for citizens to further isolate themselves within their own ideological homeland. For not only did social media sites propose a service of constantly updated partisan propaganda, but the number of sources available to be added to the flow of language was now so vast that "keeping up" with the news became a pointless endeavor. Relativism, once the bane of the right, became the right's modus operandi: "Well, we have alternative facts." In such a context, competition arose, not between different political groupings, but within the same group in order to hold more of the attention of an audience whose point of view was already fixed. Hence, radical propositions became increasingly easy to sell, not because they were more convincing than less radical perspectives, but because they were more entertaining. One beneficiary of this development was what has become known as the alt-right and one of its most successful practitioners was Alex Jones, whose web-based Info Wars broadcast a mix of radical intolerance and conspiracy theories to millions of followers, while adroitly flogging sponsors' products backed up by the personal on-air testimony of Jones himself. It was Rush Limbaugh's EIB network on steroids.

And so it was that when the Department of Justice began looking into the illegal importation practices of the Gibson Guitar Company, they unwittingly handed to the alt-right and mainstream conservative media all the elements they needed to weave a narrative of "government overreach."

The Gibson guitar factory raid, version one: what actually happened

In 2009, federal agents entered the Gibson guitar factory in Nashville, Tennessee, seizing wood used to make instruments and documents relating to the purchase and importation of that wood. The iconic American instrument maker was accused of violating the Lacey Act, a century-old conservation law originally conceived to protect native game animals and birds from the harmful effects of introducing foreign species which might upset the local ecosystem. In 2008, it was amended to include plant species, including plant products like wood. The law effectively makes illegal the importation of products from countries where the cultivation and/or exportation of those products would violate the home country's domestic laws. The goal was to combat deforestation – the biggest single contributing factor to global warming – in places where enforcement of environmental laws was insufficient. Basically, the US government was attempting to prevent American companies from participating – even indirectly – in deforestation occurring in other parts of the world.

This policy was an interesting mix of political realism and a long-term commitment to combat global warming and loss of biodiversity. The realistic aspect can be seen in the law's manifest mistrust of foreign governments to enforce their own laws. As the Department of Justice's official announcement of their settlement with Gibson explains,

> Since May 2008, it has been illegal under the Lacey Act to import into the United States plants and plant products (including wood) that have been harvested and exported in violation of the laws of another country.
>
> (US Department of Justice, 2012)

While it may be tempting to read the law as a manifestation of a kind of jurisdictional imperialism on the part of the United States – after all, the US has basically declared itself competent to enforce laws of other countries in their stead – the policy is actually a politically realistic acknowledgment of the fact that governments of countries where exotic tonewoods are produced have historically been prone to permit illegal logging in order to make short-term economic gains.

As it turns out, the wood seized at Gibson's Nashville factory is a perfect example of exactly the sort of practice Congress was trying to discourage by amending the Lacey Act. The ebony used for guitar fretboards came from Madagascar, a country that has been severely impacted by overharvesting. Malagasy law had attempted to limit the amount of trees that could be cut down, but after a military coup in 2009, the local economy took a nosedive and the new government, desperate for tax revenue, decided to allow the sale of ebony again, despite the fact that such practice was in clear violation of their own laws. So when Gibson claimed that they had all the paperwork to prove that their purchase had received the blessing of Madagascar's government (which it had) the Lacey Act's provision for US enforcement of foreign laws kicked in and Gibson was held responsible for violating a law that the local government refused to enforce.

Why, then, was the US Congress so eager to protect forests in other countries? In fact, the 2008 amendment's goal is to fight global warming by denying such governments the economic incentive to pillage their own forests. Again, as the DOJ explains,

> Congress extended the protections of the Lacey Act, the nation's oldest resource protection law, to these products in an effort to address the environmental and economic impact of illegal logging around the world.
>
> (US Department of Justice, 2012)

While global warming is not explicitly mentioned in the DOJ's announcement, this is within the sphere of "environmental impact" to which they refer. Indeed, according to *Scientific American*,

> By most accounts, deforestation in tropical rainforests adds more carbon dioxide to the atmosphere than the sum total of cars and trucks on the world's roads.
>
> (*Scientific American*, 2012)

Thus, the 2008 amendment to the Lacey Act makes the connection between irresponsible policy in Africa and instrument making in Tennessee.

This connection may seem somewhat far-fetched or at least difficult to establish and one could imagine the purchasers of wood arguing that they should not have to carry the burden of tracing the source of all their materials back through the entire chain of distribution to the actual source of the trees that produced them, but that is exactly what the law requires. At the same time, awareness of what is at stake in the logging industry is widespread among instrument makers. Gibson's main competitors have gone so far as to undertake publicity campaigns explaining their practices in terms of responsible use of natural resources (see, for example, Taylor Guitar's "Ebony Project" or more recently, Martin Guitar's joining up with the Rainforest Alliance). Moreover, the DOJ has documented with great detail how a representative of Gibson traveled to Madagascar, was told about the legal constraints involved with buying wood locally, was shown the ebony in question and was told specifically that it would be illegal to purchase it, went home to the United States and informed his superiors, and nevertheless that wood ended up in the Nashville factory.

Given the amount of documentary evidence against them and the extremely low likelihood of a trial resulting in an outcome favorable to Gibson, it is hardly surprising that the company quickly came to an agreement with the Department of Justice in order to minimize both the cost of litigation and the severity of the prospective punishment. In the end, the guitar-maker got an excellent deal. According to the terms of the agreement, they would pay $350,000 in fines and relinquish their claims to the wood. To put the amount of the fine into context, despite the fact that the company has since gone into bankruptcy, their annual earnings in the years following the factory raid fluctuated around $2 billion. That is to say, the fine represented about 0.02% of their annual earnings at that time.

So from a legal point of view, the story goes something like this: a company that sought to avoid complying with federal regulations designed to protect the environment was caught in the act; they were given a financial slap on the wrist and required to host events aimed at increasing awareness of issues related to forest preservation; they then carried on making their iconic instruments in America and the government moved on to other cases. It would seem like a clear win for the feds and for the environment. But that is not how it played out in the conservative media.

The Gibson guitar factory raid, version two: how the successful enforcement of an environmental law was transformed into a narrative of government overreach

At the time of this writing, in 2018, that is, nearly a decade after the events that happened in Nashville, a Google search of the Gibson factory raid will churn up a range of sources claiming to relate what happened, a clear majority of which portray the raid as an aberration of justice and a prime example of governmental overreach. Without even clicking on the links, we read expressions such as, "abuse-of-power scandal from President Obama's first term," "Government run amok," or how "lumber union protectionists incited [a] SWAT raid" on the factory. Evidently, the story of what happened has captivated the public mind, but the most popular narrative is not about how the company deliberately tried to benefit from the fragile political situation in a developing country in order to pillage its forest to obtain cheap material for producing products sold primarily in the West; on the contrary, the narrative which has grown out of the events is one of the federal government using phony claims about climate change as an excuse to punish American companies for employing American workers.

This is precisely what then Gibson CEO Henry Juszkiewicz claimed:

> It has nothing to do with conservation and it had nothing to do with how scarce or not scarce the rosewood or ebony is. It has to do with jobs.

According to Juszkiewicz's argument, had the ebony been shaped into finger-boards in Madagascar, Gibson would not have been subject to regulation under the Lacey Act. Therefore, he reasons, the point of the DOJ's intervention was to encourage American companies to outsource their work to foreign countries. In other words, President Obama was trying to promote employment in Africa at the expense of workers in the United States.

But Juszkiewicz's position is actually one of the more reasoned and moderate ones. For example, two years after the fact, one Youtuber opined,

> Gibson raided by the Feds. This is a little extreme. What happened to our liberties. I produced this video in response to our out of control tyrannic government. We are now at an all time Historical low. Police state and the disrespect to our Republic, Constitution and the will of the people.
>
> (Caldwell, 2011)

This sort of sentiment is typical of web-based conversations on the topic. Clearly, the story has been integrated into a larger American narrative of anarchism and resistance to tyranny. This tradition is deeply rooted in American history, going back through Henry David Thoreau's "Civil Disobedience" and the "Declaration of Independence" to religious dissidence in the 17th century. Later developments undoubtedly had less noble intentions, including Southern states' rights advocates in the antebellum period, Civil War secessionists and later segregationists warning the federal government to butt out of their local affairs. But there are more admirable strains as well, including Martin Luther King's thoughtful refusal to obey unjust laws or grassroots environmentalists in the Hudson Valley standing up to international corporations like General Electric, who were unabashedly engaging in ecological criminality. In other words, the story line of the honest little guy fighting against the big, oppressive government is always looming in the background in America, ready to be used as the interpretive prism for any events that seem to lend themselves to that sort of reading. The Gibson factory, full of American blue-collar workers whose place of employment was suddenly shut down on the orders of federal agents was a perfect setting for a story of governmental oppression. What's more, the emotional intensity of the meta narrative is as high as the perceived proximity of the threat: if the feds can show up unannounced in Nashville, the argument goes, maybe your town is next. By contrast, the alternative interpretation of the same events offered by the government lacks pungency:

> We target corporations and individuals who are removing protected species from the wild and making a profit by trafficking in them. (US Fish and Wildlife Service in response to inquiry by CNN)

In order to measure the actual impact of this unruly mass of discourse is another matter, I decided to examine only videos available on YouTube and try to see what proportion of language produced was dedicated to which narrative. The idea was to provide a quantitative basis for analyzing what John Wargo, professor of environmental law at Yale, has called "narrative advantage." (Wargo, 2011) I take this to mean that various narratives are in competition to win over the public to their side. Advantage is achieved when one narrative is more believable and in fact more believed than another. This may not, and in this case does not, correspond to factual reality. The main point is for the listener or viewer to be able to see him/herself as part of the story. Therefore, the main question for the recipient of discourse is, "Where do I fit in?" It is my contention that the logic-based discourse of the various governmental agencies involved in the Gibson case – the Departments of Homeland Security, Justice and Agriculture, in addition to the US Fish and Wildlife Service – failed to provide viable points of entry into the narrative that would have allowed the public to see the relevance of the government's action in a positive way.

There are presently 49 videos dedicated to this case available on YouTube, 46 of which support the narrative of "government overreach," the rest being relatively neutral and none actually defending the actions of the government.

Looking at the actual sources of information, two in particular account for nearly half the overall number of views: Fox News and Alex Jones' Info Wars (see Figure 1.1). Meanwhile, Henry Juszkiewicz is interviewed on over half of the available videos (25), so that the development of the "Gibson as victim of government overreach" narrative was a joint effort on the part of the company and a complicit media. (Juszkiewicz was also invited by Senator Rand Paul to testify in the US Senate.)

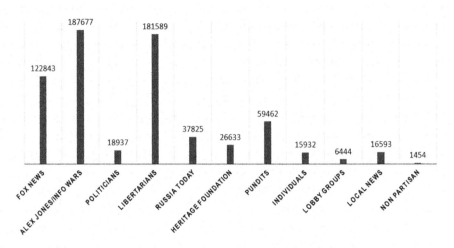

Figure 1.1 Number of views on YouTube.

Running through all the partisan reporting of the case is a common story line. A typical report begins with a portrait of Gibson's most famous guitars (the Les Paul or SG) and a quick listing of some of the most famous musicians who have played them (Paul McCartney or B.B. King). Next, the camera turns to the factory workers, a group comprised of people of different races and sexes – an idyllic image of the American workforce diligently going about its business. At this point, the company's CEO describes how one day armed federal agents made a surprise appearance, shutting down the factory and proceeding to search the premises. The journalist then announces dramatically that the object of the investigation is neither drugs nor terrorism but (after a dramatic pause) ... wood. The camera then returns to Juszkiewicz, who expresses his innocent shock and the report concludes that the government has indeed gone awry, leaving the viewer with the impression that there must be some hidden motive for such a disproportionate use of force.

The sources diverge in identifying what the hidden agenda really is, though the suggestion that Juszkiewicz's being a Republican donor is frequently evoked as a likely reason for having been targeted when other companies that use the "same wood" were not. Indeed, the Gibson CEO offers three main arguments for his innocence. First, he says, Gibson has always used the same wood, so why now? Second, other companies use the same kind of wood, so why us? And third, Gibson has documents proving that the Malagasy government authorized the sale, so how can it be illegal? The point, of course, is to imply that the enforcement of the Lacey Act's 2008 amendment was a kind of subterfuge to catch the innocent company off guard.

Juszkiewicz is careful to leave the remainder of the narrative development to the media, who then proceed to dramatize the events and imbue them with anti-tyrannical ideology. A simple survey of the titles of the reports is insightful and six thematic categories emerge: government overreach ("Government run amok – Gibson Guitar factory raid," "Runaway Government – The Spectacle of Homeland Security's Raid on Gibson Guitar," "Gibson Guitars Raided by SWAT Team: Gov't Gone Wild"), incomprehension ("Ted Nugent On Gibson Raids: Illogical, Anti-American, and Contrary to Claims of Creating Jobs," "Gibson Guitar Raid Unnecessary," "Gibson Guitars raid madness"), the shocked public ("Tea Partiers Outraged by Gibson Raid," "Public Reacts to Feds Raid on Gibson Guitars," "The Lacey Act Declarations Form! Are you kidding me?"), violence ("FED ATTACKS GIBSON," "Gibson Guitar Company 'Attacked' by FEDs," "Stringing Up Gibson Guitar by Rand Paul"), illegality of government action ("Overcriminalization in America: Tuning out Justice," "Judge Napolitano Slams DOJ Over Gibson Guitar Raid: 'Unjustifiable, Use Of Force Was Criminal'," "Gibson Guitar-Legal Extortion," "Green Police Mafia Raid Gibson Guitars"), and finally the "real" motive ("Still no charges months after armed raid on Gibson Guitars," "Blackburn: President Obama Should Come Clean on Gibson Guitar Raid," "Was Gibson Guitars Also Targeted by the IRS?," "Gibson Guitar Raids – Another Case Of Unfair Targeting By Obama Admin?," "Obama's Gestapo Raids Gibson Guitars for Being a Republican Donor").

To better comprehend how the "tyrannical government" theme is developed linguistically, I constituted a corpus of some 55,000 words, the total content of the transcripts of all the videos. Then, using the Brown corpus as a reference and Antconc software as the analytical tool, word frequencies and their relative importance (keyness) were discerned. One of the most significant semantic fields that is revealed is that of military operations. For example, the adjective-noun-verb combination of "federal" (103 occurrences)/"raid" (92)/"target" [as verb] (26) clearly conveys the notion of a military operation being carried out in a civilian context. Here we are dealing with hyperbole, for in some sense the inspection did constitute a raid that was indeed carried out by federal agents. However, this narrative element is then reinforced by the use of "semiautomatic" or "automatic weapons" (14 occurrences) and "bulletproof vests" (37) – not to mention isolated occurrences of "jackbooted," "at the barrel of a gun," "Nazi" and "Stalin"! At this stage, we have passed into the domain of fiction. Equally inappropriate from a strictly factual point of is the use of the term "SWAT (Special Weapons And Tactics) team" (37 occurrences).

One indication of the degree to which viewers are predisposed to believe such a story can be found in the fact that many of the same sources that promote the SWAT team narrative also provide photographs of the actual event, in which three or four average people wearing khaki pants or jeans and polo style shirts are seen to be carrying clipboards and bubble wrap and taking photos – hardly a group of hardened soldiers advancing in formation. But if the effectiveness of such narrative construction needed further proof, nothing would be more convincing than Gibson's issuing of a commemorate instrument to immortalize the tragic events and cash in on its popularity. The "Government Series II" Les Paul guitar sells for a little over a thousand dollars and was designed to celebrate "an Infamous Moment in Gibson History."

Conclusion

On a certain level, of course, one can hardly blame Gibson for making the best of a difficult situation, both in terms of media coverage and sales opportunities. And as far as the Department of Justice goes, one could also argue that they successfully performed their role as law enforcers and that it simply is not their vocation to inform the public of the well-founded ecological basis of the laws they are tasked to enforce. Nevertheless, the result in this case is that having won the legal battle, they seem to have lost the public opinion war. The question then arises as to whether it may be necessary for proponents of laws like the Lacey Act to address the public awareness dimension of the situation in addition to the strictly legal one.

To return to the phenomenon of populism that was referred to at the beginning, the communication gap seen here between the federal agencies and the conservative media is easy enough to recognize and write off as not the responsibility of the government to sell, but the result of this situation can no longer be said to be without consequences for the legal community. As mentioned previously, the poor image of the Environmental Protection Agency (EPA) in pro-Trump milieus has certainly lent credence to the decision to dismantle the administration from within by nominating an avowed anti-environmentalist as its head. And given the impact of linguistic practices on achieving narrative advantage, it is no coincidence that since Mr. Pruitt's arrival, the use of fact-based expressions such as "climate change" has been suppressed in official communication in favor of vaguer terminology. So if the EPA under Obama failed to convince the public of the need to discourage companies from taking part in processes that lead to deforestation, for instance, what can be expected of the Trump era EPA?

Notes

1 See Mann and Ornstein, *It's Even Worse…* for a full analysis of the change of tactics adopted during Speaker Gingrich's "100 days."
2 See for example, *Media Control, The Spectacular Achievements of Propaganda*.

References

Chomsky, Noam. 2002. *Media Control: The Spectacular Achievements of Propaganda*, New York: Seven Stories Press.
"Deforestation and its extreme effect on global warming." 2012. *Scientific American*, www.scientificamerican.com/article/deforestation-and-global-warming/
Goldberg, Bernard. 2001. *Bias: A CBS Insider Exposes How the Media Distort the News*, Washington, DC: Regnery Publishing Inc.
Guitar, Martin. 2016. "Martin Guitar joins the rainforest alliance #followthefrog campaign to raise awareness of forest sustainability," www.martinguitar.com/

about/news/martin-guitar-joins-the-rainforest-alliance-followthefrog-campaign-to-raise-awareness-of-forest-sustainability/

Mann, Thomas E. and Norman J. Ornstein. 2016. *It's Even Worse Than It Looks: How the American Constitutional System Collided with the New Politics of Extremism*, New York: Basic Books.

Sinderbrand, Rebecca. January 22, 2017. "How Kellyanne Conway ushered in the era of 'alternative facts'," *The Washington Post*, www.washingtonpost.com/news/the-fix/wp/2017/01/22/how-kellyanne-conway-ushered-in-the-era-of-alternative-facts/?utm_term=.adc5dd430991.

Taylor Guitars. "The Ebony Project," www.taylorguitars.com/ebonyproject

United States Department of Justice. August 6, 2012. "Gibson Guitar Corp. Agrees to resolve investigation into Lacey Act Violations," www.justice.gov/opa/pr/gibson-guitar-corp-agrees-resolve-investigation-lacey-act-violations.

United States Fish and Wildlife Service. 2006. 18 USC 42–43 16 USC 3371–3378 Lacey Act.

Wargo, John. March 12, 2011. "Reflections and Lessons," *Environmental Politics and Law* (EVST 255), YaleCourses, www.youtube.com/watch?v=fvbHwDujydM&list=PLeCFWdLZpnW9MYYSbVQq2Wh_NFIDP-ckF&index=24.

Appendix: Video reports used in corpus listed in descending order according to the number of views

Partisan:

www.youtube.com/watch?v=V5IYGroW1nA "The Great Gibson Guitar Raid: Months Later, Still No Charges Filed" ReasonTV/Published on February 23, 2012, 6:03/161,571 views

www.youtube.com/watch?v=2E-tXQ6kQoU&t=53s "CEO of Gibson: Feds Told Us to Leave U.S.," The Alex Jones Channel/Published on Sep 2, 2011, 14:25/104,084 views

www.youtube.com/watch?v=kxrriETsDTc "Feds raid Gibson guitar," RT/ Published on Sep 1, 2011, 9:15/37,825 views

www.youtube.com/watch?v=u6uWYoKZd4c&t=3s "Gibson Guitar-Legal Extortion," GLOOG1 (Fox News)/Published on August 12, 2012, 6:20/ 37,210 views

www.youtube.com/watch?v=JExaZHOfxfY "Government run amok – Gibson Guitar factory raid," Maureen Dowling (Fox News)/Published on Apr 8, 2014, 5:16/32,664 views

www.youtube.com/watch?v=96QOaEUnPY0 "Dana with Gibson CEO – Henry Juszkiewicz," FM NewsTalk 97.1/Published on August 26, 2011, 9:17/ 31,359 views www.youtube.com/watch?v=aUilBDkiGG0 "Green Police Mafia Raid Gibson Guitars," The Alex Jones Channel/Published on August 26, 2011, 9:53/29,828 views

www.youtube.com/watch?v=iLZUGFlCYck "Public Reacts to Feds Raid on Gibson Guitars – Infowars Nightly News," The Alex Jones Channel/Published on Sep 2, 2011, 3:41/28,945 views www.youtube.com/watch?v=O0znHGl1998 "Gibson Guitar CEO Speaks Out," The Heritage Foundation/Published on October 20, 2011, 5:04/26,633 views

www.youtube.com/watch?v=DMaUdwlVNfA "Beck interviews Gibson CEO," MrJseidl/Published on Sep 1, 2011, 7:28/25,850 views

www.youtube.com/watch?v=miDswgS21qs "Ted Nugent On Gibson Raids: 'Illogical, Anti-American, and Contrary to Claims of Creating Jobs'," NDblogvideos (Fox News)/Published on Sep 21, 2011, 3:13/23,679 views

www.youtube.com/watch?v=n829Au1y_s8 "Alex Jones: Gibson Guitar Company 'Attacked' by FEDs," Nwotaser (Info Wars)/Published on August 30, 2011, 25:41/16,614 views

www.youtube.com/watch?v=H5No0Sk9NIo "Henry E. Juszkiewicz, Gibson Raid Press Conference, Aug. 25, 2011," Nashville Scene/Published on August 25, 2011, 28:24/15,618 views

www.youtube.com/watch?v=9gqbhIanoN4 "Justin Hayward on Gibson Factory Raids," Moody Blues/Published on Sep 20, 2011, 4:49/11,366 views

www.youtube.com/watch?v=3HTJaoewJew "Gibson Guitar CEO says 'government raided wood we have used for 17 years.'," palgo573 (Fox News)/Published on Sep 1, 2011, 6:11/11,072 views

www.youtube.com/watch?v=99l8ktMYjwI "Feds Raid Gibson Guitar Company," LibertarianDailyNews/Published on August 26, 2011, 1:49/10,955 views

www.youtube.com/watch?v=pweY5b0WaiY "Newt on the Gibson Guitar Raids," Newt Gingrich/Published on Sep 16, 2011, 1:53/10,474 views

www.youtube.com/watch?v=GOMnGROs31M "Judge Napolitano Slams DOJ Over Gibson Guitar Raid: 'Unjustifiable, Use Of Force Was Criminal'," Eduardo89rp (Fox News)/Published on May 30, 2013, 5:23/8,178 views

www.youtube.com/watch?v=0mNJy0x1-P8 "Was Gibson Guitars Also Targeted by the IRS?," The Alex Jones Channel/Published on May 28, 2013, 8:01/8,160 views

www.youtube.com/watch?v=9RNqJPN0DjI "Testimony From Henry Juszkiewicz, CEO of Gibson Guitars at PROPERTY WRONGS Hearing – 10/12/11," Senator Rand Paul/Published on Nov 7, 2011, 7:48/7,764 views

www.youtube.com/watch?v=WHCE0AIF-Y8 "Ten years in jail for moving dirt? Gibson guitars swat team raided & other Tyranny," ill318 (Fox News)/Published on Sep 10, 2011, 7:03/6,736 views

www.youtube.com/watch?v=9K8IDGUTrQk "Gibson Guitar CEO Responds to Federal Raid," NRATV/Published on August 29, 2011, 8:46/5,258 views

www.youtube.com/watch?v=l_2FQY12GpM&t=19s "The Lacey Act Declarations Form! Are you kidding me?," SentryNombre/Published on Sep 6, 2011, 13:41/4,566 views www.youtube.com/watch?v=5WpEEYzAuF0 "Obama's Gestapo Raids Gibson Guitars for Being a Republican Donor," NFriction (Fox News)/Published on May 28, 2013, 5:23/1,750 views

www.youtube.com/watch?v=HWQ6q0p4t-Y "Still no charges months after armed raid on Gibson Guitars," libertylover522 (Fox News)/Published on Apr 14, 2012, 2:27/1,264 views

www.youtube.com/watch?v=dDkDyC2ybuY "Overcriminalization in America: Tuning out Justice," NACDLvideo/Published on January 22, 2015, 6:32/1,186 views

www.youtube.com/watch?v=FahGD4t_HmE "Runaway Government – The Spectacle of Homeland Security's Raid on Gibson Guitar," RealClear Radio Hour/Published on May 5, 2014, 28:45/1,056 views

www.youtube.com/watch?v=3hVRWFwo3aw "Gibson Guitar CEO visits Capitol Hill," HumanEvents/Published on Sep 9, 2011, 11:30/950 views

www.youtube.com/watch?v=vLg1iq5BgHs "Gibson Raided for Sporting (Indian) Wood," Lionel Nation/Published on Sep 6, 2011, 2:54/812 views

www.youtube.com/watch?v=fch5-LiOXQw "Gibson Guitars raid madness 24th August 2011 YouTube," LibertarianDailyNews/Published on August 27, 2011, 14:54/807 views www.youtube.com/watch?v=oWGLwhz1Wik "Gibson Guitars Raided by SWAT Team: Gov't Gone Wild," countryboy1949 (local news)/Published on October 11, 2011, 2:23/685 views

www.youtube.com/watch?v=6AYH5rbaJRo "Strumming A Scandal? RPT: White House Targeted Gibson Guitars In Raid," Mass Tea Party - Wake Up America! (Fox News)/Published on May 28, 2013, 3:04/528 views

www.youtube.com/watch?v=FgRNewIx6rI "Stringing Up Gibson Guitar by Rand Paul," Biff Burroughs/Published on Sep 5, 2013, 11:23/400 views

www.youtube.com/watch?v=zRGl7CsU_b0 "Gibson Guitar Raids – Another Case Of Unfair Targeting By Obama Admin?," Mass Tea Party – Wake Up America! (Fox News)/Published on May 31, 2013, 3:08/294 views

www.youtube.com/watch?v=LIUq_OC3Gn4 "Justice Department Raids Gibson," Milewskige (Hannity Fox News)/Published on Sep 18, 2011, 6:13/290 views

www.youtube.com/watch?v=BrJXxTbGnSI "Henry Juszkiewicz – The Lacey Act and Gibson Guitars – interview – Goldstein on Gelt – January 2013," Douglas Goldstein/Published on January 22, 2013, 16:12/260 views

www.youtube.com/watch?v=01Y5EQKqiZI "Blackburn: President Obama Should Come Clean on Gibson Guitar Raid," RepMarshaBlackburn/Published on May 31, 2013, 3:19/255 views

www.youtube.com/watch?v=JWlzOazV6lg "Tea Partiers Outraged by Gibson Raid Tnreporttv/Published on October 5, 2011, 1:29/234 views

www.youtube.com/watch?v=wbwvGfnwQBg "Feds Raid Gibson," Jase C (We Rock Network)/Published on February 14, 2012, 3:55/126 views

www.youtube.com/watch?v=BFRWuM31uso "FED ATTACKS GIBSON," Drewswebsite (Focus on the family)/Published on Apr 24, 2012, 10:48/105 views

www.youtube.com/watch?v=3vnuuyAfCJA "Marrero: Gibson Guitar Raid Unnecessary," Tnreporttv/Published on October 7, 2011, 1:56/56 views

www.youtube.com/watch?v=2psvQhXbC8o "Infowars Nightly News Special Report on Gibson Guitar Raid," Veritaze/Published on Nov 16, 2011, 3:38/46 views www.youtube.com/watch?v=ywy7YsH99rM "Blackburn Questions Motives In Gibson Guitar Raid," RepMarshaBlackburn (Fox News)/Published on May 31, 2013, 3:16/44 views

www.foxnews.com/transcript/2011/09/12/friday-lightning-round-gibson-guitars-raid.html "Friday Lightning Round: Gibson Guitars Raid," Fox News/Published April 05, 2012, (unknown number of views – subsequently removed from site)

Non-partisan:

www.youtube.com/watch?v=94xHRj6cSCE "Gibson Guitar Agrees to Settle Lacey Act Violations," WZTV FOX 17/Published on August 6, 2012, 1:45/547 views

www.youtube.com/watch?v=i1X73Ixerzw "Guitar Planet and Lacey Act," Thomas Harrigan (NAMM)/Published on Nov 21, 2011, 5:44/455 views

www.youtube.com/watch?v=q51DuLoa4ws "Gibson Guitar Corporation Paying Fines Over Wood Imports," FinancialNewsOnline/Published on August 6, 2012, 1:01/257 views

www.youtube.com/watch?v=hd7IiEsmVDs "Tom Bedell at Willcutt Guitars discusses the Lacey Act," Willcutt Guitars/Published on May 22, 2016, 5:01/195 views

2 Trial by (social) media
Anglo-Saxon and Italian practices in the digital age

Douglas Ponton and Marco Canepa

Introduction

The USA, England and Italy have all adopted an adversarial judicial system, one of whose central ideas is that a fair trial requires the complete 'cognitive virginity' (Friedman 1994: 33) of the person passing judgment on facts relating to the crime (jurors in England and America, professional judges in Italy). The evidence is presented to these figures by counsels for the prosecution and defence, and the verdict must be based solely on the grounds of evidence properly admitted at trial. Knowledge such as that found in the Net or Social Media, arguably, could jeopardize the impartiality of judge and jury.

In the digital era, it is common for high profile trials to attract intense public interest across social networks, thus threatening cognitive virginity, and resulting in the phenomenon known as 'trial by media', which may affect what goes on in court (Janoski-Haehlen 2011, Waters and Hannaford-Agor 2017). It is also, of course, true that, as Resta (2009: 21) points out, media scrutiny of criminal proceedings is everywhere 'considered essential to democracy'. However, as he also says (ibid):

> Interest in crime news is generally high, and attracts public curiosity, especially if prominent persons, sex, and mystery are involved […] a criminal trial […] easily turns into a spectacle, which has entertainment value and therefore gives newspapers and broadcasters strong incentives to provide it.

The tendency for judge and jury to be susceptible to outside influence, including that of the media, has received critical attention (e.g. Landsman and Rakos 1994, Wrightsman 2010), and there is also evidence to suggest that our opinions are shaped by what we read (Gilbert et al. 1993). We therefore argue, in this chapter, that there is a case to be made for extending the focus of legislation to include the persuasive effects of Social Media. We also suggest that Italy would do well to imitate Anglo-Saxon practices in this respect.

Trial by media in Italy

There are significant differences between how these matters are regulated, in America and Britain, on the one hand, and in Italy on the other. In 2013, the American Bar Association published its 'Formal Opinion 462',[1] which cautions against the dangers of Social Media, especially in the area of the judges' real or perceived impartiality. In the English system, cognitive virginity is a matter of major concern. At the outset of a trial jurors are warned that they must not discuss the case with anybody, read newspapers, check issues or points of law on the internet, post on social media, etc.

In the Italian system there are no similar provisions, and the phenomenon of trial by media is extremely common. High profile political figures regularly feature on prime time shows, defending themselves against various accusations that would, in other contexts, be considered *sub judice*. Programmes dealing with figures involved in true crime also attract wide audiences, since such narratives both feed, and feed off, the public's taste for sensational news items (Grabe et al. 2010). National media of all kinds take the cases up, providing, through interviews, a platform to victims and/or the accused or key witnesses. This happened, for example, in the notorious murder case against Anna Maria Franzoni (charged with killing her child in 2002, and eventually convicted), where her lawyer arranged for her to appear on the popular chat show, *Maurizio Costanzo Show*.[2] Another instance was that of the American student Amanda Knox, who became an authentic celebrity following the murder of her roommate, in 2007. In the case of Knox, the notion of trial by media is especially relevant, as it would appear that the guilty verdict depended, at least in part, on the role of Social Media. Witnesses were not sequestered before the verdict, and there was nothing to prevent their exposure to the lurid details of the crime. The personalities of Knox and her boyfriend, duly sensationalized by the media, were internationally known and discussed. Knox was painted as a devil with an angel's face, obsessed with sex, drugs and alcohol. Photos that would be normal on any twenty-year-old's MySpace account were given salacious interpretations, and all of this meant that the guilty verdict expressed conformity with the specific narrative circulating in the media, and across Social Media, before the trial took place (Mirabella 2012).

The Cosby case

Our paper focuses on a recent notorious case of global interest, which saw the popular Afro-American comedian and cultural icon, Bill Cosby, accused of diverse cases of sexual assault. At its peak, the Cosby Show's success went beyond the bounds of mere entertainment: commentators have claimed, for example, that it 'help[ed] in improving race relations by projecting universal values that both whites and blacks could identify with' (Downing 1988, Innis and Feagin 1995: 692). Its popularity in South Africa, indeed, has been identified as a factor in bringing about the end of apartheid (Krabill 2010). The show has been credited with promoting trans-racial human values, exploring fatherhood, and tackling social issues such as sexism and machismo (Dyson 1989, in Innis and Feagin 1995: 695). It has been criticized for presenting a vision of American society that downplays the racial problems that still exist (Jhally and Lewis 1992), and for featuring a family apparently above the economic difficulties felt by most Americans (Frazer and Frazer 1993).

As the central character and charismatic star of the show, Cosby's fame and popularity were immense (Gray 1989: 376). However, in 2015, he was arrested and charged with sexual assault, in a case that dated back to 2004. In a media storm that saw the involvement of the #MeToo movement against sexual assault, many other women came forward to accuse him.[3] He was tried twice, in June 2017 and April 2018, and our data focuses on representations in Social Media which appeared before the two trials.

Naturally, it is not possible to advance the claim that the guilty verdict in the second trial can be ascribed, definitively, to the effects of the media storm generated by the case. The corollary is also true, however; it cannot be convincingly argued that there is no connection between the discourse generated in society at large about a case, and decisions taken in the legal domain.

Methodology

In the inter-disciplinary spirit of Wodak's discourse-historical approach (Wodak 2001), this chapter integrates relevant background knowledge in the form of contributions from an Italian judge, currently working in his own country, who has first-hand experience with the Anglo-Saxon model. As influential as the discourse-historical approach has proved, it is problematic adapting the model for a smaller scale study. Though our paper meets most of the eleven criteria laid out by Wodak (ibid.: 69–70), it stops short of fully adopting the model. While intertextuality, for instance, is seen as crucial in the original model, it is less relevant for our study. It is also questionable whether the paper belongs in the genre of Critical Discourse Analysis. As Wodak puts it (ibid.: 70), the aim of the discourse-historical method, as of all CDA, is to 'change certain discursive and social practices', but it is already acknowledged, at least in Anglo-Saxon contexts, that trial by media constitutes a problem. The critical dimension may consist in the suggestion that members of the Italian legal system should do likewise, but this cannot be proven by means of linguistic analysis of the texts in question.

Wodak's model is useful for its insistence on a detailed, ethnographic picture of the socio-historical context, which underlies any closer approach to the interpretation of specific, embedded texts. Our account below of the different legal contexts and their positions vis-à-vis Social Media fulfils Wodak's eighth criterion (ibid.: 70), i.e. 'historical context is always analysed and integrated into the interpretation of discourses and texts'. At the level of linguistic analysis, the method is eclectic, allowing the analyst considerable freedom in selecting 'theories and methods.which are helpful in understanding and explaining the object under investigation' (ibid.: 69), and we focus mainly on discourse framing

Table 2.1 Solving for the intended interpretation

Goal: What is the intended interpretation?
Data base: The sentence uttered; the time, place and circumstances of the utterance; the speaker's beliefs about the listener; general knowledge.
Boundary conditions: Various tacit agreements between speaker and listener about how language is to be used.
Mental operations:
1 Build a candidate interpretation.
2 Test the candidate interpretation against the boundary conditions.
3 If it passes all the tests, accept it as the intended meaning.
   Otherwise begin at 1 again.

Source: from Clark 1978: 298

and the interpretation of pragmatic inferences. We adopt, for analysis, what Sperber and Wilson (1996: 21) call 'an inferential model of communication', using a model of Gricean inference (Grice 1981, 1989) based on an educated 'reading-between the lines', or 'problem-solving' approach to the extraction of meaning from linguistic utterances (Clark 1978), as well as the application of Grice's well-known conversational maxims of Quantity, Quality, Relation and Manner (Grice 1989: 28). The diagram above from Clark's early work, though it represents a starting point for later research in situational pragmatics, will be sufficient for our purposes (Table 2.1).

The boundary conditions in blog discourse consist in users' knowledge of the linguistic conventions governing this particular context, and also relate to the way shared knowledge must be applied to make sense of the contributor's intended meaning.

In terms of identity theory, the discursive construction of an online persona is explored in the terms of Bucholtz and Hall (2004, 2005), though their model, which sees identity as dependent on interaction, needs adaptation in the context of the Cosby case, which concerns the identity of a public figure, or persona, and its construction through social media (Turkle 2005). Two aspects of Bucholtz and Hall's approach are relevant; firstly, identity is not seen as an 'internal psychological phenomenon', a sort of 'true self' (Barker and Galasinksi 2001, Schwartz et al. 2011), but rather as a 'social and cultural' construct (Widdicombe and Wooffitt 1995, Wooffitt 2005). For a media figure, there may, arguably, be at least two senses in which it is possible to speak of identity; the public perception of the person in question, and their identity 'off camera' (Giesen 2006: 356). In media studies generally, what is at stake is not the *person* (seen as possessing a real, psychological, individual, inherent or intrinsic identity), but the *persona*, which is mutually understood, by self and other, as a kind of performance, a fragment of an identity adopted for a specific purpose in a specific social context (Kollock and Smith 1999, Crystal 2004: 50–51, Partington 2006, Heyd 2008).

Before his fall from grace, Cosby's 'identity', in this sense, was that with which his on-screen persona was most closely associated; an ideal family man, a generous and kind, though at times justly strict, father, a successful doctor and amusing, devoted husband. As Entman and Rojecki (2000) point out, despite the melting pot myth, race relations in America are still marked by tension and emotional distance between black and white. Cosby would appear to be a good example of their category of 'African American stars', who 'demonstrate bankable crossover appeal'; this, they say, is 'mainly in broadly comic or super-masculine action hero formats that recollect traditional stereotypes of clowning minstrels or menacing brutes' (ibid.: 11, see also Carter 1988). This chapter, in effect, shows a character's ideal, on-screen 'persona' collapsing under the pressure of testimonies to the alleged realities of his 'true self'. Cosby's transformation in the popular imagination, from comic hero to sexual predator, could be seen as representing a shift from the category of clown to that of menacing brute (Mastro 2003). The second important notion from Bucholtz and Hall's study, in fact, is that identities frequently depend on 'others' perceptions and representations (2005: 585). The identity with which we are concerned relates to how Cosby is represented in media and Social Media, and not with his own self-representation.

The adversarial system

Even though the adversarial system derives from the common law tradition, the English, American *and* Italian criminal legal systems are, on principle, adversarial. In 1988, Italy changed its criminal procedure rules and abandoned the inquisitorial model, that derived from civil law traditions, in favour of an adversarial one. The main feature of this system is that the person or panel judging the guilt or innocence of the defendant, rendering a verdict of conviction or acquittal (the jury in the English and Welsh Crown Court, the judge in Italy, hereafter referred to as the *judicial decision-maker*) should base their decision on judicial evidence alone. All the evidence, circumstantial evidence, proofs and expert opinions are displayed by the prosecutor and the counsel for the defence before this person or panel, who pass judgment only on the grounds of these findings (Slapper and Kelly 2003).

In the inquisitorial model, the judge also plays a role in the investigation and will consequently, by the trial, already have a deep grasp of the evidence relating to the case. By contrast, in the adversarial system, investigations are generally carried out by police, and the prosecutor takes over the case at trial, in order that the judicial decision-maker will not have prior knowledge of the facts. They are also forbidden to consider any other sources of information than the evidence properly admitted during the trial, displayed by counsels for the defence and prosecution. The counsels thus play a key role in bringing evidence to the trial, examining and cross-examining witnesses, presenting their side of the truth to judge or jury and, meantime, challenging the other party's version of events. The adversarial model, then, is based on the idea of two opposing sides stating their case to an impartial body, which will convict only if the prosecution's case is proved according to a certain standard (Elliott and Quinn 2016: 445).

The formal legal truth, therefore, emerges from this double-sided struggle; from the effort of counsels, on the one hand, to establish a version of events (they have the burden of production and the burden of persuasion) and, on the other, to argue and mystify their counterparts' statements, in accordance with court procedure and rules of evidence. This formal legal truth may diverge from substantive truth, but the divergence is merely the consequence of having a complex, multi-purpose system, in which actual truth, and what legally follows from it, comprises but one value among a variety of important values competing for legal realization (Summers 1999).

It is important to note that, even though the Italian code of criminal procedure has embraced the tenets of an adversarial system, these principles were essentially undone by the Constitutional Court, which placed a very high value on the search for substantive truth at trial, the so called 'real truth' (Pizzi and Montagna 2004). This permits the judge to adopt a more active and inquisitorial role, as they are allowed to ask witnesses questions and undertake further investigation at the end of the trial; judges' use of the internet and Social Media, therefore, may be seen in this light.

Anglo-Saxon and Italian legal contexts

In a trial-by-jury model such as that of the United States or Britain, jurors attend the trial, listen to the evidence and finally return a verdict, deciding among the twelve of them. The decision is based, as in every adversarial system, on the evidence displayed, the judge having no say. In this model, the judge's role consists mainly in decisions about the penalty imposed on the defendant after the conviction, or following a guilty plea. During the trial, the judge will decide on all matters of law that have arisen during the trial. The principle is that 'the law is for the judge, and the facts are for the jury' (Thayer 1898: 187).

In the Italian system, by contrast, delivering judgment is up to the judge. The Italian system has no counterpart to the jury, although there is a panel consisting of eight judges, called the 'corte di assise' (assizes court), which mainly handles murder cases. Here six lay judges sit alongside two professionals, but this differs from a jury because they work jointly, making decisions together on every point of law and matter of fact, collaborating on the verdict and the penalty.

On principle, Italy's adoption of the adversarial system should mean that decisions will be made by the judge only on the grounds of properly admitted evidence. Though the judge, as has been said, has a more active, inquisitorial role than his/her British counterpart, it is clear that any decision should be based only on judicial findings, and specifically on what has been said in the courtroom.

In terms of 'trial by media', the focus in Italy is on the right of the parties, mainly the defendant, whose right to privacy must be protected from a too inquisitive media. Politicians embroiled in an investigation, for example, may request legal provisions that limit the use by the media of courtroom evidence, such as wiretapped conversations.

The lack of concern with the issue of cognitive virginity may be due to several factors. Firstly, Italian justice is mostly in the hands of a professional and/or technical judge who, in theory, should be able to maintain impartiality in the face of strong media pressure, and to distinguish judicial evidence and opinions appropriately expressed in the courtroom from those circulating in media and Social Media. Some studies have questioned this, demonstrating that professional judges are often unable to disregard inadmissible evidence, with negative effects both for judges' and jurors' decisions (Wistrich et al. 2005, Vidmar 2011). Secondly, as mentioned above, in an Italian trial the concern is to establish the 'real truth', and there is therefore more tolerance towards the notion of a judge being exposed to external sources of information.

The Cosby case: analysing the data

In 2015, two years before Cosby's first trial, a fellow actor named Joseph C. Phillips, who had appeared with him in the Cosby Show in 1984, wrote a lengthy blog entry in which he discussed his feelings about the controversy surrounding the star.[4] We have selected this piece, and the following readers' comments section, as representing the voluminous discourse on Social Media generated by the affair.

We have suggested above that there are two contexts nowadays in which the guilt or innocence of a subject are decided, the official legal context and an unofficial counterpart, the tribunal of public opinion. The latter may have always existed, but in the age of Social Media it has unprecedented access to information about ongoing trials, as well as a forum by means of which opinions can be expressed, argumentation advanced, and persuasion achieved (Zachara 2014: 224). In our text, the discursive frame for discussion about Cosby is that of innocent/guilty, and is established by an emphatic heading containing the text: OF COURSE BILL COSBY IS GUILTY!

By contrast with discourse in a legal context, contributors to this debate are not bound by any legal requirements: bloggers simply state their views and engage with each other in informal language. Beneath the photo are buttons by means of which the blog can be shared across other forms of Social Media (Facebook, Twitter), as well as an indicator showing the number of times this has been done. Through Social Media, therefore, this mass of spontaneously ex- pressed opinion will circulate and be read, reacted to, possibly re-tweeted or shared on Facebook, and thus potentially reach an incalculable audience worldwide (Blommaert and Varis 2015: 60).

In the terms of Kress and Van Leeuwen's (1996: 57) notion of 'vertical elongation', the distribution of text and image is significant: 'What is most important or otherwise dominant goes on top, what is less important or domi- nant is relegated to the bottom'. The first semiotic item processed by the reader here, therefore, is the text, with its statement of Cosby's guilt. It is positioned immediately above a colour face-shot of Cosby in his prime; smiling, hand touching the peak of his cap in a welcoming gesture. By presenting such an image – and not one, for example, of the elderly actor in a more vulnerable, human pose – the writer presents him in a positive light. We are looking at Bill Cosby, the star of the Cosby Show, symbol of racial integration, 'America's dad'.[5] In effect, part of the writer's intention in this piece is to protect Cosby's image from further damage, so that he and, by extension, Americans generally, can continue to cherish memories of their fallen icon.

The text continues, with positive evaluations (Hunston and Thompson 2000) of Cosby during the time the two worked together:

> I was blessed in that regard, and even more blessed that I found my idol as clever, kind, and brilliant as I had imagined

The writer then tells the story of his own coming to terms with Cosby's guilt:

> this Bill was involved in illegal drugs and illicit sex, fornication, and perhaps more.

This time, the evaluation is not found in explicitly evaluative adjectives, but rather construed via what Martin and White (2005) call expressions of invoked attitude; in other words, because the character is involved in activities that society generally deplores, there is an implicit negative judgement here. Via the use of the passive voice, the severity of his actions is further diminished, at least to a degree: it is, arguably, less culpable to 'be involved in something' than 'to do' something (Trew 1979). Phillips concludes his text with a direct appeal to Bill Cosby, not to confess, to make up for the harm he has caused, etc., but rather, to retire from the scene, so that something of his legacy may survive the scandal:

> Bill, you have a family that loves you, a wife who is devoted to you; you have more money than you can spend. Please, go live a quiet country life. Allow those of us who truly love you to preserve just a bit of our enchantment.

Applying Clark's model to extrapolating the writer's meaning here, in terms of Cosby's guilt or innocence, we can paraphrase it as follows: Cosby is guilty (the writer does not, for instance, advise him to fight to clear his name in the courts), therefore he should retire from the scene. He should not face legal punishment, because the actor's legacy is more important than the ends of justice. Clark speaks of 'tacit agreement' between speaker and hearer, and an implicit conclusion such as this will be accepted only by readers that share the writer's scale of ethical/normative values. As we shall see (Table 2.2 below), this is not universally the case:

If we apply Grice's maxim of Relation to Faraone's first sentence (1–4), we have an implicit meaning, as follows: sexual abuse is a common feature of the acting industry/Hollywood, and Bill Cosby's actions must be seen as exemplifying this (= Cosby is guilty). There is also a covert reference to slipping victims Quaaludes in drink, as this is one of the 'forms' that such abuse may take (4). Thus, the 'truth' that Faraone wishes to hear Joseph demand from Cosby

Table 2.2 Blog contributions

Line	Text	Inference
	Elizabeth Faraone·	
1	Art Students League	3–4 BC is representative of this
2	I really think the majority of	behaviour
3	people in Hollywood (especially	4 these may include drugging
4	child actors) have been forced to	victims
5	accept the abuse of the acting	5–6 BC is guilty
6	industry, in all of the forms that it	8–9 J's opinions are "crazy"
7	takes. When Joseph says he wants	
8	to hear the truth from Bill, rather	
9	than that he wants him to go into	
	hiding so he can continue to live	
	in his fantasy world, I will know	
	Joseph is on the road to better	
	mental health.	
	Jody Daniel·	
10	Disc Jockey (DJ) at The	
11	Churchward Pub	
12	right? I expected what he was	
13	going to say was, bill, its not to	12–13 BC is guilty; he has "an
	late to speak the truth and own	issue"
	your ish! But thats not what	
	he said.	
	Lori Scalon	
	Jody Daniel -	
14	I KNOW! I can't believe this	
15	author. "Bill go live a quiet life in	14–15 BC is guilty
16	the country" wth?!How about...	17–18 an appropriate
17	"Bill, go finish up	punishment
18	yourdegenerate existence in a	
	10×10 cell getting raped against	
	your will!!!"	

(5–6), relates to his involvement in such actions, i.e. that he was involved in repeated abuse of women wishing to enter the acting industry. In (6), 'he' refers to Phillips, who wants to continue living in a 'fantasy world', i.e. one in which he can maintain intact the image of Cosby as an icon. Underlying Faraone's contribution is an assumption that Cosby is guilty. This is her bed-rock position, even though, it must be remembered, the actor had so far not stood trial – there is, therefore, no legal basis for her assumption, which must be based on hearsay and rumours in the media (unless she herself has first-hand experience in the matter, which is improbable). Jody Daniel's contribution builds on the first, aligning herself with Faraone via her opening word, 'right' (11), and implying that Bill should, effectively, speak the 'truth' (12). The exact contours of 'the truth' here are, as in the first contribution, imprecise, though here it is connected with Cosby having 'an issue', which he should acknowledge. It is therefore clear that Daniel, too, believes that Cosby is guilty. The final contributor picks up some of these inferences. By capitalisation (I KNOW!) she signals strong alignment with the previous two contributions, and makes explicit the aspect of the discourse that she has most trouble with: 'Bill, go live a quiet life in the country' (14–15). The acronym wth?! (what the hell?) signals her disagreement with the proposition. That Cosby is guilty, for her, is implied by the fact that she proposes a more appropriate punishment for him, in which, parenthetically, there is an explicit representation of the crime he is alleged to have committed (18), as well as by the explicit negative evaluative adjective 'degenerate' (17).

Though Cosby's identity can be said, in the terms of Bucholtz and Hall, to 'emerge' from these interactions, its precise contours do not; rather, like the meanings associated with elements of the linguistic code, they also need to be deduced, or inferred. What is clear is that for all three of the commentators and, to a lesser degree, for Phillips himself, Cosby's identity is, to some extent, that of a sexual predator who has ab/used his position as an American icon to procure gratification.

Conclusion

Freedom of expression is widely regarded as one of the pillars of democracy; however, in the age of Social Media this refers to something more than the old idea of freedom of the press. It signifies the right for everybody to comment on news, to post their opinions on reports in the press or media, to share information; to participate, unchecked, in online debate about political or judicial matters. The question, then, is how new media match up against the idea that judicial decision-makers must be shielded from knowledge of cases in progress, apart from that derived from evidence properly admitted at trial. The Cosby case represents an instance of trial by media in that, as we have seen, there was considerable debate about his innocence or guilt in the immense public forum constituted by Social Media, before the case was ever heard in court. By choosing such a high profile, recent case to illustrate the influence of Social Media on the legal process, our intention was to provoke debate about the issues involved, especially in the Italian context.

In Italy, as we have seen, cognitive virginity is not a matter of concern, and there is no provision for keeping judges safe from external influence. As a result, they might well have a close acquaintance with a case they are asked to decide on, based on other sources of knowledge than judicial findings. Naturally, judges are supposed not to take such knowledge into account, but it is questionable how far this is possible, given the extensive media coverage which sometimes accompanies trials in Italy. For example, in the cases of Knox and Franzoni, it is plain that a public tribunal had already passed judgement long before the trials received formal, legal verdicts.[6] We suggest, then, that the Italian legal system would do well to consider moves, as in the Anglo-Saxon context, to limit the possible negative influence of Social Media on the legal process. The arrival of new media implies a range of new challenges to traditional patterns of social organisation, including legal systems, and this needs to be recognized by legal systems globally if the goals of impartiality and the right to a fair trial are to be preserved.

Notes

1 American Bar Association. Online at: www.americanbar.org/content/dam/aba/administrative/professional_responsibility/formal_opinion_462.authcheckdam.pdf (last accessed 10/05/2018).
2 www.theguardian.com/media/2002/jul/24/pressandpublishing.internationalnews.
3 The Guardian. Online at: www.theguardian.com/world/2018/apr/26/bill-cosby-guilty-trial-sexual-assault (last accessed 10/05/2018).
4 Of course, Bill Cosby is guilty! Online at: http://josephcphillips.com/2015/07/of-course-bill-cosby-is-guilty/ (last accessed 10/05/2018).
5 NBC News. Online at: www.nbcnews.com/storyline/bill-cosby-scandal/bill-cosby-was-once-america-s-dad-now-he-s-n869396 (last accessed 11/05/2018). The photo is not reproduced here for copyright reasons.
6 Injustice in Perugia. Online at: www.injusticeinperugia.org/media.html (last accessed 25/06/2018).

References

Barker, Chris and Galasinski, Dariusz. 2001. *Cultural Studies and Discourse Analysis: A Dialogue on Language and Identity*. London, Thousand Oaks California and New Delhi: Sage.
Blommaert, Jan and Varis, Piia. 2015. *Enoughness, Accent and Light Communities: Essays on Contemporary Identities*. Tilburg: Tilburg University.
Bucholtz, Mary and Hall, Kira. 2004. Language and Identity. In Duranti, Alessandro (ed.) *A Companion to Linguistic Anthropology*. Malden and Oxford: Blackwell (369–395).
Bucholtz, Mary and Hall, Kira. 2005. Identity and interaction. A sociocultural linguistic approach. *Discourse Studies*, 7: 4–5 (85–614).
Carter, R. G. 1988. TV's black comfort zone for whites. *Television Quarterly*, 23: 4 (29–34).
Clark, Herbert H. 1978. Inferring what is meant. In Levelt, Willem, Johannes, Maria and Flores d'Arcais, Giovanni, B. (eds) *Studies in the Perception of Language*. London: Wiley (295–322).
Crystal, David. 2004. *Language and the Internet*. Cambridge: Cambridge University Press.
Downing, John D. H. 1988. The Cosby Show and American radical discourse. In Van Dijk, Teun and Smitherman-Donaldson, Geneva (eds) *Discourse and Discrimination*. Detroit: Wayne State UP (6–73).
Dyson, Michael. 1989. Bill Cosby and the politics of race. *Z Magazine 2: 3* (26–30).
Elliot, Catherine and Quinn, Frances. 2016. *English Legal System*. Harlow, London and New York: Pearson.

Entman, Robert M. and Rojecki, Andrew. 2000. *The Black Image in the White Mind: Media and Race in America*. Chicago: University of Chicago Press.

Frazer, June M., and Frazer, Timothy C. 1993. 'Father Knows Best' and 'The Cosby Show': Nostalgia and the sitcom tradition. *Journal of Popular Culture 27* (163–172).

Friedman, Lawrence M. 1994. *Crime and Punishment in American History*. Basic Books: epub.

Giesen, Bernhard. 2006. Performing the Sacred: A Durkheimian Perspective on the Performative Turn in the Social Sciences. In Alexander, Jeffrey C., Giesen, Bernhard and Mast, Jason L. (eds) *Social Performance: Symbolic Action, Cultural Pragmatics and Ritual*. Cambridge: Cambridge University Press (325–368).

Gilbert, Daniel T., Tafarodi Romin W. and Malone, Patrick S. 1993. You can't not believe everything you read. *Journal of Personality and Social Psychology 65*: 2 (221–233).

Grabe, Maria Elizabeth, Zhou, Shuhua and Barnett, Brooke. 2010. Explicating sensationalism in television news: Content and the bells and whistles of form. *Journal of Broadcasting and Electronic Media, 45*: 4 (635–655).

Gray, Herman. 1989. Television, Black Americans, and the American dream. *Critical Studies in Mass Communication, 6*: 4 (376–386).

Grice, H. Paul. 1981. Presupposition and conversational implicature. In Cole, Peter (ed.) *Radical Pragmatics*. New York: Academic Press (167–181).

Grice, H. Paul. 1989. *Studies in the Way of Words*. Cambridge Massachusetts and London: Harvard University Press.

Heyd, Theresa. 2008. *Email Hoaxes: Form, Function, Genre Ecology*. Amsterdam and Philadelphia: John Benjamins.

Hunston, Susan and Thompson, Geoff (eds). 2000. *Evaluation in Text: Authorial Stance and the Construction of Discourse*. Oxford: Oxford University Press.

Innis, Leslie B. and Feagin, Joe R. 1995. The Cosby Show: The view from the black middle class. *Journal of Black Studies, 25*: 6 (692–711).

Janoski-Haehlen, Emily M. 2011. The Courts are all a Twitter: The Implications of Social Media Use in the Courts, 46 Val. U. L. Rev. 43. Available at: http://scholar.valpo.edu/vulr/vol46/iss1/2 (last visited 04/10/2017).

Jhally, Sut, and Lewis, Justin. 1992. *Enlightened Racism: The Cosby Show, Audiences, and the Myth of the American Dream*. Boulder, CO: Westview Press.

Kollock, Peter and Smith, Marc A. (eds). 1999. *Communities in Cyberspace*. London and New York: Routledge.

Krabill, Ron. 2010. *Starring Mandela and Cosby: Media and the End(s) of Apartheid*. Chicago and London: University of Chicago Press.

Kress, Gunther and Van Leeuwen, Theo. 1996. *Reading Images: The Grammar of Visual Design*. London: Routledge.

Landsman, Stephan and Rakos, Richard F. 1994. A preliminary inquiry into the effect of potentially biasing information on judges and jurors in civil litigation. *Behavioral Sciences and the Law, 12* (113–126).

Martin, James R. and White, Peter R.R. 2005. *The Language of Evaluation: Appraisal in English*, Palgrave Macmillan: London and New York.

Mastro, Dana E. 2003. A social identity approach to understanding the impact of television messages. *Communication Monographs, 70*: 2 (98–113).

Mirabella, Julia G. 2012. Scales of justice: Assessing Italian criminal procedure through the Amanda Knox trial. *Boston University International Law Journal, 30*: 1 (230–262).

Partington, Alan. 2006. *The Linguistics of Laughter: A Corpus-Assisted Study of Laughter-Talk*. London and New York: Routledge.

Pizzi, William T. and Montagna, Mariangela. 2004. The Battle to Establish an Adversarial Trial System in Italy. *Michigan Journal of International Law*, 25: 2 (429–465).

Resta, Giorgio. 2009. *Trial by Media as a Legal Problem. A Comparative Analysis*. Naples: Editoriale Scientifica.

Schwartz, Seth J., Luyckx, Koen and Vignoles, Vivian L. (eds). 2011. *Handbook of Identity Theory and Research*. New York, Dordrecht, Heidelberg and London: Springer.

Slapper, Gary and Kelly, David. 2003. *The English Legal System*. London, Sydney and Oregon: Cavendish.

Sperber, Dan and Wilson, Deirdre. 1996. *Relevance, Communication and Cognition*. Oxford and Cambridge, Massachusetts: Blackwell.

Summers, Robert S. 1999. Formal legal truth and substantive truth in judicial fact-finding – their justified divergence in some particular cases. *Cornell Law Faculty Publications*, Paper *1186*.

Thayer, James B. 1898. *Preliminary Treatise on Evidence at the Common Law*. Boston: Little, Brown and Co.

Trew, Tony. 1979. Theory and ideology at work. In Fowler, Roger, Hodge, Bob, Kress, Gunther and Trew, Tony (eds) *Language and Control*. London: Routledge and Kegan Paul (94–116).

Turkle, Sherry. 2005. *The Second Self: Computers and the Human Spirit*. Cambridge, Massachusetts and London, England: MIT Press.

Vidmar, Neil. 2011. The psychology of trial judging. *Current Directions in Psychological Science*, 20: 1 (58–62).

Waters, Nicole, L. and Hannaford-Agor, Paola. 2017. Jurors 24/7: The impact of new media on jurors, public perceptions of the jury system, and the American criminal justice system (unpublished). Online at: http://www.ncsc-jurystudies.org/~/media/Microsites/Files/CJS/What%20We%20Do/Jurors_%2024-7_REV011512.ashx (last accessed 04/10/2017).

Widdicombe, Susan and Wooffitt, Robin. 1995. *The Language of Youth Subcultures: Social Identity in Action*. Hemel Hempstead: Harvester Wheatsheaf.

Wistrich, Andrew J., Guthrie, Chris and Rachlinski, Jeffrey J. 2005. Can judges ignore inadmissible information? The difficulty of deliberately disregarding. *University of Pennsylvania Law Review*, 153 (1251–1345).

Wodak, Ruth. 2001. The discourse-historical approach. In Wodak, R. and Meyer, M. (eds) *Methods of Critical Discourse Analysis*, London: Sage (63–95).

Wooffitt, Robin. 2005. *Conversation Analysis and Discourse Analysis: A Comparative and Critical Introduction*. London, Thousand Oaks California and New Delhi: Sage.

Wrightsman, Lawrence S. 2010. Persuasion in the decision making of U.S. Supreme Court Justices. In Klein, David and Mitchell, Gregory (eds) *The Psychology of Judicial Decision Making*. Oxford: Oxford University Press (57–73).

Zachara, Malgorzata. 2014. Private voices of public diplomacy: How digital technology shapes the image of states and societies. In Robson, Garry and Zachara, Malgorzata (eds) *Digital Diversities: Social Media and Intercultural Experience*. Newcastle: Cambridge Scholars Publishing (212–230).

3 Legally dead, illegally frozen? The legal aspects of cryonics as discursively constructed online by providers and the media

Kim Grego

Background

Cryonics is defined as

> The practice or technique of cryogenically preserving a person's body with the aim of reviving it in the future; esp. the cryogenic preservation of a person with an incurable disease until such time as a cure is found (first attested: 1966) (OED, s.v. CRYONICS).

As such, it is a practice that mixes viable existing technology, i.e. cryopreservation (as used for example to preserve tissue, organs, eggs, sperm, embryos, etc.) with currently unattainable objectives such as resuscitation from death. Its hybrid nature makes it scientifically questionable yet highly fascinating at a popular level. This is well reflected in the number of publications that have dealt with it since its inception, in the 1960s. *PubMed*, for instance, hosts 18 texts containing the search term 'cryonics,' published between 1979 and 2018. The *British Medical Journal* has six texts citing cryonics in its database dated between 1840 and 2018. *LexisNexis*, on the other hand, returns a list of 2666 newspaper articles containing the word 'cryonics' between 21 November 1971 and 12 September 2018. The popular interest in the possibility of 'living again' equals the indifference of the academic community toward it.

Currently, only five companies worldwide offer cryonics services: Alcor Life Extension (US), Cryonics Institute (US), KrioRus (Russia), Oregon Cryonics (US) and TransTime (US).[1] Of these, according to Cryonics Institute 2017, as of April 2017 Alcor Life Extension (Alcor) and Cryonics Institute (CI) take the lion's share, with 150 and 151 cryopreserved bodies respectively; TransTime only has three, while KrioRus caters for Eurasian clients, having 51 of them preserved on their premises. Oregon Cryonics (2017) declares it has 6 preserved patients.

What does the law say, then, about cryonics? Not much or, actually, close to nothing, if we consider the United States, where four out of five providers are based. Although discussions are taking place, at both the academic (e.g. Huxtable 2018) and the popular (e.g. Purtill 2017) levels, as to whether and how the practice should (or should not) be regulated, there is currently no comprehensive state or federal law concerning it. Oregon, a state that is particularly sensitive to end-of-life issues (it was the first to introduce physician-assisted suicide in its 1994 Death with Dignity Act), passed House Bill 3345 on nontransplant anatomical research recovery organizations (NARROs) in 2013. Oregon Cryonics says of itself that it

> is licensed through the State of Oregon as a Nontransplant Anatomical Research Recovery Organization (NARRO). This license allows us to make use of the Uniform Anatomical Gift Act (UAGA) to legally accept body and tissue donations.[2]

While the body is donated for free, the body preservation service is presented by the company as a separate service, for which the donor can be charged.

Incidentally, while the law in the US, where cryonics is mainly practiced, does not say much about how to regulate it, Canada's British Columbia is the only country to have an (anti-) cryonics law, dated 2004:

> Prohibition on sales, and offers of sale, of arrangements relating to cryonics and irradiation.

> 14 A person must not offer for sale, or sell, an arrangement for the preservation or storage of human remains that is based on cryonics.[3]

Although widely debated in popular sources, it appears little discussed (and mainly with suspicion) in academic contexts, including linguistics, where very little background literature on cryonics is currently to be found. Previous work by the author focused on the marketing aspects of cryonics popularization (Grego 2017).

Aims, methods and corpus

The research question aims at exploring how the legal aspects of cryonics are discursively constructed by cryonics services providers and by the media.

Two corpora have been assembled, one containing texts from the websites of cryonics services providers that deal with the legal aspects of the practice, and one of newspaper articles. The first corpus, Providers, was assembled manually. KrioRus's website is mostly in Russian, though the English version includes a FAQ page featuring two interesting sections: Legal and political aspects and Cultural aspects.[4] Unfortunately, these sections open up in pages entirely in Russian, so they could not be included in the corpus. TransTime's website is made up of six single-page sections in addition to the homepage, with very little information, which does not seem to have been updated since at least 2016. Since no specific legal information is provided, TransTime could not be considered either. As for Oregon Cryonics, it is a non-profit organization founded in

2005 that only recently (2016) started to offer cryopreservation services, though it does not offer full-body but head-only cryopreservation; for these reasons, it has also been excluded from the study for the moment. Cryonics Institute (CI) and Alcor Life Extension (ALE), on the contrary, report extensive legal information subdivided into various sections and subsections. A total of 16 texts dealing with legal aspects were thus collected from the CI website (tokens: 23,450; words: 20,278; normalized type/token ratio or NTTR: 86%), while 34 texts make up the ALE subcorpus (tokens: 80,203; words: 66,893; NTTR 83%) (see Primary sources in the References for the complete list of texts considered). The second corpus, News, was retrieved from *LexisNexis*, using CRYONICS AND LEGAL as search terms. It comprises 378 texts collected between 24 Jun. 1984 and 10 Apr. 2018[5]. The number of tokens is 335,046; words are 285,296; the NTTR is 85.15%.

Methodologically, while *SketchEngine* (Kilgarriff & Rychlý 2003) has been used for wordlist compilation and keyword extraction, this is intended as a short qualitative linguistic study interpreted from a Critical Discourse Analysis/Critical Discourse Studies perspective (Fairclough 1992, 2003, 2018; Wodak & Meyer 2001; Rajah 2018). This approach has been considered suitable for the purpose of this research, since CDA is defined as

> a form of practical argumentation: argumentation from a set of premises to a claim about what should be done. According to Fairclough and Fairclough (2012), the premises in practical argumentation are: a circumstantial premise which represents an *existing state* of affairs, a Goal premise which specifies an *alternative state* of affairs as goal on the basis of a Value premise (the values and concerns one is arguing from) and a Means-Goal premise which claims that the *advocated line of action* in the conclusion (or Claim) of the argument is a means of achieving the goal. The values and goals in CDA follow from its critical aims, including for instance the value of social justice and the goal of a *just society* (Fairclough 2018: 17 on dialectical reasoning, emphasis added).

Such a definition implies that ethical directions lie at the basis of this approach, which is oriented toward uncovering social injustice against a *status quo* that withholds information and rights from the people due to an imbalance in social power. While this is considered a fitting perspective to analyse such a debatable issue as cryonics, we will see below (Discussion and Conclusions) how providers of this service can make use of a discourse constructed using phrases and expressions that are very similar to those we can find in the above definition.

Results and discussion

The two corpora collected include texts dealing with a number of topical legal issues, including many concerning contracts and agreements and the sale of services for the preservation of corpses that are still, as seen, not or not entirely regulated by the law. Among these, fraud and the notion of (legal) death seemed two interesting themes to start with as a first approach to addressing the legal aspects of cryonics, if only because they are two issues frequently raised not only by critics of the practice but, as will be seen, by providers themselves. The following subsections, therefore, analyse how they are linguistically constructed in the Providers and News corpora, hoping to return relevant results for the purposes of the present investigation.

Cryonics is fraud

Understandably, one of the main points on which CI and ALE both insist is that cryonics – and the related services that they provide for money – is not fraud. It is thus not surprising that both companies should devote considerable space on their websites to argue against any accusations of the kind.

The Cryonics Institute subcorpus

CI does so in a specially dedicated subsection of its 'About cryonics' section, called 'Common myths about cryonics.' Myth number 10 is titled 'Cryonics is a scam or rip off.' CI chooses to create a contrast between the informal terms in the title ('scam' and 'rip off') and the image it creates using promotional strategies.

> CI is *non profit* and as such *its books are open to public scrutiny.* Our organization is run by and for our members. Our Board and officers provide their often expert services on a volunteer basis. *We do not make money from cryonics - and we don't want to. We want to improve the chances of revival for ourselves and our families.*

> The Cryonics Institute's mission is to keep patients in indefinite suspension until *science* can find a way to revive them, not to get rich. Our members and patients (including Robert Ettinger, the Father of Cryonics and members of his family) believe this will come to pass and that we will all get a second chance at life. However, *science currently does not have the means to revive these patients, which gives rise to the accusation this is all a scam or ripoff.* On the contrary, no one at CI profits from the organization or the members' dues. We have just two full-time employees and the rest of our Board of Directors and management team contribute their professional experience and time on a strictly volunteer basis. *Monies collected are used to maintain operations and keep our patients* in safe, stable and indefinite suspension until the time comes that they can be successfully revived. A bulk of those costs include the expense of liquid nitrogen, which needs to be replenished on a regular basis. Additionally, we keep our expenses *to a minimum in order to make cryostasis as affordable as possible* for our members and to maintain operations for as long into the future as it takes for successful revival.

As far as revival, our members and patients *are fully aware there is no absolute guarantee or conclusive proof that this grand experiment will work – yet.* This is what we are all counting on – that science will eventually find the means for revival and that we will all get a second chance at life.[6]

In the reply to the scam accusation, CI builds an image of itself, discursively and especially lexically as uninterested in money ('non profit'), and not actually carrying out work – which would involve an economic return – but acting on a free basis ('volunteer'), and fiscally transparent ('its books are open to public scrutiny'). To reinforce the concept, they clearly state that they 'do not make money from cryonics – and [...] don't want to,' and that any monies they collect is for maintenance and services only ('Monies collected are used to maintain operations and keep our patients'). And these expenses are even kept 'to a minimum in order to make cryostasis as affordable as possible,' so an almost missionary conduct is depicted here, with their final aim being 'to improve the chances of revival for ourselves and our families,' which implies that life is their ultimate goal – a hard to contest value in the Western world. On top of that, they specify that they want all this for themselves and their families, which also appeals to the traditional US value of individual freedom or 'modern individualism, which has its greatest manifestation in the American *right of privacy*' (Antelmi 2007: 111). The implication is that, even if they were doing something debatable, it would not affect anyone else except themselves and their dear ones. These are furthermore 'fully aware there is no absolute guarantee or conclusive proof that this grand experiment will work – yet,' so they are acting consciously and, supposedly, willingly. Two more words contribute to shaping their discursive construction: the evaluative adjective 'grand,' projecting an ambitious and visionary aura on cryonics practitioners as pioneers of science, and the adverb 'yet,' which very simply but also quite effectively limits the inconclusive proof existing so far to a matter of time – how much, they do not say. So where does the doubt that cryonics might be fraud come from? According to how CI builds its argument linguistically, it comes from science ('science currently does not have the means to revive these patients, which gives rise to the accusation this is all a scam or ripoff'), a grammatical subject representing a vague abstract notion (that of the scientific community in general), which is failing those who believe in revival by not having found a means to realize it yet. It is this, their failure ('which'), that 'gives rise' to the accusation that cryonicists are scammers. That very science, guilty of showing them in a bad light, is also twice more called into question in this short text as being charged with making sure that cryopreserved people can live again ('until science can find a way to revive them,' 'science will eventually find the means for revival'). A final note should regard the use of the term 'revival,' which is preferred by CI to its synonym 'resuscitation.' By making careful linguistic choices as such, CI shapes a discourse revolving entirely around life, since 'revival' etymologically points to living again, as opposed to 'resuscitation,' which casts the shadow of coming back from death. Death is indeed never mentioned; 'suspension' is the word chosen for cryopreserved corpses, which are in turn never called such, but always referred to as either 'people' or 'patients,' i.e. terms usually applied to the living.

The Alcor Life Extension subcorpus

ALE too openly deals with the same issue in its 'About Cryonics' section, under a subsection titled 'Cryonics Myths.' Contrarily to CI, they address it immediately, as their number-one myth to debunk:

> Myth 1: Cryonics is *consumer fraud.*
> By definition, fraud involves *deception* for *financial* gain. This myth fails on both counts.
>
> First, cryonics is not based on deception. To the contrary, it is both *scientifically credible* (see the Scientists' Open Letter on Cryonics) and supported by the extant scientific literature (see PubMed for a list of some published journal articles on cryonics). *There are no known credible technical arguments that lead one to conclude that cryonics, carried out under good conditions today, would not work.*
>
> Second, cryonicists are *not motivated by financial gain.* The history of cryonics is full of individuals who made great sacrifices for the benefit of cryonics, and (so far) bereft of people enriched by it. Alcor has no company owners to profit from cryonics, salaries are modest, and the Board of Directors serves *without pay.* Cryonics *is known for* consuming the time and resources of its supporters rather than enriching them.
>
> The *reality* is that Alcor is run by people who think cryonics can *save lives* and who want cryonics available for themselves, their friends, their loved ones, and the world in general.[7]

Similarities with the CI's text are numerous. The same image of cryonicists as selfless and uninterested in money – 'Cryonics is known for consuming the time and resources of its supporters rather than enriching them' – is also constructed by ALE. In line with their preference for more formal terms, they define themselves as 'not motivated by financial gain.' Just like CI, though, they go as far as to make missionaries out of cryonics supporters, 'who made great sacrifices for the benefit of cryonics, and (so far) bereft of people enriched.' Corporate-wise, the discursive construction is made along similar lines, with Alcor having 'no company owners to profit from cryonics,' 'modest' salaries and an unpaid Board of Directors. The US cultural factor, here, could be represented by the hint at the superhero-like nature of cryonicists using juxtaposed expressions like 'The reality is' and 'can save lives [...] themselves, their friends, their loved ones, and the world in general' in the same sentence: they stand accused of fraud, they are actually heroes. Again, a discourse of life is carefully put together that never mentions death but only life, and only in terms of saving it.

Unlike CI, however, a culprit for the alleged fraud accusations is not identified, as they prefer to oppose these accusations argumentatively, as in a real trial. Indeed, differently from CI, ALE's approach employs the use of (pseudo) legal language, starting from their preference for the term 'consumer fraud' in the description of the myth. Other specialized terminology employed, providing an overall more formal tone to this text with respect to the CI one, includes 'deception,' 'financial gain,' 'extant scientific literature.' In fact, the argument that ALE puts forth in its defence is different from CI's in two ways. Firstly, as it is entirely based on a definition ('By definition, fraud involves deception for financial gain'), it relies heavily on the linguistic definitory strategy often employed in legal discourse to clarify terms and concepts for laypeople, but definitions always carry ideological implications and thus reveal the author's stance (Antelmi 2007). Secondly, when it states that 'There are no known credible technical arguments that lead one to conclude that cryonics, carried out under good conditions today, would not work,' it adopts the rhetorically means of the argument from ignorance (Jäger 2001: 55), or

> appeal to ignorance. Sometimes it is also called lack-of-knowledge inference, negative evidence or negative proof. [...] It is based on ignorance, or so-called negative evidence.
>
> (Walton 1995: 1)

As such, ALE's argument also violates van Eemeren and Grootendorst (1987: 285)'s dialectical rule II ('Whoever advances a standpoint is obliged to defend it if asked to do so').

The News corpus

The expectation was that the possibility of cryonics being a fraud would be widely discussed in the media as a kind of ethical debate that might potentially apply and thus be of interest to a large number of people. In fact, a study of the corpus of newspapers collected for this research revealed a slightly different situation. The word SCAM only appears once in the News corpus, namely in an article in the Irish edition of *The Sun* of 21 November 2016:

> The Catholic added: 'I don't believe cryonics is against God's will. People think we're a *scam* but that's just not true. We don't make any money.'
>
> (Beal 2016: 19, emphasis added)

The informal term cannot be said to be used in connection with cryonics in the press, since even its single appearance in the *The Sun*, possibly the most popular British tabloid, only features in direct reported speech. The issue of the legality of cryonics in fact does emerge in the corpus, but mainly in connection with other

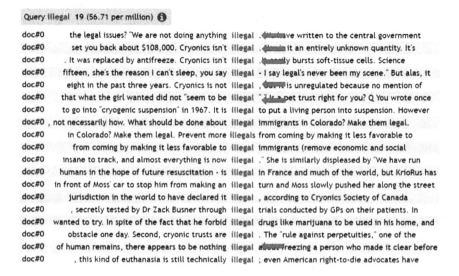

Figure 3.1 Concordances of ILLEGAL in News corpus

more neutral terms such as FRAUD and ILLEGAL. Numbers, though, do not show a quantitative concern with the (il)legal aspects of cryonics, as FRAUD* and ILLEGAL only appear 19 times each. Qualitative scrutiny, furthermore, confirms that, for example, out of the 19 times ILLEGAL occurs in the corpus, six times it was used in connection with a negation or a negative word, resulting in expressions having the meaning of 'not illegal' (Figure 3.1).

The legal aspects revolving around cryonics also emerge from the frequency, this time quite high, of the word LEGAL (f.: 460). They seem to regard specific cases, though, and not the legality of cryonics in itself, which could be expected since, as seen in the Background section above, the practice is far from regulated. A *SketchEngine* word sketch of the term shows that the nouns most frequently right-collocating with it are '(LEGAL) BATTLE' (f.: 48), '(LEGAL) ACTION' (f.: 19) and '(LEGAL) DEATH' (f.: 20). While the first two collocations confirm that specific lawsuits make the news as they arise due to the lack of cryonics laws, the third collocation, 'LEGAL DEATH' emerges as particularly interesting because it both isolates one of the main focal points in such law cases (i.e. when is a person allowed to be cryopreserved?), and the underlying legal, ethical, religious and ultimately philosophical concept behind it, i.e. what death is and what kind of death cryonics considers.

Cryonics between life and life

Because DEATH was also a word carefully avoided by providers in the previous sections on fraud accusations, it appeared especially interesting as the other theme to analyse in this study.

The Providers corpus

Since it seemed that, when dealing with the accusation of fraud, cryonics providers do not like to refer to the concept of death, it was expected that in the rest of the corpus they would not insist on it either. Indeed, DEATH* is not a very popular word in the CI subcorpus, with only 41 occurrences, or 1748.40 frequency per million (FPM), as expected. Similarly, although the ALE collection includes a larger number of texts (34), death is also not very frequent (f.: 220 or 2743.03 FPM). What is interesting, though, is that in both subcorpora its most recurrent modifier is LEGAL, as in LEGAL DEATH, which is also the first multi-word key term (in CI, f.: 8, 341.15 FPM; in ALE: f.: 83, 1034.87). This possibly means that, whenever they have to deal with death, providers do so from the legal point of view. In other words, the implication could be that, no matter how much cryonics providers prefer to avoid discussing death when marketing their services to their public, they are nonetheless compelled to do so at least in one case, i.e. where the law is concerned. As a result, their marketing dilemma is that, since they do not consider death a permanent state, they do not like to mention it, but they cannot start providing their services *legally* until it occurs. Hence the necessity of mentioning it at least in legal terms, i.e. as in the phrase LEGAL DEATH. The presence of this term seems to serve two purposes: on the one hand, it is used in a specialized way, for example in contracts and in agreements to correctly protect both customers and themselves from incurring in illegal practices or situations. On the other, it contributes to shaping their discourse on cryonics, since providers only use it as a specialized term and in specialized contexts, in this way setting it apart from their usual discursive construction of 'no real death,' and making it stand out as a bureaucratic requirement, an annoying necessity, a mere formality to go through beforehand in order to access the promising developments that may occur by choosing cryonics. Being dead according to the existing law is therefore a requirement that, although unwillingly or disagreeing with the concept in theory, cryonics providers still need to abide by before fulfilling their obligations to their end users. Nevertheless, legal death, in spite of its being a legal issue, is usually established not by a lawyer but by a doctor. Not surprisingly, then, the second most frequent modifier of DEATH in the Providers corpus is CLINICAL, as in CLINICAL DEATH (in CI, f.: 3 or 127.93 FPM; in ALE: f.: 8, 99.75 FPM), a definition more often associated with a medical understanding of death, which tends to correspond to its legal counterpart, though not in all cases. The distinction between the concepts of legal and clinical death is indeed complex and still debated by the academic community itself: 'although brain death is nowadays widely accepted as a criterion for death, there is no global consensus on the definition and diagnostic criteria of brain death' (Ettema 2016: 399). In times of scientific advances and innovative medical technologies, it is then constantly being renegotiated, often ending up in courts when existing laws still do not cater for such novel situations.[8] What is confirmed is that, in the Providers corpus, DEATH as a term shows very few occurrences for companies that deal with corpses. One would expect that, if death as a word and as a subject is avoided, the discourse would revolve around life. Looking at its counterpart, however, it is clear that that is not the case. The term LIFE is even less frequent (in CI, f.: 28 or 1194.02 FPM; in ALE, f.: 126 or 1571.01 FPM). The lower frequency in ALE is made even lower by the fact that in this case the word life is contained in the name of the company, ALCOR LIFE EXTENSION FOUNDATION, which occurs 31 times (386.52 FPM). The scarcity of LIFE is surprising, as it contradicts the results from a previous study by the author on the marketing of cryonics (Grego 2017), which showed that indeed life is a central theme in cryonics promotion. However, when considering that these texts were collected from a legal – and not a marketing – perspective, the quantitative limit makes more sense. A qualitative review shows that the most frequent collocates of LIFE are INSURANCE and POLICY, as in LIFE INSURANCE (in CI, f.: 4 or 170.58 FPM; in ALE, f.: 22 or 274.30 FPM) and LIFE INSURANCE POLICY in the CI subcorpus (f.: 6 or 255.86 FPM) and in the ALE subcorpus (f.: 9 or 112.22 FPM): when mentioning life, cryonics providers are not promoting themselves, but merely adding technical information to their legal documents about a possible way of paying for their services. Overall, life and death, in this subcorpus, seem relegated to a specialized legal usage, and assigned the status of minor technicalities.

The News corpus

The corpus of news was expected to be more emphatic in its tones, in line with its popular nature. Despite its containing texts from tabloids as well as quality newspapers, though, rather than emphasis what it seemed to show is wonder at cryonics and its alleged possibilities. Death is not insisted upon: the lemma DEATH* is found 708 times (2113.14 FPM) in the corpus, so with a frequency strikingly similar to that of the Providers corpus. When it comes to the legal notion of death, however, the frequency of LEGAL DEATH drops to 20 occurrences or 59.69 FPM: about one sixth of CI (341.15 FPM) and one seventeenth of ALE (1034.87 FPM). The quantitative datum appears understandable, given that most of the legal documents in the Providers corpus are agreements and contracts, thus very specialized texts. The debated correspondence or difference between legal and clinical death is only mentioned in passing in News, but is not, quantitatively speaking, at the core of it: CLINICAL DEATH only features nine times (26.86 FPM), while the more specific medical definition BRAIN DEATH also appears, with a frequency of six times or 17.91 FPM. Interestingly, the latter is even premodified by LEGAL, in what is perhaps a novel collocation (see Figure 3.2), revealing a novel definition: 'As death is now defined legally as brain death' (Ho 2002).

One difference with the Providers corpus lies, instead, in the juxtaposition of the concepts of life and death. As a collocation, LIFE AND DEATH occurs 15 times (44.77 FPM) in the news articles, so very sparsely, but never occurs in Providers, where the only and/or-collocate of LIFE is HEALTH (as in LIFE AND HEALTH),

Query 6 (17.91 per million) ⓘ

doc#0   and the heartbeat stop, followed by *brain* death when electrical activity in the brain ceases.

doc#0   activity in the brain ceases. Only after *brain* death has transpired does cellular death, when all

doc#0 , ensue. As death is now defined legally as *brain* death , cryopreservation can be started before

doc#0   of cryonics say waiting for legal *brain* death harms the patient's chances of a successful

doc#0   experts claim that waiting for legal *brain* death hurts patients' chances of a successful "

doc#0   definition of death from heart failure to *brain* death . Attempts to preserve heads with machines

Figure 3.2 BRAIN DEATH in News corpus

appearing 8 times (99.75 FPM) and in the ALE subcorpus only, again evidencing that providers wish to avoid mentioning death and certainly not in conjunction with life, their ultimate aim.

Talking about LIFE*, this is about twice as more frequent in News (f.: 874 or 2608.59 FPM) than it is in both the Providers subcorpora (in CI, f.: 28 or 1194.02; in ALE, f.: 126 or 1571.01 FPM), again with the specification that 108 of the 874 occurrences (322.34 FPM) in News feature in the provider's name ALCOR LIFE EXTENSION FOUNDATION, only slightly less than in ALE's own subcorpus. Life is therefore what the newspaper texts focus on and, while they are not so emphatic as expected, popular sources are understandably more concerned with raising hope of life after death in their readers, with what sounds like a newsworthy enough topic (Galtung and Ruge 1973). Differently from the Providers corpus, even if the News corpus too was collected aiming to include the legal perspective (see Aims, methods and corpus above), the collocates of LIFE return a different picture. No longer associated with insurances or policies, in News, LIFE appears in collocations such as HUMAN LIFE* (f.: 17 or 50.74 FPM), ETERNAL LIFE (f.: 15 or 44.77 FPM), EXTEND* LIFE* (f.: 12 or 35.82 FPM) or 'LONG LIFE' (f.: 5 or 14.92 FPM), where the interest is clearly directed at the possibilities inherent in cryonics and not at how to finance them. In particular, HUMAN LIFE* and EXTEND* LIFE* are employed when discussing science/technology, LONG LIFE in medical contexts, and ETERNAL LIFE if ethical, philosophical or religious considerations are made. Quantitatively, the collocations of LIFE dealing with the technological aspect of cryonics are the most numerous, and this is confirmed by the first multi-word key term in the News corpus being LIQUID NITROGEN (f.: 174 or 519.33 FPM): people want to know – or newspapers think they want to know – the 'how do they do it?' behind cryonics. Thus, semantically, life in this corpus appears connected with a sense of wonder at the possibilities of technology.

Discussion and conclusions

This short investigation aimed to uncover how the legal aspects of cryonics are discursively constructed by cryonics service providers and by the media. To do so, two specific themes were selected for analysis that seemed fundamental when beginning to address the legal aspects of cryonics, and strictly interconnected: the notions of fraud and of (legal) death. While fraud was discussed first, it soon became clear that it cannot be thoroughly addressed without (linguistically) going through death first. This is because cryonics providers do not sell anything different from a form of corpse preservation, similar to embalmment. In fact, some providers do not actually 'sell' anything, but provide a service for free and the money they receive from their end users goes towards maintenance (materials, power, venue, etc.). From a legal point of view, then, although the practice may be very much under regulated, there would seem to be no question of their performing illegal acts, as evidenced above in *Cryonics is fraud* – The News corpus when discussing ILLEGAL.

Most legal disputes on cryonics have in fact been raised over contractual matters, and not between the providers and the end users (of course or, perhaps, not yet), but between the former and the families or heirs or legal representatives of the latter. Indeed, many of the cases in question are reported by CI and ALE themselves in their websites, especially those in which they won (e.g. see ALE's 'Alcor's Legal Battles' section[9]). Other concerns on the legitimacy (but not necessarily on the legality) of cryonics have regarded the way providers promote it, i.e. by possibly instilling a false hope in resurrection that is not based on currently viable science. However, '[i]f a critical conception of 'law,' coupled with a CDS approach, expands the borders of what we perceive as legal discourse, then discourses that engage with questions of *legitimacy* might also be regarded as inherently *legal* in nature (Rajah 2018: 484, emphasis added).' This is the reason, for example, behind the British Columbia anti-cryonics law of 2004, prohibiting the 'sale' or even the 'offer for sale,' which evokes the idea of soliciting, of corpse preservation through cryonics – yet not its sheer practice. A further type of preoccupation lies in the practices usually performed very swiftly by cryonics providers near and/or immediately after death, aimed at the best preservation of the corpse in the time elapsing before its cryogenic storage – a period when time is of essence but also when legal disputes with families tend to arise, jeopardizing the chances of good preservation (and thus of possible resuscitation). In extreme scenarios, even the 'preventive' termination of life in ideal conditions is envisaged in order to guarantee the best options of cryopreservation (cf. Minerva and Sandberg 2017) – only, under many legislations in many countries, said preventive termination of life is still considered to be murder, and carries a sentence. The marketing of cryonics and its step-by-step procedures are two issues that would definitely be worth further investigation from the legal viewpoint. They, too, however, rely on and revolve around the notion of legal death, which thus appears as the central node to most cryonics-related issues.

Turning to this, previous research (Grego 2017) on the scientific dissemination of cryonics observed that cryonics discourse, although about (supposedly restoring) life, presupposes a notion of death, but this is ideologically framed, socially constructed and constantly renegotiated (Fairclough 1992, 2003, 2018;

Wodak & Meyers 2001) as civilizations and their technologies evolve. It is then configured as potentially misleading and, therefore, raises an underlying ethical debate. If this is the case, it means that power relations are involved, expressed in ways in which the strong actors tend to oppress (in this case maybe just mislead) the weak ones and, when misleading discourse occurs, Critical Discourse Studies can certainly provide support in addressing it.

In particular, the notion of death as a mere technicality – they call it 'legal' or 'clinical death' as if it were a minor bureaucratic obstacle to non-death or eternal life – conveyed by providers is skilfully constructed as a fight against a ruling hegemonic position held and maintained by mainstream authority, i.e. those who believe that legal death is the end of it all. In this fight, the cryonics companies paint themselves in the eyes of their potential customers as those whose mission (metaphorically but also literally, in corporate terms) is to challenge this hegemonic power relation in the name of (individual) freedom of thought and action: they might have a key to an opportunity that is being kept from the people, and they are willing to give it to them. In so doing, however, cryonics providers use a discursive construction that is surprisingly not dissimilar from the underlying aim of Critical Discourse Analysis as defined, for example, by Fairclough (2018: 17) and reported in Background above: *legal* death represents 'an existing state of affairs'; cryonicists present and offer 'an alternative state of affairs,' in the name of 'social justice' with 'the goal of a just society.' What, then, is the difference between the scope of cryonicists and that of critical discourse analysts? Are cryonicists not doing exactly the kind of uncovering of social injustice that critical discourse analysts do? The possible difference could emerge when considering that CDA relies on a

> Value premise (the values and concerns one is arguing from) and a Means-Goal premise which claims that the advocated line of action in the conclusion (or Claim) of the argument is a means of achieving the goal.
>
> (ibid.)

In the legal discourse of cryonics as it emerges from its providers' texts (but not from the media), neither premise is satisfactorily met. Firstly, because the values and concerns cryonicists are arguing from may not be so ethical as in CDA, if they are moved by the intent of financial gain, which they claim is not the case, but has been the subject of several lawsuits against them.[10] Secondly, the argument they put forward to achieve their Means-Goal, is definitely flawed according to the rules of dialectic, since it is an argument from ignorance which, as seen above in *Cryonics is fraud* – The Alcor Life Extension subcorpus, ultimately falls among those 'arguments from negative evidence [...] often [...] mistrusted, and assigned a second-class status in logic' (Walton 1995: 2). In other words, if we move from Richard Weaver's (1953: 15) definition of rhetoric as complementary to dialectic, or 'truth plus its artful presentation,' then the discourse of cryonicists mimics CDA frames but, when observed in detail with CDA instruments, it runs the risk of emerging not as dialectic but as rhetorical, i.e. to be more artful presentation than truth.

Notes

1 A fifth company is expected to open in New South Wales, Australia, in 2019 (Southern Cryonics 2018).
2 About Oregon Cryonics, www.oregoncryo.com/aboutOC.html.
3 Cremation, Interment and Funeral Services Act, Statute of British Columbia of 13 May 2004, Chapter 35, Part 3, Article14.
4 KrioRus, FAQ, http://kriorus.ru/en/faq.
5 Of these, 58 deal with the case of J.S., a 14-year-old British girl who died on 17 October 2016 and asked to be cryopreserved; as the case involved parental permission and ended up in court, it was widely reported by the media.
6 About Cryonics, Common myths about cryonics, www.cryonics.org/about-us/myths/ (emphasis added).
7 About Cryonics, Cryonics myths, https://alcor.org/cryomyths.html#myth1 (emphasis added).
8 World-famous cases include those of Terry Schiavo (d. 2005) in the US, Piergiorgio Welby (d. 2006) in Italy and, lately, an anonymous minor (d. 2016), the first under-age person to be granted the right to die on request in Belgium under a recent update to its legislation.
9 'Alcor's Legal Battles,' https://alcor.org/Library/html/legalbattles.html.
10 The cases the providers report are essentially those they have won, but cf. Burton 2018 for one of the latest lawsuits brought against ALE for preserving only the head and not the entire body of a customer.

References

Primary sources

Cryonics Institute

1 A Guide to Cryopreservation Contracts
2 Advance Directives
3 Articles of Incorporation
4 Authorization by Children
5 Authorization by Parents
6 Avoiding Autopsy for Cryonics
7 By-Laws of the Cryonics Institute
8 Certificate of Religious Belief and Religious Objection to Autopsy
9 CI Membership Worldwide
10 Common Myths about Cryonics
11 Cryonic Storage Agreement - MEMBER
12 Cryonic Storage Agreement - NON MEMBER
13 Cryonic_Suspension_Agreement
14 Emergency Situations
15 MEMBERSHIP_Annual
16 MEMBERSHIP_Lifetime

Alcor Life Extension

1 Alcor Trust Main Agreement
2 Alcor Trust Funding Agreement

References from the News corpus

Beal, James. 2016. Frozen in a vat with five others. *The Sun*. Irish edition. 21 November: (19).
Ho, Andy. 2002. Keeping the dead 'alive' – legislation needed here. *The Straits Times*. Analysis section. 26 March.

General references

Antelmi, Donella. 2007. Manifest ideology and hidden ideology in legal language: Definitions and terms. In Garzone, Giuliana and Sarangi, Srikant (eds). *Discourse, Ideology and Specialized Communication*, Bern: Peter Lang (101–117).
Burton, Lucy. 2018. Cryogenics firm sued for freezing man's head instead of whole body. *The Telegraph*, 9 September. www.telegraph.co.uk/business/2018/09/09/cryogenics-firm-sued-freezing-mans-head-instead-whole-body/.

Cryonics Institute. 2017. *The CI Advantage*. http://www.cryonics.org/the-ci-advantage/.

Ettema, Erik. 2016. Brain death. In ten Have, Henk (ed.). *Encyclopedia of Global Bioethics*. Dordrecht: Springer (1–10).

Fairclough, Norman. 1992. *Discourse and Social Change*. Cambridge: Polity.

Fairclough, Norman. 2003. *Analysing Discourse: Textual Analysis for Social Research*. London: Routledge.

Fairclough, Norman. 2018. CDA as dialectical reasoning. In Flowerdew, John and Richardson, John E. (eds). *The Routledge Handbook of Critical Discourse Studies*. London and New York: Routledge.

Galtung, Johan and Ruge, Mari. 1973. Structuring and selecting news. In Cohen, Stanley and Young, Jock (eds). *The Manufacture of News: Deviance, Social Problems and the Mass Media*. London: Constable (62–73).

Grego, Kim. 2017. *Marketing life after death: Cryopreservation in the hope of resuscitation*. Paper presented at XXVIII AIA Conference, Worlds of Words: Complexity, Creativity, and Conventionality in English Language, Literature and Culture. University of Pisa, Pisa, 14–16 September 2017.

Huxtable, Richard. 2018. Cryonics in the Courtroom: Which interests? Whose interests? *Medical Law Review 26(3)*: 476–499.

Jäger, Siegried. 2001. Discourse and knowledge: Theoretical and methodological aspects of a critical discourse and dispositive analysis. In Wodak, Ruth and Meyer, Michael (eds). *Methods of Critical Discourse Analysis*. London: Sage (32–62).

Kilgarriff, Adam and Rychlý, Pavel. 2003. *SketchEngine*. Brighton: Lexical Computing.

Minerva, Francesca and Sandberg, Anders. 2017. Euthanasia and cryothanasia. *Bioethics 31*: 526–533.

Oregon Cryonics. 2017. Cases. www.oregoncryo.com/caseReports.html.

Oxford English Dictionary online. 2011. 3rd edition.

Purtill, Corinne. 2017. Inside the highly experimental, loosely regulated world of for-profit body donation. *Quartz*. 21 February. https://qz.com/914490/theres-a-completely-legal-reason-this-american-dentist-has-an-office-full-of-human-heads/.

Rajah, Jothie. 2018. Legal discourse. In Flowerdew, John and Richardson, John E. (eds), *The Routledge Handbook of Critical Discourse Studies*. London and New York: Routledge.

Southern Cryonics. 2018. *Homepage*. https://southerncryonics.com/.

van Eemeren, Frans and Grootendorst, Rob. 1987. Fallacies in Pragma-Dia-lectical Perspective. *Argumentation 1*: 283–301.

Walton, Douglas. 1996. *Arguments from ignorance*. University Park PA: Pennsylvania State University Press.

Weaver, Richard. 1953. The Phaedrus and the nature of rhetoric. In Weaver, Richard (ed.). *The Ethics of Rhetoric*. Chicago: Henry Regnery (3–26).

Wodak, Ruth and Meyer, Michael (eds). 2001. *Methods of Critical Discourse Analysis*. London: Sage.

4 The fuzzy line between media and judicial discourse

Insights from the Pinto-López Madrid Case

Gianluca Pontrandolfo

Introduction

Lawyers, judges, courts and legal institutions in general are increasingly represented by mainstream media and are often depicted through conventional representations, which are part of the symbolic repertoire used by media producers and available to consumers, often influencing the ways legal actors are shown and perceived by audiences. These models or stereotypes colour the way that representatives of the legal profession are depicted in the media, and influence the way in which issues involving them are framed (Robson 2007). Legal and judicial cases reported in the media generally follow a script, in that specific and 'traditional' roles are assigned to participants, thus influencing or distorting the information conveyed to the audience. In addition to these stereotypical representations, which are determined by the cultural environment of the countries concerned, there is nowadays a growing tendency towards the mediatization of justice: judicial cases receive huge media attention and become the object of massive public interest or even social campaigns.

As Boyd demonstrated in the analysis of the controversial judicial case involving Amanda Knox in Italy (2013, 2016), a further level of distortion and misrepresentation of the judicial world take place in media representation. This is due to an inner discursive incompatibility between the technical language and rational argumentation of the law, and the common-sense, emotive discourse of the media, especially in countries where such cases are not handled by specialized journalists with a legal background (Portier Duparc and Pech, 2007; Carretero González and Úlcar Ventura, 2011; see also Breeze, Gotti and Sancho Guinda, 2014). The clash between the technical issues of the legal sphere and the emotional and sensationalist aspects of the media produces an interesting discursive intersection, which has been scarcely investigated in the literature (see Bhatia and Bhatia 2017: 33–34).

The present chapter aims at exploring the multifaceted relationship between law, language and the media through the lens of a Spanish judicial case. The focus relies on the media depiction of the 'characters' of a prototypical case with a view to studying how identity – understood here both as the personal and social role played by each social actor in the case – and ideology (Fairclough 2013: 56–68) – strictly connected with the notion of power and manipulation (see Orts Llopis, Breeze and Gotti, 2017) – interact with the legal/judicial environment.

The results of the corpus-based analysis conducted in the study will shed light on the reasons why the case under investigation has attracted media attention and contribute to providing a picture of how lawyers, judges, prosecutors and defendants are portrayed in the press. As will be demonstrated in the analysis, cultural representations and non-legal factors (such as gender) do play a role in shaping and perpetuating our view of the world.

The story

Mr. Javier López Madrid is a rich and famous man of Spanish society, president of the OHL and friend to Felipe, King of Spain. Ms. Elisa Pinto is a renowned dermatologist.

The case starts in 2012 when Dr. Pinto (43 years old) becomes the dermatologist of the López Madrid family (Javier is 47) and they have an affair.

In 2013, they both start to be threatened by telephone calls: she is accused of being unfaithful and of harassing him; on his part, he also receives calls in which he is insulted for being unfaithful to his wife and to his daughter. Mr. Pepe Villarejo, a police inspector, lawyer, businessman, is hired as private detective to avoid an 'explosion' of the case.

On December 2013, someone buys a telephone card supposedly belonging to Mr. López Madrid and starts to violently insult the dermatologist. Dr. Pinto reports the case to the police, stating that she is being threatened (murder threats, harassment, stabbing) and she hires private security. At the same time, he reports her to the police, claiming that she is insane and he is living in a horror movie.

Two paradoxically opposite judicial proceedings are held: one in the *Juzgado 39 de Instrucción de Madrid* for the harassment and aggressions allegedly inflicted on Elisa Pinto by Javier López Madrid; the other in the *Juzgado 26 de Instrucción de Madrid* dealing with the alleged harassment and threats made by Elisa Pinto against Javier López Madrid and his environment. Evidence is brought before the Court: Dr. Pinto brings SMS, pictures, audio recordings, gifts, whereas Mr. López Madrid shows 52 emails.

In April 2014, the *Guardia Civil* and the *EMUME* (the service of assistance to women and minors) carry out a series of investigations, which lead to the accusation of Dr. Elisa Pinto as it appears that the telephone calls received by Mr. López Madrid were made by her. In July 2015, additional investigations by the police obtain the same results: evidence leads to her. Dr. Pinto's thesis is that the police (although the case has been investigated by the Guardia Civil) is protecting Mr. Pepe Villarejo and she also accuses him of being her aggressor.

In the meantime, the case is gaining increasing media attention: Alejandra, the daughter of Dr. Pinto's mentor (Mr. Joaquín Soto Melo), declares that Pinto also had an affair with her father so the scandal begins to circulate.

In 2016, the judge Mrs. Belen Sánchez (*Juzgado 39*) files the case on the basis that Dr. Pinto's declarations are unreliable whereas in the *Juzgado 26* the case is still open.

On October 2017, the *Audiencia Provincial* of Madrid, with an appeal function, suspects elements of criminal offence: the hard disks of both Dr. Pinto and Mr. López Madrid are analysed. Messages from Queen Letizia of Spain are found in Mr. López Madrid's hard disk, which is a further ingredient for the mediatization of the case.

The judicial case is still open and has inevitably attracted media attention. *En el thriller de la doctora Pinto y López Madrid nada es lo que parece* [In the thriller of Dr. Pinto and Mr. López Madrid nothing is what it seems] is the title of one of the articles[1] analysed in this chapter, stressing the fact that this judicial case is full of half-truths and lies. The following sections investigate the case from a discursive, corpus-based perspective.

The study

The Pinto-López Madrid case has all the ideal ingredients of a perfect informative cocktail: sex, money, power and the media and Crown 'sewers,' confirmed by the fact that the scandal overwhelmed the Spanish social press.[2]

The chapter aims to explore the multifaceted relationship between law, language, power and media by means of an investigation of the communicative and rhetorical strategies used by the media to represent the social actors of the judicial case.

Research questions, hypothesis and expected results

A number of interconnected research questions guide the study:

1 How is the judicial case portrayed in the media?
2 How is the dichotomy Pinto vs. López Madrid (man vs. woman) portrayed in the press? Are there gendered representations?
3 How are law and the judicial world represented in the media?

The main hypothesis sustaining the study is that, in line with van Leeuwen (2008), the discursive strategies[3] deployed in representing social actors underlie ideological frameworks and these representations influence future social actions and interactions (see Breeze 2018) with the media having a key role in this process (Fairclough 2003, Wodak 2015).

In terms of expected results, a negative representation of López Madrid – by means of a set of negative attributes and associations – is expected to be found as a strategy aimed at reinforcing the process of alignment against him in the texts/ society. Moreover, the sensionalistic[4] discourses of the tabloid press (Conboy 2006, Johansson 2008) will have a powerful persuasive effect on the newspapers' readers (more generally on Spanish society). The details of the story will be used by the media to undermine readers' sympathy for López Madrid and to take sides with Dr. Pinto, also in line with the media and the public emphatic reaction supporting a member of a 'disadvantaged group,' i.e. a woman (see Monzó-Nebot 2017).

Material and methodology

In order to test the hypothesis, a small monolingual corpus of Spanish newspapers articles dealing with the case has been compiled. Texts do not belong exclusively to the traditional press (*El País, El Mundo, La Vanguardia, ABC*) but also – and more interestingly – to magazines and other press sources specialized in gossip, often labelled as 'tabloids' (*El Confidencial, Vanity Fair.es, 20 minutos, Hola, El español*).

The articles' selection has been carried out by searching some keywords or seeds (such as 'El País' + 'López" 'Pinto") on the newspapers' webpages. The composition is described in Table 4.1.

As far as the methodology is concerned, a combination of quantitative and qualitative analysis, as well as corpus-based and -driven tests, has been considered as an adequate strategy to investigate a number of discursive features, selected for offering interesting insights into the research. The method of analysis, which triangulates different approaches (Marchi and Taylor 2018: 6–8), falls within Corpus-Assisted Discourse Studies (CADS, see Partington et al. 2013) in that, apart from wordlists and concordancing, intuitions for research also arise from reading the actual parts of the data set in their wider and complex contexts of production.

Keyness analysis, which has been the first step of an exploratory discourse approach to the corpus (see Gabrielatos 2018), has been carried out comparing the wordlist of the Pinto López corpus with that of a reference corpus containing general articles extracted from *El País* (66 texts extracted in 2014 totalling 282,696 tokens).

Analysis has been performed by means of WordSmith Tools (v. 5.0, Scott 2008).

Results

The research started with an exploratory (corpus-driven) approach by means of a keyword analysis – that is to say, checking for words which occur with unusual frequency in the corpus (see Scott 1997: 236, Gabrielatos 2018: 225) – and then

Table 4.1 Composition of the Pinto López Madrid corpus

	EP-EM-LV-ABC (traditional press)	EC-VF-20m-H-Esp (popular/tabloid press)
txt	20	14
tokens	18,294	18,878
tot	37,172	

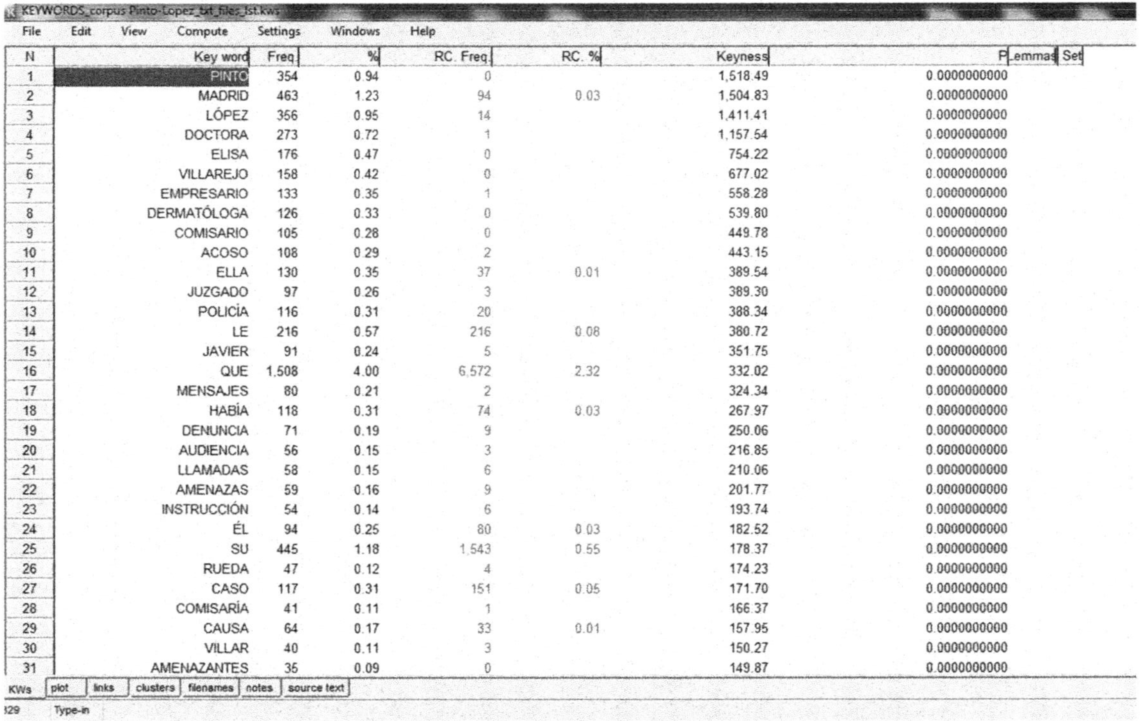

N	Key word	Freq.	%	RC. Freq.	RC. %	Keyness	P	Lemmas	Set
1	PINTO	354	0.94	0		1,518.49	0.0000000000		
2	MADRID	463	1.23	94	0.03	1,504.83	0.0000000000		
3	LÓPEZ	356	0.95	14		1,411.41	0.0000000000		
4	DOCTORA	273	0.72	1		1,157.54	0.0000000000		
5	ELISA	176	0.47	0		754.22	0.0000000000		
6	VILLAREJO	158	0.42	0		677.02	0.0000000000		
7	EMPRESARIO	133	0.35	1		558.28	0.0000000000		
8	DERMATÓLOGA	126	0.33	0		539.80	0.0000000000		
9	COMISARIO	105	0.28	0		449.78	0.0000000000		
10	ACOSO	108	0.29	2		443.15	0.0000000000		
11	ELLA	130	0.35	37	0.01	389.54	0.0000000000		
12	JUZGADO	97	0.26	3		389.30	0.0000000000		
13	POLICÍA	116	0.31	20		388.34	0.0000000000		
14	LE	216	0.57	216	0.08	380.72	0.0000000000		
15	JAVIER	91	0.24	5		351.75	0.0000000000		
16	QUE	1,508	4.00	6,572	2.32	332.02	0.0000000000		
17	MENSAJES	80	0.21	2		324.34	0.0000000000		
18	HABÍA	118	0.31	74	0.03	267.97	0.0000000000		
19	DENUNCIA	71	0.19	9		250.06	0.0000000000		
20	AUDIENCIA	56	0.15	3		216.85	0.0000000000		
21	LLAMADAS	58	0.15	6		210.06	0.0000000000		
22	AMENAZAS	59	0.16	9		201.77	0.0000000000		
23	INSTRUCCIÓN	54	0.14	6		193.74	0.0000000000		
24	ÉL	94	0.25	80	0.03	182.52	0.0000000000		
25	SU	445	1.18	1,543	0.55	178.37	0.0000000000		
26	RUEDA	47	0.12	4		174.23	0.0000000000		
27	CASO	117	0.31	151	0.05	171.70	0.0000000000		
28	COMISARÍA	41	0.11	1		166.37	0.0000000000		
29	CAUSA	64	0.17	33	0.01	157.95	0.0000000000		
30	VILLAR	40	0.11	3		150.27	0.0000000000		
31	AMENAZANTES	35	0.09	0		149.87	0.0000000000		

Figure 4.1 Keywords in the Pinto López Madrid corpus

switched to a targeted (corpus-based) approach, where particular types of items were selected for concordance analysis.

Figure 4.1 confirms the close relationship between keyness and aboutness (Gabrielatos 2018: 225): the first 30 keywords actually identify the core elements of the judicial case and can be classified into three main areas, which will help to answer the research questions of the study and be the object of the following subsections: a) the characters of the story (Pinto, Madrid, López, Villarejo, empresario, dermatóloga, etc.); b) the facts of the case (acoso, ella, le, mensajes, denuncia, llamadas, amenazas, instrucción, amenazantes, etc.); and c) the legal world (comisario, Juzgado, Policía, Comisaría, etc.).

The characters of the story

The aim of this section is to analyse the discursive construction of the Pinto vs. López-Madrid dichotomy and to see if this contrast elicits the ideological underpinning of media discourse on the 'social actors' (van Leeuwen 2008: 23–54) of this judicial case.

A first query of the surnames of the two characters directly involved in the case shows that their presence in the texts of the corpus is balanced. A high frequency of *empresario* and *doctora/dermatóloga* is a remarkable feature of the corpus; an in-depth analysis of the contexts in which they occur reveal that the use of these job nouns does not seem to be a social remark nor to have an explicit ideological connotation. They are used as a cohesive device, i.e. a lexical anaphora, to avoid the repetition of their names. However, the use of these terms may also be interpreted as a rhetorical strategy employed by the media to implicitly manipulate audience attention. The idea behind these titles is that this is a high-society case in which the private lives of famous professional individuals are brought into focus in the public space. Social actors are therefore represented in terms of the identities and functions they share with others (in van Leeuwen's terms, 'functionalisation' as a subgroup of 'categorisation' 2008: 40–42). In line with this view, this could be part of the 'sensationalism'[5] characterising tabloids and increasingly broadsheets as well (Bhatia and Bhatia 2017: 33), a strategy to involve the readers and catch their attention.

As far as the use of *hombre* [man] and *mujer* [women] is concerned, it is worth stressing that most of the time they refer to third characters in the story, such as Villarejo or Silvia Villar Mar (López Madrid's wife) and are not used to refer to

Table 4.2 The characters of the story

Pinto	354
López Madrid	347
empresario (entrepreneur)	133
doctora (doctor)	273
dermatóloga (dermatologist)	126
hombre (man)	25
mujer (woman)	52

Table 4.3 Personal pronouns in the Pinto
López Madrid corpus

yo (I)	17
tú (you)	3
él (he)	94
ella (she)	130
me (me)	66
te (you)	27
le (him/her)	216

Pinto and López Madrid. The lack of explicit identity and the depersonalization conveyed by these general words is also a strategy to portray – for example – the man who stabbed Dr. Pinto.

One of the key linguistic elements allowing the study of the contrast between the two characters is the use of personal pronouns in the narration of the events of the judicial case, which can be interpreted as signs of polarization between Pinto and López Madrid and provides an insight into how the press and the media see the two characters in general.

The use of personal pronouns, within the naming strategies adopted by the press, provides interesting insights into the semantics of solidarity and power (Hook 1984: 183) and the gendered identity constructions of social actors (Potts and Weare 2018).

First, it is important to consider these pronouns in the context of the polyphony (Garzone 2016) which characterizes these texts. Newspapers heavily rely on reported speeches, which are declarations made by the characters in the story and later used in court. Many texts composing the corpus, especially those pertaining to tabloids (e.g., *El Español*), entirely rely on transcriptions so the role of direct and indirect speech is pivotal when distinguishing between, say, verbal aggressions and reported narrative speeches.

The pronouns in Table 4.3 can be analysed in antithetic couples (*yo* vs. *tú*, *él* vs. *ella*, *me* vs. *te* vs. *le*) which strengthen the contrast between the two characters.

The first opposition does not add any particular discursive effect to the narration of the events, whereas the second (*él* vs. *ella*) reveals a first unbalanced picture. *Él* is mostly used to refer to López (more than a marginal character like Villarejo) and a common cluster is *contra él* (against him); *ella*, that is more frequent than *él*, is used to tell the story of Dr. Pinto and it usually occurs with action verbs (imperfect or present tense). The analysis of the latter opposition (*me, te, le*) confirms that the focus of the story is the woman, since most of personal pronouns refer to her, which may be interpreted as an implicit stance taken by the media, who take sides with her.

As a matter of fact, if *me* is generally used in the pattern *me* + imperfect (see Table 4.5) to tell the story, *te* is strongly associated with verbal aggressions, mostly threats against Dr. Pinto (see Table 4.4). A further confirmation is the use

Table 4.4 Examples of the use of the personal pronoun *te* in the corpus

Violence against HER (13)	*Violence against HIM (4)*
(1) "Vamos a pinchar a tus hijos"; "**Te** vamos a matar"; "Volveremos a pinchar**te** a ti y a tus hijos **te** vamos a destrozar la vida [...]" (VF) [We are going to stab your children; we are going to kill you; we will stab you and your children again, we are going to ruin your life [...]]	(4) "Nosotros **te** vamos a dar lo que mereces la cárcel y la fama en la prensa. La paliza **te** la dará tu suegro o tus amigos por traidor [...]" (VF) [We are going to give you what you deserve: prison and fame in the press. Your father-in-law or your friends will beat you for being a traitor]
(2) "Elisa, déjame en paz; la Policía **te** va a venir a ver" (Esp) [Elisa, leave me alone; the police are going to find you]	(5) "**Te** recordarán como un loco que quiere matarla" (MSN) [People will remember you as a mad person who wants to kill her]
(3) "Si vuelves a coger un teléfono o una cabina, **te** vas a meter en un lío gordísimo" (Esp) [If you call me again or get closer to a phone booth, you will get yourself into serious trouble]	(6) "Eres un loco y tus perversiones **te** pasarán factura" (MSN) [You are mad and your perversions will take their toll]

of the personal pronoun *le* referring most of the time to her in clusters like (se *le* acercó [he moved closer to her], *le* dijo [he told her], *le* clavó [he stuck to her]) where the active subject is the man and the passive patient is the woman, who suffers his threatening acts.

A closer look at the concordances of *te* reveals that out of 17 instances – ten were excluded for being not relevant – 13 hits expressed violence against her and only four violence against him. As shown in Table 4.4, a negative semantic prosody is associated with the woman, which is corroborated by a semantic preference for the future tense expressed by means of the periphrasis *ir a + infinitivo* (going to) showing the intention to do something (*te* vamos a matar [we are going to kill you]) or the negative imperative (No *te* metas [Don't stick your nose in], No *te* acerques [Don't get closer]).

The use of *me*, which grammatically may refer to both her and him, confirms the unbalance in the presentation of the news. Out of 66 instances, 45 refer to her and only 21 to him.

Me refers to the story Dr. Pinto told the Police and the Court in her report (*denuncia*), highly charged with negative and passive attributes (verbs denoting aggressions and threatening: *atar* [tie], *doler* [hurt], *amenazar* [threaten], *acuchillar* [stab], *arruinar* [destroy]). Analysis of the concordances reveals the harassment suffered by the woman and does not elicit any harassment on his part. In fact, when *me* is used by López Madrid, it is generally framed within sexual remarks

Table 4.5 Examples of the use of the personal pronoun *me* in the corpus

SHE (45)	HE (21)
(7) "**Me** decía que **me** iba a atar, que **me** tenía que doler. Que cuando dolía se disfrutaba más" (VF) [He said that he would kill me and it should hurt, that he enjoyed my suffering]	(10) "**Me** estoy tocando para ti. **Me** estoy abriendo para ti. Anoche **me** corrí para ti". "Estoy súper excitado, súper caliente". "Quiero oír tus gemidos doctora". (VF)[I'm touching myself for you. I'm opening up for you. Last night I came for you. I'm horny, I want to hear your moans, Doctor]
(8) "Lo único que quiero es que haya limpieza en las investigaciones y que este señor pague por lo que está haciendo, porque **me** ha arruinado la vida" (EM) [I only want that the investigations shed light on the case and that this man pay for what he is doing, because he is destroying my life]	(11) "Elisa, déjalo ya, deja de acosar a la gente, **me** has hecho un daño tremendo; eres más lista que yo, pero no que la Policía" (Esp) [Elisa, stop it, stop accusing people, you harmed me badly; you are smarter than me, but not smarter than the police]
(9) "**Me** han amenazado, **me** han acuchillado y nadie ha investigado. Nadie **me** ha ayudado y **me** han dejado sola" (Esp) [He has threatened me, they stabbed me and nobody has ever investigated. Nobody has helped me, they just left me alone]	(12) "**Me** he tratado de portar contigo como una persona normal. No trates por ningún momento de ser la más lista. Olvídate de mí y de mis amigos. No sé qué pretendes. No entiendo qué más daño me quieres hacer" (Esp) [I tried to treat you like a normal person. Don't you try to be the smartest. Forget about my friends and me. I don't know what you want from me. I don't know how can you harm me more than you already did]

(as in example (10)) or personal reflection on how his life has changed because of the whole story.

The corpus-based analysis of the personal pronouns shows that media manipulate the information in reporting the details of the case. The discursive focus is the woman, considered as the weaker part (the victim/innocent) who suffered aggressions from the man (the guilty person), although – theoretically and judicially – both received the same threats.

The discursive construction of the two social actors of the case by the media is influenced by gender stereotypes; through their story telling, journalists consciously or unconsciously persuade readers creating a narrative that encodes ideology (see Potts and Weare 2018).

Table 4.6 The legal facts in the Pinto López Madrid corpus

*acoso** (harassment(s))	109
*agresión/** (aggression(s))	56
*amenaza** (threat(s))	117
apuñalamiento (stabbing)	29
*correo** (email(s))	19
*denuncia** (report(s))	170
*mensaje** (message(s))	90
*sex** (sex/sexual)	67
víctima (victim)	24
*acusa** (accuse(d))	9

The facts and their legal implications

The second corpus-based investigation, based on the previously identified key-words, concerns the facts of the case and their legal implications (the 'social action' in van Leeuwen's terms, 2008: 55–74). Table 4.6 summarizes the main terms, which have been scrutinized by concordancing with a view to studying their semantic behaviour.

The analysis shows that the majority of the terms relate to alleged offences suffered by Dr. Pinto. The high frequency of certain legal terms in the corpus associated with the woman (such as *acoso, amenaza, denuncia*, etc.) is indicative of a strong emotional reaction by the media and, consequently, the audience, who take her side because she is portrayed as a victim. As a matter of fact, the term *víctima* (which is not a full-blown legal term to be used in judicial documents) is only once associated with him: the remaining 23 instances are referred to her. The same occurs with the unbalanced distribution of *acusad**, used in the feminine gender only once (*acusada*) and in eight instances with the masculine gender (*acusado*) and with the term *denuncia*: the pattern *denuncia contra* co-occurs with him six out of eight times.

The whole story is construed around a number of negative events with legal consequences (*acoso* + *sexual, agresión, apuñalamiento, correo, mensajes, lla-madas*, etc.) suffered by the woman. The legal details provided in the articles are presented in a way that the reader inevitably associates the bad character with him and the poor/good one with her.

However, it is interesting to observe the co-occurring patterns of the adjective *supuest** (57) and *presunt** (31) (alleged) which raise a series of doubts about the declarations made by Dr. Pinto, whose credibility is undermined. Actually, these adjectives co-occur with nouns such as *sicarios* [hired killer], *apuñalamiento* [stabbing], *aggresor* [aggressor], etc. which are used to describe threatening acts suffered by the woman. The high frequency of the conjunction *pero* [but] (79) can also be interpreted in line with this reporting strategy aimed at highlighting the doubts which surround the case. The fact that the case has not been solved, the mystery surrounding the truth, the involvement of the Crown, are all

Table 4.7 The legal 'characters' in the Pinto López Madrid corpus

*juez** (judge(s))	48
*tribunal** (court(s))	6
*Juzgado** (court(s))	124
Audiencia Provincial (Court of Appeal)	56
Fiscal (prosecutor)	14
policía (police)	117
*abogad** (lawyer(s))	60
*letrad** (lawyer(s))	8
*ley** (law(s)	1
*denuncia** (report/(s))	103
*auto** (decree(s))	23
justicia (justice)	8

ingredients contributing to attract and seduce a wider readership, instilling a constant sense of curiosity.

From a textual and discursive point of view, this is what Bhatia and Bhatia (2017: 33) call a 'hybrid genre,' that is to say, a mix of information-giving and entertainment functions. The exaggeration of some details of the case and the speculations made in reporting the facts can be seen as manipulation of the truth of the story in focus, which remain unknown, and this is achieved by means of lexico-grammatical and rhetorical resources and strategies used to make the judicial case attractive to a much wider audience.

The legal world

In order to answer the last research questions (how law and the judicial world are represented in the media) legal terms have been queried and scrutinized.

Surprisingly, references to the legal and judicial world are neutral and do not reveal ideological alignment with one or the other party. Legal entities and figures (*abogado, fiscal, juzgado*, etc.) and legal acts (*autos, denuncias*) are seen as 'super-partes' sources of power whose authority is not questioned by newspapers.

The only exceptions are the term *jueza* (a female judge)[6] (see Table 4.8) and *policía* (Table 4.9) which tend to have a strong semantic prosody (negative connotation).

Harsh criticism is patent in the comments related to the judge who filed the case, criticized for closing too quickly the investigations: surprisingly she decided to file the case (ex. 13), she omitted important facts (ex. 14), she refrained to carry out due investigations (ex. 15).

Similar negative comments are addressed to the police, accused of not doing anything during investigations (see ex. 18 in Table 4.9).

The legal aspects of the case and the description of the judicial procedure are not described in the articles composing the corpus, possibly due to the inner difficulty in grasping the technical aspects of the case. The media focus tends to

Table 4.8 Examples of *la jueza* in the corpus

---

(13) Pero si es intrigante que el comisario no se presentara, más sorprendente es aún que **la jueza** no esperara al regreso de Villarejo y decidiera archivar el caso en marzo de 2016, lo que llevó a la abogada de Pinto a recurrir el archivo y, por fin, poner a la dermatóloga frente al comisario, primer logro alcanzado esta mañana por parte de Elisa y su abogada. (VF)
[If it is surprising that the inspector did not show up, it is even more surprising that the judge did not wait for Mr. Villarejo's return and just decided to file the case in March 2016, which led Dr. Pinto's lawyer to appeal the decision and finally bring the dermatologist to the inspector, first result reached this morning by Elisa and her lawyer]

(14) Así lo afirma la defensa de Pinto en un extenso recurso en el que pide al Juzgado de Instrucción número 39 de Madrid que revoque el archivo del procedimiento y lleve a cabo diligencias "esenciales" e "imprescindibles" para aclarar los hechos que han sido omitidos por **la jueza** instructora, Belén Sánchez. (Esp)
[This is what Dr. Pinto's defence stated in a long appeal in which she required the re-opening of the case to the Juzgado de Instrucción n. 39 of Madrid with the aim of conducting investigations considered as "essential" and "indispensable" in order to shed light on the facts that have been omitted by the instructing judge, Mrs. Belén Sánchez]

(15) Su abogada, Ana Blanco, recurrió al entender que **la jueza** se inhibió de practicar diligencias requeridas, no pudiéndose esclarecer el caso que ahora se reabre (EM)[Her lawyer, Ms. Ana Blanco, appealed the decision on the basis that the judge refrained to carry out the necessary investigations and therefore hindering the understanding of the case which now is open again]

Table 4.9 Example of *policía* in the corpus

---

(18) Pero la **Policía**, en lugar de inmovilizar el coche, tomar huellas, hacer las pesquisas en la zona y comprobar las cámaras de seguridad, no realiza nada"
(Esp)[But the Police, instead of immobilising the vehicle, taking fingerprints, carrying out the investigations in the area and checking the security cameras, did not do anything.]

---

be placed on the reactions of the two characters, especially Pinto's: their private matters are the real object of intense media attention.

This is confirmed by some concordance lines: También era el principio de un *viacrucis judicial* que la dermatóloga y el empresario llevan viviendo desde entonces [This was the beginning of a judicial 'way of the cross' that the dermatologist and the entrepreneur have been living since then], El caso sigue *en manos de la Justicia* [The case is still in the hands of the Justice]. The use of two evocative metaphors – both religious in a way, if Justice (with a capital letter) is considered as an allegorical personification of Lady Justice – contributes to arousing the curiosity of the readers, leaving a mysterious halo around the case.

Concluding remarks

The corpus-based analysis carried out in this study has confirmed the main hypothesis guiding the research: the media representation of the case is biased by an ideological stance, which draws on pre-existing representations of social categories (men vs. women). As a matter of fact, the analysis has demonstrated an unbalanced representation of the two actors of the story: the media tend to focus more on Dr. Pinto (considered as the weak party) than on Mr. López Madrid (considered as the 'guilty' party). The dichotomy between the two social actors (Pinto vs. López Madrid) is emotionally charged since negative comments and evaluation tend to be associated with the behaviour of the man.

What emerges from the analysis is the reinforcement of a binary representation of good and evil, the identification of 'she' versus 'he,' namely a gendered representation on the part of the media. The emotional dichotomies established between the two parties, discursively manipulated by the newspapers, serve to raise the emotional temperature of the reports. This reflects the logic of the popular press, in which issues can always be resolved through an appeal to supposedly universal human values on an affective level (Breeze 2018: 66). Highly emotive framing and aggressive language are perfect ingredients to involve readers and indirectly invite them to take sides with one of the 'characters of the story.' Moreover, the discursive presentation of the issues coalesces perfectly with what Conboy (2006: 26) describes as the tabloids' 'ideological pact with readers' in which their characteristic 'textual display of intimacy' with readers (2006: 10) reinforces their ideological alignment with social actors of contemporary society (see Breeze 2018: 66).

The analysis has also revealed the power of the media in manipulating the facts of the case; this involves a re-contextualization of the story in a manner that will attract a wider readership. In line with what Bhatia and Bhatia found in the case of the Panama Papers in India, this controversial case has offered the media an opportunity to combine the seriousness of judicial reporting with an emotional spin on famous stories to manipulate objectivity in their reporting (2017: 33–34).

The research conducted can obviously be completed by comparing the differences between traditional and popular press, a dichotomy which has remained in the background in this study, to see if traditional broadsheets are more neutral compared to tabloids and if the gendered representation is typical of one of the two types of press. In addition to this, an interesting perspective could be provided by analysing the judicial documents of the case, with a view to checking the level of manipulation performed by the media.

The case has offered interesting insights into the intersection between media and judicial discourses, an area that will definitely gain weight in the years to follow, especially after the growing trend towards the mediatization of justice. In fact, court cases are receiving huge media attention worldwide, awakening a massive public interest and closer attention needs to be paid to these new hybrid discourses.

Notes

1 www.elespanol.com/reportajes/20171117/262843717_12.html [accessed 22/ 09/2018].
2 https://elpais.com/elpais/2017/10/21/eps/1508537116_150853.html [accessed 22/09/2018].
3 'Discourse' is conceived here as 'context-dependent semiotic practices which are both "socially constituted and socially constitutive"' (Wodak 2009: 89).
4 'News media often manipulate unverified claims, hearsay, or unconfirmed half-truths to influence public opinion in an attempt to sensationalize even legal constraints' (Bhatia and Bhatia 2017: 29).
5 'Discursive manipulation in mass media is generally seen as a function of editorial bias, which makes use of a number of different strategies for different effects. The most prominent of these is sensationalism, primarily seen in tabloids, but often selectively used in broadsheets as well, depending upon the nature, timing, and newsworthiness of the news item. [...] In sensationalism, every-day happenings reported in the news are exaggerated to present a biased impression. [...] The main motivation for sensationalising news reports is to increase readership in order to collect higher revenues in advertising, which sometimes leads to less objective reporting. [...] Some of the most glaring examples [of manipulation] are provided by political and film celebrity scandals, especially as regards their personal misdemeanours. The private lives of famous individuals are increasingly being brought into focus in the public space, thus creating interesting opportunities for genre-mixing and embedding' (Bhatia and Bhatia 2017: 33–34).
6 For an interesting perspective on identitarian language, including the (ideological) use of the term 'jueza' in Spanish, see the article by A. Grijelmo 'Los lenguajes identitarios' published by El País on 24/04/2019: https://elpais.com/elpais/ 2019/04/11/ideas/1554995417_416895.html [accessed 12/05/2019].

References

Bhatia, Vijay K. and Bhatia, Aditi. 2017. Interdiscursive manipulation in media reporting: the case of the Panama Papers in India. In Orts Llopis, María, Breeze, Ruth and Gotti, Maurizio (eds). *Power, Persuasion and Manipulation in Specialised Genres. Providing Keys to the Rhetoric of Professional Communities*. Frankfurt am Main: Peter Lang (29–50).
Boyd, Michael. 2013. Representation of foreign justice in the media: the Amanda Knox case. *Critical Approaches to Discourse Analysis across Disciplines* 7 (3): 33–50.
Boyd, Michael. 2016. From news to comment: Tracing text trajectories in news reporting about Amanda Knox. In Gies, Lieve and Bortoluzzi, Maria (eds) *Transmedia Crime Stories: the Trial of Amanda Knox and Raffaele Sollecito in the Globalised Media Sphere*. Cham: Palgrave (139–164).
Breeze, Ruth. 2018. 'Enemies of the people': Populist performances in the Daily Mail reporting of the Article 50 case. *Discourse, Context and Media* 25: 60–67.
Breeze, Ruth, Gotti, Maurizio and Sancho Guinda, Carmen (eds). 2014. *Interpersonality in Legal Genres*. Bern: Peter Lang.

Carretero González, Cristina and Úlcar Ventura, Pilar. 2011. Noticias jurídicas en prensa: propiedades lingüísticas y técnicas. *Icade. Revista cuadrimestral de las Facultades de Derecho y Ciencias Económicas y Empresariales*, n. 83–84. Especial 50 Aniversario ICADE: 59–79.

Conboy, Martin. 2006. *Tabloid Britain: Constructing a Community through Language*. London: Routledge.

Fairclough, Norman. 2003. *Analysing Discourse: Textual Analysis for Social Research*. London/New York: Routledge.

Fairclough, Norman. 2013. *Critical Discourse Analysis. The Critical Study of Language*. Second edition. London/New York: Routledge.

Gabrielatos, Costas. 2018. Keyness analysis: Nature, metrics and techniques. In Taylor, Charlotte and Marchi, Anna (eds). *Corpus Approaches to Discourse: A Critical Review*, London/New York: Routledge (225–258).

Garzone, Giuliana. 2016. Polyphony and Dialogism in Legal Discourse: Focus on Syntactic Negation. In Tessuto, Girolamo, Bhatia, Vijay K., Garzone, Giuliana, Salvi, Rita and Williams, Christopher (eds). *Constructing Legal Discourses and Social Practices. Issues and Perspectives*. Newcastle: Cambridge Scholars Publishing (2–27).

Hook, Donald. 1984. First names and titles as solidarity and power semantics in English. *IRAL 22 (3)*: 183–189.

Johansson, Sofia. 2008. Gossip, sport and pretty girls. *Journalism Practice, 2 (3)*: The Future of Newspapers: 402–413.

Marchi, Anna and Taylor, Charlotte. 2018. Introduction. Partiality and reflexivity. In Taylor, Charlotte and Marchi, Anna (eds). *Corpus Approaches to Discourse: A Critical Review*, London/New York: Routledge (1–15).

Monzó-Nebot, Esther. 2017. 'Silence will break my bones': The presentation and representation of victims and perpetrators at the service of just-world views in judicial discourse. In Orts Llopis, María, Breeze, Ruth and Gotti, Maurizio (eds). *Power, Persuasion and Manipulation in Specialised Genres. Providing Keys to the Rhetoric of Professional Communities*. Frankfurt am Main: Peter Lang (131–159).

Orts Llopis, María, Breeze, Ruth and Gotti, Maurizio (eds). 2017. *Power, Persuasion and Manipulation in Specialised Genres. Providing Keys to the Rhetoric of Professional Communities*. Frankfurt am Main: Peter Lang.

Partington, Alan, Duguid, Alison and Taylor, Charlotte. 2013. *Patterns and Meanings in Discourse: Theory and Practice in Corpus-assisted Discourse Studies (CADS)*. Amsterdam/Philadelphia: John Benjamins.

Portier Duparc, Pascale and Pech, Laurent. 2007. The portrayal of the judicial process in the French and Irish media. In Masson, Antoine and O'Connor, Kevin (eds). *Representations of Justice*. Bern: Peter Lang (95–114).

Potts, Amanda and Weare, Siobhan. 2018. Mother, monster, Mrs, I: A critical evaluation of gendered naming strategies in English sentencing remarks of women who kill. *International Journal for the Semiotics of Law – Revue internationale de Sémiotique juridique 31* (1): 21–52.

Robson, Peter. 2007. Developments in law and popular culture. The case of the TV lawyer. In Masson, Antoine and O'Connor, Kevin (eds), *Representations of Justice*. Bern: Peter Lang (74–94).

Scott, Mike. 1997. PC analysis of key words – and key words. *System, 25 (2)*: 233–245.

Scott, Mike. 2008. *Wordsmith Tools version 5.* Stroud: Lexical Analysis Software.

van Leeuwen, Theo. 2008. *Discourse and Practice: New Tools for Critical Analysis.* Oxford: Oxford University Press.

Wodak, Ruth. 2009. The discourse-historical approach. In Wodak, Ruth and Meyer, Michael (eds). *Methods of Critical Discourse Analysis.* London: Sage (87–121).

Wodak, Ruth. 2015. *The Politics of Fear. What Right-wing Political Discourses Mean.* London: Sage.

5 Ideological positioning in Amnesty International human rights web-based documents

Gerald Delahunty

Introduction

The human rights movement over the last 200 years has led to the creation of a great many organizations whose purpose is to encourage powerful organizations and groups, legal or not, to abide by the human and humanitarian rights articulated in the Universal Declaration of Human Rights (UDHR) and the various Geneva Conventions (GC) (Neier 2012; Sikkink 2017). This chapter investigates the intertextual relations among five closely related Amnesty International (AI) genres, the UDHR, and the GCs, especially Protocols I and II. It examines the relations among the participant roles implicated by these AI documents and how they are ideologically (re-) positioned across the documents and the linguistic choices that enact these relationships. I provide brief discussions of human and humanitarian rights and AI, participant discourse roles, and my assumptions about ideology. I then briefly describe the seven legal and AI documents, the conception of intertextuality I invoke, how it is linguistically and visually manifested in the documents, and then how it (re-)positions the discourse participants. I conclude with a discussion of the intertextual relations among the documents.[1]

Background

This study is part of ongoing work on the genres AI uses to support human and humanitarian rights and redress their violations. Until now I have focused on the analysis of a corpus of one of these genres, which I refer to as the "appeal letter," or just the "appeal," which I introduce below with its compatriot documents.

Terminology

I use "text" to refer to linguistic representations and "document" to refer more generally to representations that may incorporate text, photos, and/or other forms of representation intended to be interpreted as coherent wholes (Hodges 2018).

Human and humanitarian rights

Human rights are fundamental rights articulated in legal instruments enacted by authoritative international bodies such as the United Nations and are designed to protect individuals and groups "from severe political, legal, and social abuses" (Nickel 2017). They derive from "widely cherished" values of respect, power, enlightenment, well-being, wealth, skill, affection, and rectitude (Chen 2015: 251–252). Human rights include social, economic, environmental, civil and political rights, as well as group protections of women, children, racial and ethnic minorities, and sexual identities. These values and their protections are proclaimed in the United Nations Charter, the UDHR, the International Covenant on Civil and Political Rights (ICCPR), the International Covenant on Economic, Social, and Cultural Rights (ICESCR), the Covenant on the Rights of the Child (CRC), the UN Convention Against Torture, and a broad range of other instruments. Some of these instruments are regional international agreements, e.g., the European Convention for the Protection of Human Rights and Fundamental Freedoms, the American Convention on Human Rights, the African Charter of Human and Peoples' Rights, and the Arab Charter on Human Rights.[2] These rights are enforced, more or less effectively, by international tribunals such as the International Court of Justice (ICJ), the International Criminal Court (ICC), the European Court of Human Rights, the Inter-American Court of Human Rights, and the African Court of Human and Peoples' Rights. AI documents primarily invoke the UDHR.

Humanitarian rights are articulated in the Hague and Geneva Conventions and the latter's Additional Protocols. They are designed to protect sick and wounded combatants and civilians in both international and national armed conflicts. They also protect those who assist the sick and wounded as well as their vehicles and facilities.

Amnesty International (AI)

AI is the best-known NGO currently working on behalf of human rights. It claims to be "a global movement of more than 7 million people who take injustice personally … campaigning for a world where human rights are enjoyed by all."[3] It has offices in Africa, Australia, Asia, Europe, the Middle East, and in North and South America. It was awarded the Nobel Peace Prize in 1977.

AI was founded in 1961 to work on behalf of "Prisoners of Conscience," defined as

> someone who has not used or advocated violence but is imprisoned because of who they are (sexual orientation, ethnic, national or social origin, language, birth, colour, sex or economic status).[4]

AI initially campaigned on behalf of freedom of speech, though this focus has been substantially broadened since 1961. It has also adapted to changing communications media – from hand- or type-written appeals to mobile apps. It is currently represented online by multiple webpages put up by various regional offices, e.g. Amnesty International USA, AI Canada, and AI Australia. The AIUSA main webpage characterizes its work as research, mobilization, and advocacy on behalf of people whose human and/or humanitarian rights have been violated, whether by governments or non-state actors.[5]

AI's reports have earned a reputation for consistency and accuracy in detailing human rights abuses and related situations. This reputation is based on the careful collection and multiple checking of information for its reports on specific situations. It has earned AI the ability to work "directly with the U.N. system while maintaining an independence" (Chen 2015: 83). Recommendations in its reports are addressed to the relevant government(s), the UN Security Council, the international community, and other relevant actors, e.g., armed groups.[6]

Participant roles: Goffman's categories

Goffman (1981) distinguishes various roles that discourse producers and recipients may adopt. Though Goffman's schema has been criticized (e.g. Goodwin and Goodwin 2007), it is widely used in discourse analysis and is sufficient for my current purposes.

Producers

a   Animator: individual active in the role of utterance production.
b   Author: someone who has selected the sentiments that are expressed and the words in which they are encoded.
c   Principal: someone whose *position* is established by the words that are spoken, someone whose beliefs have been told, someone who is committed to what the words say (Goffman 1981: 144–145, emphasis added).

It is often impossible to identify individuals playing these roles, e.g. only one of the seven documents described below is attributed to an individual producer, and even this attribution is problematic. Documents such as the UDHR, though presumably crafted and produced by individuals, are the responsibility of institutions – the UN, the states signatory to the Geneva Conventions, and so on – which are therefore positioned by being "committed to what the words say."

Recipients

a   Addressee: person(s) to whom the utterance is addressed.
b   Ratified recipient: has status as a ratified participant in the encounter.
c   Intended recipient: those whom the "speaker" intends to hear/read and understand the utterance (can take in eavesdroppers or bystanders).

d   Recipient in general: those who hear/read the utterance, irrespective of what the "speaker" intends or is even aware of.

As discussed below, these roles are variously distributed by the different genres.

Ideology

Though most scholars these days assume that ideology may be positive, negative, or neutral, much discourse analytic research focuses on ideologies that the analysts find objectionable. AI, in keeping with the traditional negative understanding of ideology, seems to regard its own discourses as non-ideological, as evidenced by a recent AI Letter Writing Guide[7] that cautions writers to "Be factual in your appeal … *Do not discuss ideology or politics*" (emphasis added), and its current Urgent Action letter writing guidelines say that

> AI seeks to uphold human rights in a manner of impartiality and independence from any government, political faction, *ideology*, economic interest or religious belief.[8] *(emphasis added)*

These imply that AI views its activities as impartial and independent, and neither ideological nor political.

There are, of course, conceptions of ideology that allow us to see the discourses and actions of legitimate, eleemosynary, liberationist, and life-affirming groups as ideological; for example, Featherman (2015). Verschueren (2012) defines ideology as

> any basic pattern of meaning or frame of interpretation bearing on or involved in (an) aspect(s) of social "reality" (in particular in the realm of social relations in the public sphere), felt to be commonsensical, and often functioning in a normative way. (p. 10)

Eagleton (2007: 45, italics in original) provides a set of characteristics of ideology that are operationalizable for the purposes of the current research. Ideologies are *unifying, action-oriented, rationalizing, legitimating, universalizing* and *naturalizing*. Because the UDHR and GCs are elements of international law, and laws are normative by definition, I follow Verschueren in adding *normative*.

The seven documents under investigation here manifest all these characteristics of ideology.

Unifying

As the UDHR and GCs are instruments of international law, they apply to everyone, and are thereby unifying. The UDHR Preamble proclaims "the inherent dignity and the equal and inalienable rights of all members of the human family."

Tharoor (2000), rebutting claims to the contrary, argues that HRs are indeed universal. The AI documents attempt to "synchronise a community … so that they are all talking about the same thing in the same way" (Snyder 2015: 216).

Action-oriented

The UDHR not only proclaims but also prescribes the exercise of those rights. Its Preamble states that "every individual and every organ of society … shall strive … to promote respect for these rights." The GCs explicitly prescribe certain actions, e.g. regarding the treatment of prisoners of war, and proscribe others, e.g. torture. The AI genres are attempts to persuade their various classes of addressees by appeal and protest to redress violations of human/humanitarian rights.

Rationalizing

"False consciousness" notions of ideology regard the rationalizing function as attempting to provide logical, ethical, or legal bases for hidden agendas. A neutral view of ideology sees the rationalizing function as providing "more or less systematic attempts to provide explanations and justifications that might otherwise be the object of criticism" (Eagleton 2007: 51–52). The UDHR justifies itself by appeal to the "fundamental human rights" and "the dignity and worth of the human person and in the equal rights of men and women" (Preamble). The GCs are based on "principles of humanity, impartiality, and neutrality" (ICRC Summary of Geneva Conventions and Additional Protocols).[9] The AI documents justify their evaluations of the actions of governments and individuals on the bases of the UDHR and the GCs and their associated procedural norms, e.g. the AI report characterizes the situation in Eastern Ghouta, Syria as violating international human rights, humanitarian rights, and criminal laws (67–71).

Legitimizing

Legitimizing is akin to rationalizing. It differs in that it seeks to invoke legal authority for its object. The legal authority of the UDHR and GCs derive from their ratification by the vast majority of the world's countries in accordance with the procedures of authoritative bodies, such as the UN. AI legitimizes its documents and actions by invoking the UDHR and GCs, and the other international legal instruments mentioned above. It also invokes local legal proceedings and rulings, e.g. a US District Court, the Iraqi Court of Cassation, the Inter-American Court of Human Rights, the International Violence Against Women Act, and by displaying the number of times each letter is sent.

Universalizing

Human rights as declared in the UDHR are explicitly universal, as are the provisions of the GCs and other conventions. The AI documents are presented as universal by invoking the universality of human rights and humanitarian laws. We must note, though, that while the UDHR is characterized as "universal" and thus applying to all people, peoples, and governments, some countries have not ratified it and others have crafted alternative declarations (e.g. the Cairo Declaration on Human Rights in Islam). AI appeals urge governments to "follow international law," abolish the death penalty, "respect the right to freedom of expression, association and peaceful assembly," and refrain from "torture and other cruel, inhuman or degrading treatment or punishment."

Naturalizing

Propositions or assumptions can be naturalized by presenting them as un-controversial and accepted by both authors and audiences. Though the UDHR and GCs have been ratified by authoritative international institutions, and should be regarded as accepted law, they are not without their critics (Tharoor 2000; Neier 2012). Nonetheless, the AI documents take for granted that characterizing an action or situation as a violation of human or humanitarian rights is sufficient warrant for its evaluation and redress, e.g. "I call on you to quash Raif Badawi's flogging sentence immediately, as it is a flagrant violation of the prohibition on torture or other cruel, inhuman or degrading treatment under international law." Here, the bald assertion that Badawi's flogging violates international law is presented without supporting justification, thus implying that the claim is natural and "commonsensical." AI indexes the acceptance of its evaluations by making frequent use of a broad range of markers of presupposition, i.e. information that is presented as accepted by both author and audience, most notably, definite descriptions, e.g. "the siege," "his torture," and "the escalating attacks on the people of Eastern Ghouta," which typically license the inference that their referents exist.

Normative

As the UDHR and GCs are laws, they are inherently normative. As the AI documents invoke these legally binding declarations and covenants, they too are inherently normative. Many letters invoke "international standards" of legal procedure in their evaluations of appeal situations and in their evaluation of the redressive actions they appeal for.

Seven documents

1   The UN UDHR[10] has been ratified by the most of the world's states.
2   The Geneva Conventions and Protocols I and II have also been ratified by most of the world's states.[11]
3   *AI report* on an exigent situation in Eastern Ghouta, Syria, was published in 2015.[12]

4   *AI webpage* with a brief description of the exigent situation in Eastern Ghouta, including text and photo, requesting action.[13]

5   *AI email to volunteers/members* with a brief description of situation in Eastern Ghouta, including text and photo, requesting action.

6   *AI appeal letter* embedded in email and webpage addressed to powerful individuals, briefly describing the situation and its exigency and requesting redress.

7   *AI response email* to someone taking action in regard to situation (*Thank you, Please donate, Take other actions*). Though this document adds very little to our discussion, I include this here as it completes the intertextual cycle. I will say little more about it in this chapter.

Brief overview of the five AI documents

We can view these as problem/solution documents (Hoey 2001), re-contextualized and re-genericized for their various rhetorical purposes. And overall, the report is presented as authoritative and thus as an accurate source and basis for the other documents thereby licensing a range of inferences, particularly related to the documents' trustworthiness and to the legitimacy of their recommendations.

AI webpage

The AI webpages contain text and still photos regarding the situation described in the report. The photo is juxtaposed with the text, thereby implying that it represents a scene from that situation. The pages also contain multiple links that allow readers to TAKE ACTION to redress the situation. Clicking on one of these links takes the clicker to a page giving a related description of the situation and which embeds an AI appeal. Readers are asked to SEND this appeal, ostensibly to its named MESSAGE RECIPIENTS, e.g. "President Putin." I do not know whether it actually goes to its MESSAGE RECIPIENTS, or that the SENDs are simply tallied by AI and the tally used in AI's efforts to persuade the powerful to redress the exigent situation.

Email to volunteers/members

These emails are sent, often several in a day, to volunteers or members who have signed up to receive them. Like the webpage, they provide a précis of the report information on the situation, but unlike the webpage, they are addressed to the individual member/volunteer, e.g. "Dear Gerald" and signed by an AI official. Like the webpage, they embed an appeal letter.

Appeal letter

The appeals are addressed to powerful individuals, e.g. "President Barak Obama." They briefly characterize the violative situation and urge the addressees to redress that violation, which they typically characterize as contravening human or humanitarian rights.

Response email

Immediately upon sending the appeal letter, the sender receives an email thanking them for doing so and asking them to donate and to distribute the appeal more widely by emailing it to friends or posting it on Facebook, and the like.

Report

Reports may be mere descriptions of, typically, problematic situations, e.g. news reports, but they may also include recommendations for the solution of those problems, and perhaps exhortations to various types of recipients to adopt the proposed solution or to help bring it about. AI reports include descriptions of situations and events, evaluations of those situations/events according to AI's human rights framework, suggested responses to the evaluation, and indexes of the efforts made by their curators to establish their authority and credibility.

AI's report, "LEFT TO DIE UNDER SIEGE" WAR CRIMES AND HUMAN RIGHTS ABUSES IN EASTERN GHOUTA, can be found in AI's archive of reports and is identified as a "report" on its back cover, which also provides a précis of the reported information. No authors are listed, but the copyright belongs to AI. Presumably it was written by AI staffers skilled in curating (Snyder 2015) such reports. Curating "is always ideological, always rhetorical and often political" (209) as it always "involves human filtering and organizing" (213). The report is highly edited (unlike some of the appeal letters, which show signs of hasty drafting or incomplete command of English), with many footnotes identifying the sources of the information and the legal instruments represented. It comprises the following main sections:

The *Executive Summary* is a 2.5-page footnote-free, text-only précis of the report findings on the current situation, its history, its legal status (e.g. crimes against humanity, contravention of UN resolutions), AI sources of information, and calls to actors to meet their commitments under international law.

The *Methodology* is a 1.25-page footnote-free, text-only summary of the sources AI used in the compilation of the report, e.g. interviews with witnesses, email correspondence, other human rights organizations, satellite imagery, statements from the Syrian government, expressions of gratitude to those who contributed information.

The *Background* provides a 6.25-page text-only summary of the chronology of events that led up to the current exigent situation; it is heavily footnoted with references to sources of information, e.g. YouTube videos, Agence France Presse, emails and skype interviews with reporters and witnesses in the area, etc.

Attacks on civilians and civilian objects and the use of explosive weapons in populated areas is a 30-page section providing information on Syrian government airstrikes on cities in Eastern Ghouta, attacks with missiles and other projectiles, retaliatory attacks by non-state armed groups, and humanitarian conditions and restrictions on access to those under siege. It includes various voices in several modes – translated quotes from witnesses, information from other NGO's, e.g. Human Rights Watch, footnoted links to original sources, photos from various sources including annotated aerial photos, and satellite imagery (from Digital Globe).

Under siege in Eastern Ghouta: Humanitarian conditions and access is a 17-page section that provides a heavily footnoted overview of the situation and descriptions of conditions in which the civilians currently live, with a single photo and ending with a highlighted page on "The Impact on Women."

The *Methodology, Background, Attacks,* and *Under Siege* sections are all heavily footnoted to identify the sources of the information and links to many of those sources, presumably with the goals of establishing the report as credible – from a rhetorical point of view, establishing its ethos – and licensing the assumption that the curators and their information are trustworthy.

Disregard for international law is a five-page text-only legal brief with extensive footnoting of the various laws referenced: UN Universal Declaration of Human Rights, International Covenant on Civil and Political Rights, International Covenant on Economic, Social and Cultural Rights, Convention on the Rights of the Child, and institutions related to these, e.g. the International Court of Justice, UN Human Rights Committee. The footnoting supports the assumption that the writers are experts in international law, and that their legal analyses are reliable.

Conclusions and recommendations is a four-page footnote-free, text-only précis of the current situation and its history, its legal status, with bulleted lists of recommendations for the redress of the situation to the Syrian authorities, armed groups engaged in the Syrian conflict, the UN Security Council, and the International Community.

The last page is a statement of AI's goals and activities, the proclamation I WANT TO HELP, all against AI's signature yellow background and juxtaposed to a pair of forms for personal information headed by the statements "I am interested in receiving further information on becoming a member of Amnesty International" and "I wish to make a donation to Amnesty International."

While the report is 77 pages long, the webpage and email are designed to fit on a single screen, and with links to other pages, though notably not to the report. The appeal is quite different. It has neither photos nor links to other pages, and is generally less than a page of text. Clearly, all the information in the report cannot fit into any of these other documents, so just as clearly the producers of these documents must make adjustments to the ideological, rhetorical, and linguistic choices of information to be presented and its framing for new purposes and audiences.

Intertextuality

The concept of intertextuality derives from the work of Bakhtin whose publications were translated and developed by Julia Kristeva (1986). It has been much debated and developed by literary scholars (e.g. Miola 2004) and communications scholars (e.g. Ott and Walter 2000), as well as discourse analysts (see Hodges 2018 for a recent thorough discussion).

For the purposes of this work I think of intertextuality as the inescapable phenomenon whereby discourse elements – linguistic, visual, auditory, etc. – that are deployed in one context are reconstituted in other contexts, where they are hybridized by being re-framed and re-genrecized, typically so as to anticipate – "pre-contextualize" (Johnstone 2018) – reactions. This reconstitution re-ascribes participant roles and ideologically re-positions participants.

Intertextual traces in the seven documents

The UDHR and Geneva Convention documents are text-only (though illustrated versions are available). The AI documents, except the appeals, incorporate both text and photographs, and so the traces of intertextuality among them involve both modes. The webpage and email show versions of the same photograph of a man carrying a boy by a burning car across a debris field with a destroyed building in the background. The report contains photos of boys and young men on debris fields with destroyed buildings in the background. It also contains photos of destroyed buildings and their associated debris fields and a photo of a destroyed car on a debris field in front of destroyed buildings. While the photos in the webpage and email are almost identical – they are cropped slightly differently – the one on the webpage is rectangular and spread right across the page; the one in the email is much smaller, approximately square, and integrated into the text. While this photo could have been included in the report, it was not. Nonetheless, it re-constitutes visual themes from the report photos in ways that are more appropriate for the webpage and email genres. That is, the report is designed to be factual and authoritative in order to convince its intended recipients by visual and linguistic argument of the truth of its findings and to act as the report recommends. In contrast, the webpage and email are designed to persuade their recipients to act by appeal to facts and empathy. The photo of a man carrying a boy past a burning car accomplishes both.

The visual and linguistic resonances among the seven documents reflect their re-framing and re-genrecising, "rekeying" (Goffman 1974: ch. 3), as they are adapted to their various genres. Notably, the extensive footnoting in the report contrasts with its complete absence in the other documents, reflecting their different genres and relations among participants.

Linguistic resonances include the report's explicit characterization of the "siege" by the Syrian government and non-state armed groups as violating "international humanitarian and human rights law" (7) by depriving the residents of Eastern Ghouta of food and other necessities. "Siege" is repeated in the webpage, the email, and the appeal. The report explicitly characterizes the Syrian government's denial of "adequate food and housing" as a "breach" of international human rights law, and specifically the ICCPR, the ICESCR, and the CRC (67). The webpage and the email both describe "children and elderly people ... dying of malnutrition and lack of medication," which the appeal echoes, saying that the people of Eastern Ghouta "have been enduring hunger, malnutrition, lack of medication and escalated bombardment that has targeted civilians, homes, hospitals and markets."

As we should expect, all the AI documents, except the "Thank you/Please donate" email, include expressions representing human/humanitarian rights and characterizing a situation as problematic from a human or humanitarian rights point of view; unsurprisingly, "violation" occurs frequently across the genres. So do unmitigated statements of fact: "Civilians in/the residents of Eastern Ghouta have been trapped in a cruel siege for nearly six years" (Webpage/Email), and "Nearly half a million civilians live in areas under siege across Syria" (Report). As do directives to act: "Tell the Syrian and Russian governments to end the attacks" (Webpage and Email), and "I am calling on you to ... end all attacks on civilians" (Appeal).

The linguistic differences across the genres are also significant. The report characterizes its directives to the parties involved as "recommendations," whereas the emails to members may urge them to "demand" that authorities act to redress the violations. The webpages direct their readers using imperatives such as "demand," "urge," "tell," and "ask," while the appeal letters never demand that their addresses act, they are content to "urge," "call on," or merely "ask" that the MESSAGE RECIPIENTS redress the situation. This slippage in speech act force is surely related to the "rekeying" of the relationships between AI and the various audiences for which the genres are intended: the Eastern Ghouta report's "recommendations" are addressed to powerful entities. As AI has no control over these it cannot demand anything from them, and so the directives must be mitigated to recommendations, which seems characteristic of the report genre generally. The audiences for the webpage may be assumed to be sympathetic to human rights causes and so may be baldly directed by imperatives to "tell" the MESSAGE RECIPIENTS to act to redress the problematic situation.

The emails to AI members are addressed to "Dear (First Name)." Immediately below a directive to TAKE ACTION is the electronic signature of the executive director of AI, Margaret Huang, or of some other AI official, such as a specialist in specific areas of the world or in specific causes. Notably, while the addressee is addressed by their first name, the AI signer is identified by first and last name and underneath this by organizational title. This is an intriguing contrast, as both my first and last names are in AI's records and the AI functionary could have signed just her first name, with her first and last names and title typed beneath. I assume, but cannot be certain, that the executive director of AI does not compose these emails and that other individuals are authorized to electronically insert her signature, name, and title. This asymmetry in naming may be chosen to construct a somewhat personalized version of a form letter, but without relinquishing the authority suggested by first and last name and AI affiliation and rank. This seems to be more or less typical of philanthropic appeal letters (Delahunty 2018a; Mann and Thompson 1992).

The familiarity of the first name in the address line is supported by first person singular pronouns referring to the signer and the inclusive first-person plural pronouns, presumably referring not just to the addressee and signer, but to the addressee and all AI members, and perhaps various overhearers and eavesdroppers.

And so, by AI's discursive practices, I am positioned as one who can be addressed by his first name, as a familiar, as a co-member of an organization, and as one who is, in Goffman's terms, at least a principal, "someone whose position is established by the words that are spoken" (Goffman 1981: 144–145), and as someone who can be persuaded to adopt the emotional, factual, and moral stances indexed in the webpage, email, and appeal letter, as the appeals to pathos, logos, and ethos in those genres evidence, and to take the actions urged upon me.

The MESSAGE RECIPIENTS of the appeal, e.g., "Presidents Putin and Assad," are similarly positioned, as people who may be persuaded by the appeal to human and humanitarian rights and international norms, though like all such positioning, it is "not necessarily indefeasible" (Davies and Harré 1990: 48) and the appeals' "invitation to conform" (Davies and Harré 1990: 51) to the norms of human rights may be defeated by the MESSAGE RECIPIENTS or their surrogates deploying an alternative discourse that legitimizes their re-contextualization and re-evaluation of the problematic situation. Such alternative discourses occasionally surface explicitly as concessions in the appeal letters, but they are always rebutted by the appeals' invocation of international human rights to "trump" (Wenar 2015: 13) legitimations based on local exigencies or laws.

Needless to remark, discourse analysts, who might consider themselves "outside" the interplay of these genres and thus ideologically neutral and objective, have also positioned themselves and the selves indexed in the texts, and may in fact have a range of ideological commitments, stretching from activist to activist/analyst professionally interested in the discourses in which they are engaged. Other discourse analysts may have no commitments to the human rights agenda, but may have commitments to "objective" scientific analyses, while others may have broader liberationist commitments, e.g. to Critical Discourse Analysis, for which every analysis is irremediably ideological.

Ideological positioning

AI is an organization whose goal is to engage those who participate in its discourses, i.e., the various classes of producers and receivers of its documents, to act on behalf of individuals whose human rights have been severely infringed. As we have seen, AI and its documents meet the criteria I have identified as constituting ideological discourse. And by virtue of engaging people in the production, reception, and dissemination of those documents, it positions them as enacting the various participant roles, most importantly as principals whose beliefs have been told, and thus ideologically committed.

The AI report explicitly addresses its recommendations to the Syrian authorities, armed groups, the UN security council and the international community. These are the addressees and the ratified and intended recipients who may be persuaded of the truth of the facts and validity of the legal arguments of the report, and perhaps to act as recommended, in which case they also become principals. However, the report may be accessed by anyone with the necessary web browsing skills and, presumably, interest, of whatever sort, e.g. discourse analysts, with whatever motivations, but also by members of other similar organizations, e.g. staffers at Human Rights Watch, as there is evidence that AI uses HRW materials in its reports. These accessors are recipients in general, who also may be persuaded to act, and thus become principals.

Like the report, the webpage may be accessed by anyone with minimal browsing skills and relevant interests. While there are no named addressees, the page does address readers as "you," whose referent changes with every reader. So those webpage readers, anonymous as they are, are the addressees, ratified and intended recipients, and recipients in general of the webpage. They are exhorted to act, and if they do, they thereby become principals.

The email to a member identifies the member by first name, and that person is thereby also an addressee and a ratified and intended recipient. If the member clicks to SEND the appeal, ostensibly to its MESSAGE RECIPIENTS, they thereby become a principal.

The appeal letter is addressed to its MESSAGE RECIPIENTS and (optionally) signed by the sender, who is thereby positioned as a principal. If the MESSAGE RECIPIENTS act as the appeal requests, they too become principals.

Final thoughts

Donald Trump, speaking to the UN General Assembly on September 25, 2018, contrasted "the ideology of globalism" with the "doctrine of patriotism," thus invoking the traditional and lay understanding of ideology as necessarily nefarious. "Doctrine," of course, is blessed by religious collocations and connotations, which thereby sanctify "patriotism." This contrast is in keeping with his administration's withdrawal of the US from the UN Human Rights Council and the contentious relationship between the US and the International Criminal Court and the International Court of Justice. As human and humanitarian rights are elements of globalism, we must assume that Trump regards them also as ideological and nefarious. As nationalism is just as certainly ideological as globalism, it is clear that one person's ideology is another's sacred duty, and an ideology that is nefarious to one is liberating to another. How we evaluate the positions assigned to participants in the play of discourse will derive from our evaluations of the ideology enacted in that discourse. As analysts we must aim for as neutral a stance as possible toward the discourses we study, though advocates of Critical Discourse Analysis (CDA) would reject that possibility. Verschueren (2012: 4 and fn. 5), expresses concern about CDA analyses arguing that

> a lack of procedural systematicity may produce results that make it hard to distinguish between preconceived ideas, research findings and mere speculation

and proposes guidelines for researching ideological discourse. The discussion above is presented in the spirit of Verschueren's guidelines, keeping in mind his remark that

> [i]n actual research practice, most discourse-based studies of ideological processes start from basic *intuitions* that are not unrelated to the researcher's *involvement.* (Verschueren 2012: 21, emphases in original)

My involvement is two-fold: I am a pragmatist and discourse analyst and I am an AI member. As an analyst I strive for objectivity or at least neutrality. As an AI member, I view human rights and their discourses as ideological, but I believe that this ideology is beneficial, and assent to my position as "someone who is committed to what [AI's] words say."

Notes

1 See Delahunty (2018b) for related discussion.
2 The texts of many of these and a great many others can be accessed at www. ohchr.org/documents/publications/compilation1.1en.pdf.
3 www.amnesty.org/en/who-we-are.
4 www.amnesty.org/en/what-we-do/detention/.
5 www.amnestyusa.org/our-work/.
6 AI's reports are available at www.amnestyusa.org/tools-and-reports/reports/.
7 www.amnestyusa.org/files/pdfs/uan_guide.pdf.
8 www.amnestyusa.org/take-action/urgent-action-network/writing-an-appeal/#100.
9 www.redcross.org/content/dam/redcross/atg/PDF_s/International_Services/ International_Humanitarian_Law/IHL_SummaryGenevaConv.pdf.
10 www.un.org/en/universal-declaration-human-rights/.
11 https://ihldatabases.icrc.org/applic/ihl/ihl.nsf/vwTreaties1949.xsp.
12 www.amnesty.org/en/documents/mde24/2079/2015/en/.
13 https://act.amnestyusa.org/page/21064/action/1?locale=en-US.

References

Chen, Lung-Chu. 2015. *International Law: A Policy-Oriented Perspective.* Oxford: Oxford University Press.

Davies, Bronwyn and Harré, Rom. 1990. Positioning: The discursive production of selves. *Journal for the Theory of the Social Sciences 20*(1): 43–63.

Delahunty, Gerald. 2018a. Amnesty International (AI) and philanthropic fundraising (PF) appeals. In Götzsche, Hans (ed.). *The Meaning of Language.* Newcastle-upon-Tyne: Cambridge Scholars Publishing.

Delahunty, Gerald. 2018b. Language, ideology, and participant positioning in Amnesty International appeal letters. *Journal of Linguistics and Language Teaching 9*(2).

Eagleton, Terry. 2007. *Ideology* (2nd edn). London: Verso.

Featherman, Christopher. 2015. *Discourse of Ideology and Identity.* New York/London: Routledge.

Goffman, Irving. 1974. *Frame Analysis.* New York: Harper Colophon.

Goffman, Irving. 1981. *Forms of Talk*. Philadelphia: University of Pennsylvania Press.

Goodwin, Charles and Goodwin, Marjorie H. 2007. Participation. In Duranti, Alessandro (ed.). *A Companion to Linguistic Anthropology*. Oxford: Blackwell.

Hodges, Adam. 2018. Intertextuality in discourse. In Tannen, Deborah, Hamilton, Heidi E. and Schiffrin, Deborah (eds). *The Handbook of Discourse Analysis*. Oxford: Wiley Blackwell.

Hoey, Michael. 2001. *Textual Interaction*. London: Psychology Press.

Johnstone, Barbara. 2018. *Discourse Analysis* (3rd edn). Oxford: Wiley Blackwell.

Kristeva, Julia. 1986. *The Kristeva Reader*, Moi, Toril (ed.). Oxford: Blackwell.

Mann, William C. and Thompson, Sandra A. 1992. *Discourse Description: Diverse Linguistic Analyses of a Fund-raising Text*. Amsterdam: John Benjamins.

Miola, Robert S. 2004. Seven types of intertextuality. In Marrapodi, Michele (ed.). *Shakespeare, Italy, and Intertextuality*. Manchester, NY: Manchester University Press.

Neier, Aryeh. 2012. *The International Human Rights Movement*. Princeton: Princeton University Press.

Nickel, James. 2017. Human rights. In Zalta, Edward N. (ed.). *The Stanford Encyclopedia of Philosophy* (Spring). https://plato.stanford.edu/archives/spr2017/entries/rights-human/.

Ott, Brian and Walter, Cameron. 2000. Intertextuality: Interpretive practice and textual strategy. *Critical Studies in Media Communication 17*(4): 429–446.

Sikkink, Kathryn. 2017. *Evidence for Hope: Making Human Rights Work in the 21st Century*. Princeton: Princeton University Press.

Snyder, Ilana. 2015. Discourses of "curation" in digital times. In Jones, Rodney H., Chik, Alice and Hafner, Christoph (eds). *Discourse and Digital Practices: Doing Discourse Analysis in the Digital Age*. London/New York: Routledge.

Tharoor, Shashi. 2000. Are human rights universal? *World Policy Journal 16*(4).

Verschueren, Jef. 2012. *Ideology in Language Use: Pragmatic Guidelines for Empirical Research*. Cambridge: Cambridge University Press.

Wenar, Leif. 2015. Rights. In Zalta, Edward N. (ed.). *The Stanford Encyclopedia of Philosophy* (Spring). https://plato.stanford.edu/archives/fall2015/entries/rights/

6 Argumentation and video evidence in a legal context

A multidisciplinary case study from Brazilian military justice

André Lazaro, Vicente Riccio and Amitza Torres Vieira

Contemporary society is marked by the presence of the media, especially in the audiovisual sector. This presence, its dissemination and recent technological advances have defined a new way of interaction and knowledge of reality (Thompson 1995). Nowadays, experiences are no longer limited in time and space and facts that occur thousands of kilometres away are part of our daily lives, to be debated, discussed and judged by an undetermined number of people.

This presence is evident in several situations, such as the consumption of cultural products, television news, the establishment of communities in social networks or the dissemination of information produced by smartphones by witnesses to a specific event, among others. This plurality of situations also affects the field of law and can be observed in different cultural products, such as print journalism, audiovisual movies dealing with law (Asimow 2009, Brown 2017), as well as the presence of images and other audiovisual records in courts from different countries and legal cultures (Tait 2007, Silbey, 2008, Kahan, 2009, Sherwin 2011, Riccio et al. 2018).

The field of law and media studies is vast and involves different objects and methodologies. In the case of the present research, the study deals with the use of the audiovisual image in the process of judicial deliberation. The chapter is a case study regarding a lawsuit judged by Brazilian Military Justice originating in the aggression committed by a corporal and a private against another helpless private. The fact was recorded by smartphone and shared in the military garrison. After an official became aware of the existence of the video, an investigative procedure was instituted to investigate the case. Thus, the present study analyzes how the prosecutor, the public defender, the military federal judge and the judge-rapporteur of the Military Court, in the first and second instances, built their arguments around the images presented. The study is based on the use of textual linguistics (Koch 1986, 2011, 2015, Thompson and Hunston 2000). Analysis focused on the linguistic marks of the utterance and the direction of the argumentative force in the process in relation to video evidence. This analysis allowed for verification of the way in which admission and valuation of the image were established. In addition, the study verified how practitioners justified the nature of evidence incorporated in a legal case, demonstrative or substantive, and the arguments used to support their positions. Finally, the chapter discusses the ability of legal professionals to analyze audiovisual content brought to the case as a means of proof.

Justification/description of the problem

As stated above, contemporary society is characterized by the presence of the media, especially audiovisual media. This is no timid presence but on the contrary, ubiquitous and excessive. At all times, multiple visual stimuli surround people and "navigation" in this "turbulent sea" of images is arduous. Sherwin (2011) defines this situation as the digital baroque, that is, the situation in which there is a profusion of overlapping images of difficult interpretation. The way in which legal reasoning is established, considering factors such as life experience, cultural capital, socioeconomic origin, among others, interferes with the individuals' perceptions about the facts:

> Visual literacy means knowing how images create certain impressions and how they construct or evoke preconceived visual meanings.
>
> (Sherwin 2011: 40)

Thus, it is a tool that can provide the elements for the proper understanding of the role of the image by the legal professional, providing it with mechanisms for the neutralization of biases that can influence what their eyes may see.

It is especially important because of Silbey's (2008) tendency to reassert certain myths about the image, especially in court, in other words the belief in the objectivity of the videos, the lack of ambiguity and the transformation into a face-to-face witness of the viewer recorded on video. This belief in the objectivity of the image spawned the silent witness theory (Gardner, 1946). The basic assumption was to let the camera speak for itself and the spectator witness with their own eyes. The expansion of surveillance and surveillance cameras in public and private spaces, as well as the development of smartphones, has expanded the supply of images for judicial appraisal.

The presence of a camera in a police car reinforced the perspective of the silent theory in the Scott v. Harris decision by the Supreme Court of the United States of America. The case concerned a police chase in which police officer Scott crashed his patrol car into the vehicle of the fugitive Harris, successfully removing the suspect from the road. As a result of this incident, the suspect was left quadriplegic and sued the police officer for excessive use of force. In their defense, the police used the video of the car chase, which was the object of debate on the part of the judges of the Supreme Court. In that case, the police won by eight votes to one and it was not sent to a jury.

The important point in this decision is how the video was interpreted. Further analysis of the Supreme Court's decision points to an over-reliance on the part of the judges on the video. It was accepted as "an account of the fact" and its nuances were not addressed at the time of the trial. The vote of Judge Anthony

Scalia declaring that he was "happy to allow the videotape to speak for itself" is typical of this tendency (United States Supreme Court 2007: 378). In his conclusion, he stated that no reasonable jury would interpret the images by pointing to the disproportionate use of force. He further stated that it was the most exciting police chase since "Operation France." The only divergent vote interpreted the video differently and questioned the alleged danger to the collectivity posed by the suspect driving at high speed on a deserted road. Judge Stevens' vanquished vote was based on a new interpretation of the images and on the appreciation of other details not observed by the other members of the Court.

Considering the Scott v. Harris decision, Kahan (2009) studied four representative groups of American society to ascertain their perceptions about the video of police conduct. Based on theories of the guilt control model, the cognition of identity protection and the cultural cognition of risk, he hypothesized that people with diverse identities and commitments elaborate diverse conceptions of facts presented on video. The results of his research showed that individuals, particularly male, white, rich and linked to hierarchical and individualistic cultural visions, took the same position as the Supreme Court's majority vote. However, for a subgroup of African-Americans, women, poor and with equal values, the positioning was the opposite.

This instant validation of the image is questioned by Sherwin (2011), because seeing is not believing, although the images seem to represent reality as it is. The image must be rigorously scrutinized to avoid distorted excesses and points of view. This aspect is relevant, since there is a risk of the incorporation of the image in the context of the probative process, reaffirming its myths, namely: 1) video images are objective; 2) their meanings are obvious and unambiguous; and 3) the film transforms the observer in a witness (Silbey 2008). The strong criticism regarding the Scott vs. Harris case lies in the reaffirmation of the myths of the image by the judges.

Sherwin (2011) further reinforces this point by citing studies that have analyzed the appropriation of the visual element in the context of judicial argumentation. The comparison between the response to visual and written stimuli in judicial proceedings leads to different associations. Video-based stimuli could lead to unconscious psychological and mental associations related to elements such as memory, experience, and fantasy. Such elements would be added to the mental processing of the image so quickly as to prevent the performance of rational filters responsible for a more critical reflection on the events observed. The effect of this is to see what is expected, what is subjectively desired. Therefore, it is impossible for the film to speak for itself, since it does not present a ready and defined interpretation. The understanding of the explicit and implicit contours of the image is of fundamental importance for its correct appropriation, especially in the judicial context. Visual literacy would promote adequate competence for the understanding of the image by the legal professional.

Silbey (2008) discusses this issue by criticizing the silent witness theory. This approach reinforces the idea of an illusory witness, because the persuasive potential of the image arouses in the viewers judgments based on emotion. Visual literacy, then, is the ability of the legal professional to mobilize various cognitive resources to corroborate or weaken a seemingly dominant version of the argument presented by the video. Thus, video is another element to be subjected to cross-examination as with other types of evidence.

In order to investigate the intensity of the parties' arguments about the video evidence, Silbey developed research (2004) analyzing several cases submitted to the American Courts to assess whether the interpretation of the nature of the evidence (demonstrative or substantive) corresponded to the procedures adopted and the valuation. Substantive evidence is evidence directly related to the disputed fact. Its validity does not depend on another element, since it is sufficient to sustain a point of view. Thus, its admissibility in US law is defined by reason of its relevance and legitimacy.

Demonstrative evidence, such as flowcharts, diagrams and models, is designed to illustrate arguments or to explain another proof, when used to clarify the testimony of a witness, for example. Therefore, demonstrative evidence is not sufficient in itself but depends on another element for its validation. In the case of a diagram, it is not enough to prove a fact. Its use in court comes to the aid of other substantive evidence, such as the testimony of a witness or a set of documents, among others. Demonstrative evidence serves to corroborate substantive evidence.

Silbey's (2004) research examined how video was admitted in courts, whether in substantive or demonstrative format. The author verified the admission of the video as demonstrative proof in the majority of the judgments analyzed, without it being related to previous substantive proof. In this case, the video, which could not speak for itself in whole or in part, was valued as substantive evidence, although it did not present such characteristics.

In Brazilian Criminal Procedural Law there are no specific rules for the treatment of video evidence. Thus, the rules regarding documentary evidence are applied when video evidence is brought to the courts (Lopes Júnior 2011). There are no specific legal prescriptions concerning the adoption of this kind of evidence in the courts. Furthermore, references to the way the proof was obtained and to its nature (demonstrative or substantive) are not observed at this stage.

The use of video evidence in Brazil is based on analogy. In general, the same criteria adopted to analyze written documents are applied to video evidence in Brazil. The main issue is the understanding of the image in a legal culture with little tradition of oral debate (Riccio et al. 2018). Thus, the present study attempts to answer the following research questions: how is the argumentation of legal professionals carried out in cases involving video evidence? Or, more specifically, "how do you develop the argument about video evidence in a military criminal trial?" In order to answer such questions, the research adopts a multidisciplinary perspective, understood as the interaction between sciences for solving a problem (Philippi Júnior and Silva Neto 2010). Thus, the research incorporates concepts of law, social sciences and linguistics. These aspects are addressed in the following sections.

Textual linguistics and argumentation on video evidence

Textual linguistics aims to understand how units of speech are understood in a broader view. It is concerned with written and spoken texts in a specific context. One of the initial concerns of this field was to construct textual grammars, responsible for describing categories of words and rules in a certain language. The initial perspective gradually included a semantic orientation, focused on the meaning and the process of interpretation of the text and its components. However, the study of language as an autonomous phenomenon was retained. The pragmatic orientation began to defend the analysis of the text based on its relation with the communicative processes of a concrete society, which reveals an external orientation in the search for meaning. The external orientation was followed by an internal, cognitivist character, occupied in analyzing the mental models of operations and their types of operations. The socio-cognitive-interactionist perspective emerged from the union of these last two strands. In this approach, subjects are seen as social actors/constructors and the text as the proper place of interaction (Koch 2015). In short, the goal is to reveal the argumentative end of a specific interaction.

The understanding of the argumentative process is achieved by the analysis of the textual elements chosen by those who are interacting. These elements constitute the linguistic marks of the utterance and may consist of argumentative operators, presuppositions markers, modal indicators, evaluation markers and polyphony cases (Koch 2015). Argumentative operators are names or expressions that indicate the argumentative scale and belong to an argumentative class. The argumentative scale can be represented graphically, according to the example in Fig. 6.1.

In the lacuna present in the statement 'he dined ____ yesterday', operators can be inserted and will vary according to the intensity of the argument. It can vary from a little, describing the least of them, to everything – the strongest degree. Thus, an argumentative scale may contain several types of argumentative operators, responsible for describing the development and intensity of argumentation.

Presupposition markers introduce presupposed semantic contents. In the statement John went on to miss work, the enunciator presupposes the fact that John is a hard worker. According to Koch (2015), they are constituted by verbs indicative of state change or permanence (stay, continue, etc.), factual verbs (indicating a psychological state, such as regret) and by the rhetoric of the presupposition, characterized by the presentation of information linked to the other subsequent information. An example of using the rhetoric of the presupposition is the information "we regret the inconvenience," which is

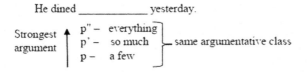

Figure 6.1 Argumentative scale

sometimes observed in commercial establishments under construction. The last term (inconvenient, pertinent to disturbances that the work may have caused) is taken for granted, although it consists of the main information (the alert for the existence of the work itself).

Modal indicators demonstrate the way something is said, since the same statement can be influenced by several modalities. Derived from studies of classical logic, the division comprises algetic (indicating need or possibility), epistemic (certainty or doubt) and deontic statements (compulsory or facultative). They usually have the use of auxiliary verbs of duty or power, as can be seen in the statements presented by Koch (1986): "it must be snowing in Paris" (algetic – possibility), "you must fulfill your duties to the firm" (deontic – obligatory) and "the enemies must be a hundred" (epistemic – doubt).

In evaluation indexes, the person responsible for the argument evaluates a fact, its context or the feeling nourished. The first is represented by subjectivity markers (Thompson and Hunston 2000) and includes names used from the value load on an act or fact. An example is the statement "he begged for forgiveness." Beg for something is an act that shows great intensity and evaluation indexes.

Domain indexes are composed by the context of understanding a fact (strategically, economically) or how it is formulated (secretly, openly, briefly). Attitudinal indicators are names and expressions that present the psychological state of the enunciator about the fact (happily, unfortunately). Those domains are common in communicative interactions.

Polyphony is the phenomenon characterized by the presence of a speech from a different perspective that may or may not have the agreement of the enunciator. The most common forms are the use of proverbs or popular sayings (two wrongs don't make a right) and in the authority argument (according to the bible, laziness is one of the capital sins). Thus, textual linguistics provides some important tools for highlighting possible distinctions between the way of arguing about video evidence in relation to other evidence, as well as characterizing the nature of the video (such as demonstrative or substantive evidence) and its valuation.

Case study

This chapter analyzes a case dealt with by Brazilian Military Justice based on a video recorded by a cell phone. The case began when an officer observed a soldier watching a video of bullying in the barracks. In the video, a corporal applied a jiu-jitsu arm-lock on a private, who cried to be released. During this interaction, a second soldier entered the scene and proceeded to suffocate the victim with a towel, at which point the screams increased in intensity. The military police used the video to open a case against the perpetrators. The video was also the key evidence to sustain a conviction in the lower court. After the sentence was appealed, the case was finally decided by the Superior Military Tribunal in Brasilia, the highest military court in Brazil, which held the lower court's conviction.

The research analyzed the arguments used in a legal case by the prosecutor, the public defender, the federal military judge and the judge-rapporteur in the Superior

Military Court, the latter being first and second instance judges. The research started from a qualitative perspective based on textual linguistics. The qualitative approach attempted to understand a social phenomenon from the meanings attributed by those who experience them (Denzin and Lincoln 1998), in order to observe and explain a singular event – in this particular case the use of video evidence in a military court.

Data analysis

Research began with the analysis of all the documents of all case files that presented some type of argumentation about the video evidence. In this group are the arguments of the prosecutor, the public defender, the military federal judge and the judge-rapporteur in the case debate. After this initial cut, the argumentative elements were codified through the categories of textual linguistics. The arguments developed by the prosecutor on the evidence took place in 23 excerpts divided as follows: nine on the testimony of the accused, victim and witnesses, seven on the video evidence and seven comprising both the testimony and the video evidence. The video evidence is not a preponderant element in the argumentative process according to the data. The argumentative resources employed by the prosecutor do not demonstrate a prevalence of the video over the other kinds of evidence brought to the case.

The analysis of excerpts dealing with video evidence or the video combined with other kinds of evidence results in the following: a) ten excerpts reinforce the substantive nature of video evidence; b) two excerpts emphasize the descriptive nature; and c) two neutral excerpts discuss the need for a forensic expert to validate the video and another demanding the full transcription of its contents. The prosecutor's view reinforces the substantive nature of video evidence.

Thus, the prosecutor reinforced the substantive nature of video evidence in the case. Excerpt 25 is particularly expressive:

> So, in order for Your Honor to have a real notion of the seriousness of the aggression, **I suggest that you watch the video in plenary and draw your conclusions**. The persuasive and summarizing power of the images surpasses everything written here.

In another excerpt, he strongly reaffirms the requirements of a condemnatory request from the video: "both authorship and materiality have been proven in the film" (excerpt 20).

According to Brazilian criminal procedural law, the prosecutor is responsible for requesting authentication of evidence. In this case, the video was not submitted to an expert's analysis to validate its authenticity. Authentication was limited to the trust deposited in the testimony of the fourth witness who "confiscated the cell phone and copied the scenes of the aggression" (excerpt 24). This authentication procedure is characteristic of demonstrative evidence whose validity is linked with specific substantive evidence. This mismatch between the admission criteria and their evaluation reinforces the use of demonstrative evidence as substantive (Silbey 2004).

The prosecutor only requested "the transcription of the audio of the film inserted in the CD of Annex 1" (excerpt 11). By doing so, he sought to transform the video evidence into documental evidence without considering important multimodal elements, such as looks, gestures and movements, essential to the appreciation of the proof (Kjeldsen 2015, Bateman 2016). The transcription was not discussed by any of the parties involved. The request for transcription reveals the difficulty of Brazilian legal professionals in dealing with video evidence. Thus, the need for visual literacy is a real issue.

The final conclusion concerning the prosecutor's argumentation in the process is the prevalence of evaluation indexes in excerpts that discuss the video alone or accompanied by other types of evidence. The video allows the prosecutor to emphasize his accusatory power. In excerpt 21, he states that "the jiu-jitsu arm-lock was *extremely* dangerous and *extremely* violent, rather than a joke." This excerpt does not allow for verifying an unconscious or conscious decision in the valuation of the video by the prosecutor.

On the other hand, the public defender adopted a different strategy concerning the video. He insisted on the thesis of no intention of harm by his clients. It was a joke with an unexpected result. Thus, his arguments aimed to avoid the video and to discuss the witnesses' testimony. The public defender discussed the video evidence in twenty-one excerpts. He stresses the testimonies brought to the case (accused, victim and witnesses) on seventeen occasions. His strategy is to disregard the video and to work with the testimonies. His thesis of a bad joke with unintended results prevails. It can be observed in excerpt 03, when he states that the defendants "applied jiu-jitsu blows, among other forms of *mild* aggression."

The defense did not argue directly about the video. In excerpts 32 and 44, the Public Defender stated that the accused allowed the filming. So, it would be reasonable to prove that a joke had been carried out. Thus, the defense focuses its arguments on: 1) the absence of intention to commit an act of violence; 2) the characterization of the action as a "joke"; 3) the "joke" as a form of military subculture; and 4) the participation of the victim in acts of this nature, including involving the accused. The transcript of excerpt 32 describes the defense's argumentative strategy:

> The idea that it was not an illicit, but a "joke," was so solid that the accused, even, let a third soldier film the incident. It is obvious that if they had a criminal potential in their conduct, they would not have allowed such evidence to be produced.

Therefore, it is possible to conclude that the public defender interpreted the video as substantive evidence. However, the defense did not exploit the potentiality of its content, and had a restricted interpretation based only on the "joke argument." There was no more forceful refutation of the arguments put forward by the prosecutor. The public defender could, for example, have questioned the authenticity of the footage, how the officer had obtained the video, or the identification of the participants in their oral support in plenary. Moreover, he could have demonstrated the controversial nature of several multimodal elements present in the video, such as the movement of participants, sounds, and the focus of the footage.

The last group of video interpreters is made up of the military federal judge at the first degree of jurisdiction and the second degree ministries from the Superior Military Court in Brasilia. Both followed the prosecutor's arguments and brought the video contents to their votes. They employed expressions to evaluate the image when discussing the facts. The federal military judge and the judge-rapporteur reinforced the arguments based on video evidence or video evidence accompanied by witnesses' testimonials (seven out of nine excerpts). The markers of evaluation presented the highest incidence among the argumentative resources, indicating intense interpretive activity, especially regarding the video.

They considered the audiovisual record as substantive proof. In excerpt 50, the first degree judge refers to the insistent requests of the victim to cease the aggression. Additionally, in excerpt 53 it is possible to highlight the second degree judge-rapporteur's argument about victim's exposure to risk. He mentioned this after watching the images in video evidence. So, he had considered the video as substantive evidence. This belief in the evidence was so firm that no judge questioned the validity of how the evidence was obtained – in this case the confiscation of a cell phone belonging to a private by a superior officer.

The video was the most relevant evidence produced in this case. For instance, one judge relies heavily on the video and affirms (excerpt 49): "the use of physical force is *very clear by the images.*" This is an evaluative index with strong emphasis on the video's content. The judge-rapporteur considered that the video depictions affirmed that the first accused was the perpetrator and the act occurred violently. The valuation of this evidence with such relevance reinforces the comments in the previous paragraph on the need for greater attention to authentication of evidence, as alerted by Silbey (2008).

The judge-rapporteur's argument in excerpt 54 demonstrates the impact of the image. He states the potential damage of the jiu-jitsu arm-lock applied against the defenseless private:

> *I can assure* you that the severity of the coup applied to the victim could have caused irreversible harm.

The use of the epistemic argument "*I can assure*" reveals a degree of certainty typical of an eyewitness.

The judges also brought their personal experiences to the case when discussing the depicted content. One judge described the jiu-jitsu hold applied by the defendant against the victim (excerpt 52):

the coup applied, the arm-lock, is potentially harmful, and the possibility of a more serious result, such as a bodily injury, was concrete.

The magistrate demonstrates knowledge of the nature of the hold, which is reinforced in excerpt 54: "This same type of blow even injured a well-known Brazilian fighter in a UFC event." These activated excerpts from his memoirs could be associated with unconscious biases (Sherwin 2011). It can be observed when the judge-rapporteur made a mental association between the act of the accused and the UFC (Ultimate Fighting Championship) event known worldwide, in which fighters are placed in a cage-shaped ring to fight against each other. Among the resources available is the arm-lock, designed to fracture the bones of the opponent's upper limb. This reference to a previous memory is common and reinforces the need for visual training of judges to avoid prejudices lying in their subconscious (Kahan, 2009).

Conclusion

The research analyzed how legal professionals built their arguments around the image in a legal case conducted by Brazilian Military Justice. From the case studied, it was possible to analyze how legal professionals in a specific case construct the nature of evidence, substantive or demonstrative. Moreover, the research analyzed the ability of legal professionals to interpret the images recorded, stored and disseminated in the video.

Considering the argumentation process, the prosecutor relied on the video to sustain the accusation. In a group of 23 excerpts, the prosecutor stresses the video content in fourteen excerpts. In his view, the video works as substantive evidence. The judges in both levels of jurisdiction follow the same pattern, relying on the video to sustain their decisions.

The public defender's argument relied on the testimony of the accused, the victim and the witnesses, corresponding to seventeen out of a total of 21 excerpts. The video was not explored or even questioned in terms of validity, visual aspects or trustworthiness, demonstrating a lack of understanding of the nature and potential of video in a legal context.

Regarding the nature of evidence, the legal professionals stressed unanimously its substantive nature. In addition, the prosecutor and the judges rated it the most relevant evidence to sustain the condemnatory decisions. The prosecutor declares its convincing power over the other evidence brought to the court. The same perspective can be observed in the statement from a judge-rapporteur affirming the potential damage from the jiu-jitsu hold recorded on video through the use of the epistemic argument "I can assure."

Finally, the need for greater visual literacy for legal professionals working in Brazil is real. The image is still an unknown field and understanding its specificities presents a considerable challenge. The development of further research incorporating the problem of legal culture, visual literacy and the use of different argumentative modes is central to the advancement of the field. This study has attempted to fill a specific gap in this huge field.

Acknowledgement

The authors would like to thank the *Fundação para o Apoio à Pesquisa do Estado de Minas Gerais (FAPEMIG)* for the financial support to the project "Video Evidence in Second Degree Courts: an empirical analysis of judicial interpretation of the image" (APQ 01236–16).

References

Asimow, Michael. 2009. *Lawyers in your Living Room: Law On Television*. Chicago: American Bar Association.

Bateman, John. 2016. From narrative to visual narrative to audiovisual narrative: The multimodal discourse theory connection. In Miller, Ben, Lieto, Antonio, Ronfard, Rémi, Ware, Stephen G. and Finlayson, Mark (eds) *7th Workshop on Computational Models of Narrative*, Article N° 1: 1–11.

Brown, Michele. 2017. *Visual criminology. Oxford Research Encyclopedia*. doi:10.1093/acrefore/9780190264079.013.206.

Denzin, Norman K. and Lincoln, Yvonna. 1998. *Collecting and Interpreting Qualitative Materials*. London, Sage.

Gardner, Dillard S. 1946. The camera goes to court. *North Carolina Law Review 24*(*3*): 233–246.

Kahan, Dan M. 2009. Whose eyes are you going to believe? Scott v. Harris and the perils of cognitive illiberalism. *Harvard Law Review 122*(*3*): 837–906.

Kjeldsen, Jens. 2015. The study of visual and multimodal argumentation. *Argumentation 29*: 115–132.

Koch, Ingedore G. V. 1986. *A questão das modalidades numa Nova Gramática da Língua Portuguesa*. Araraquara: Saraiva.

Koch, Ingedore G. V. 2011. *Argumentação e Linguagem*. São Paulo: Cortez.

Koch, Ingedore G. V. 2015. *A Inter-ação pela e Linguagem*. São Paulo: Cortez.

Lopes Júnior, Aury. 2011. *Direito Processual Penal e sua Conformidade Constitucional*. Rio de Janeiro: Lumen Juris.

Riccio, Vicente, Vieira, Amitza Torres and Guedes, Clarissa D. 2018. *Video Evidence, Legal Culture and Court Decision in Brazil*. In Tessuto, Girolamo, Bhatia, Vijay K. and Engberg, Jan (eds) *Frameworks for Discursive Actions and Practices of the Law*, 1st edn. Newcastle upon Tyne: Cambridge Scholars Publishing.

Sherwin, Richard K. 2011. *Visualizing Law in the Age of the Digital Baroque*. London and New York: Routledge.

Silbey, Jessica. 2004. Judge as film critics: New approaches to filmic evidence. *University of Michigan Journal of Law Reform 37*(*2*): 493–571.

Silbey, Jessica. 2008. Cross-examining film. *Race, Religion, Gender & Class 8*(*17*): 17–46.

Tait, David. 2007. Rethinking the role of the image in justice: visual evidence and science in the trial process. *Law, Probability and Risk 6*: 311–318.

Thompson, Geoff and Hunston, Susan. 2000. *Evaluation: An introduction.* In Thompson, Geoff and Hunston, Susan (eds) *Evaluation in Text: Authorial Stance and the Construction of Discourse.* Oxford: Oxford University Press.
Thompson, John B. 1995. *The Media and the Modernity: A Social Theory of the Media.* Stanford: Stanford University Press.
Philippi Jr., Arlindo and Silva Neto, Antonio. 2011. *Interdisciplinaridade em Ciência, Tecnologia & Inovação.* São Paulo: Manole.
United States Supreme Court. 2007. *Scott vs. Harris.* Nº 05–1631.

Section 2 - Social media for client empowerment

7 The discursive construction of Hong Kong's Civic Square in the media

Contesting social and legal perspectives

Aditi Bhatia

Introduction

At the 2011 inauguration ceremony of the Central Government Offices (CGO), then Chief Executive (CE) Donald Tsang Yam-kuen declared that the design of the complex was to be consistent "with the main themes of 'Doors Always Open', 'Land Always Green', 'Sky Will Be Blue' and 'People Will Be Connected'."[1] Tsang added that the design was not purely "an architectural feature, but also a reminder telling us to be liberal, open-minded and proactively solicit public opinion at all times" (Lin, 2014). The site has since been the focal point of key demonstrations by Hong Kong protestors, primarily under the stewardship of former CE Leung Chun-ying. In fact, the East Wing Forecourt of the CGO was rechristened by the public as the "Civic Square during the Anti-National Education movement in 2012 ... [and has since] been at the heart of different large-scale protests and many people look upon it as an open space for public gatherings" (Varsity, Chinese University of Hong Kong, 2015). This has also included the more prominent Hong Kong Umbrella Movement of 2014.

However, in the summer of 2014, the Square was officially closed off to the public, as three-metre high fences were installed around the forecourt amid the government's concern over security risks. While there has been much public dissatisfaction over the last few years surrounding this decision, the debate was resurrected in April 2017 with the arrival of Hong Kong's new CE Carrie Lam Cheng Yuet-ngor, including arguments by the outgoing CE to keep the fences intact for public safety; arguments by democracy activists to reopen the Square and return to people the right to public assembly; and middlemen from both democratic and pro-Beijing factions to reopen the Square without the right to public assembly as a gesture of reconciliation between contesting parties.

This debate has stemmed from, as well, a relatively murky understanding of whether the Square can be regarded legally as public space, or part of government premises open to the public, with members of democracy and media groups arguing that it belongs to members of the public, but members of the government claiming that the Square "is neither a public place nor a public open space, and the public does not have an absolute right of free access to it ... [it is]

primarily used as a vehicular access for the Central Government Offices."[2] In the context of this debate, this chapter will investigate the subsequent discursive construction of the colloquially termed Civic Square by contesting discourse clans[3] (Bhatia, 2015b), through the framework of the Discourse of Illusion (to which we give more light below), in which the Square is contradictorily (re) conceptualized as being both symbolic of fear and threat and the right to assembly and free speech, giving rise to powerful discursive illusions in two competing narratives proliferated through local online media.

The Discourse of Illusion

Kant (1970) argued that our minds actively participate in the construction of our realities; this process involving the creation of a coherent, yet subjective, reconstruction of the external world by drawing on past experiences and ideologies (cf. Berger and Luckmann, 1966; Bhatia, 2015a, 2015b, 2016). As such, our conceptualization of reality becomes a product of history, evolving over the course of time, apparent "not in documents or static things, but only in 'the actual run of event in experience'" (Hart, 1929, 492). This cognitive-socio-historical phenomenon Bourdieu (1990) has referred to as *habitus*, which "produces individual and collective practices ... in accordance with the schemes generated by history ... [that] tend to guarantee the 'correctness' of practices" (54). These predisposed forms of ideological behaviour, which may not be consciously controlled but still regulative, naturalize into our consciousness, becoming difficult to discern in everyday activities.

Our conceptualizations of reality are subjective *because* they are ideologically-rooted, they are no more than "a bundle or collection of different perceptions" (Hume, 1970, 278), constructed through our language and action. But it is possible to attire these subjective conceptualizations as objective truths through the means of collective consent, as we invariably employ the "principle of social validation" to ascertain "what other people think is correct" (Cialdini, 1997, 199). Authority, power struggles, and hegemony, as well as material means (e.g. language, modality etc.) play a considerable part in justification and acceptance of particular ideological conceptualizations of reality.

More specifically, this chapter is concerned with the notion of collective illusions created through public discourse (cf. Carfantan, 2003). Creators of discursive illusions (typically powerful groups in society, or discourse clans), with access to proliferative mediums (e.g. mass/social media), often employ particular semantico-pragmatic and lexico-syntactic resources to persuade audiences of the legitimacy of their conceptualizations. Thus, collective illusions arise when particular conceptualizations of reality (be it of an event, issue, phenomena, occurrence etc.) become recognized as the *dominant framework* (through endorsement from many witnesses) within which understanding of *that* reality operates (Bhatia, 2015a). Such illusions become challenging to disprove because they start representing what is true (for any particular social group) with regards to any aspect of reality.

Subjective conceptualizations of reality offered as narratives of truth become all the more persuasive because they evoke either social fear, prejudice, doubt, or happiness etc. and because they are often disguised as truths that audiences are free to accept or reject. As Perloff (1993, 12) argues, if "message recipients perceive that they are free to reject the advocated position, then, as a practical matter, they are free; and the influence attempt is regarded as 'persuasive in nature'." This process is most commonly understood in terms of Gramsci's notion of hegemony, whereby a "hegemonic class, or part of a class, is one which gains the consent of other classes and social forces through creating and maintaining a system of alliances by means of political and ideological struggle" (in translation, Simon, 1999, 25–26). In regarding this process as hegemony, then, I further elevate the earlier notion *of dominant framework* to dominant representations [or conceptualizations] of specific instances of reality, proliferated through various multimodalities, [which] go on to constitute the hegemonic discursive framework through which understanding, action and discussion is formed. What is of concern here is not necessarily the falsity or subjectivity of the representations [or conceptualizations] conveyed but rather the process through which they acquire a status of facticity/objectivity (Bhatia, 2015a, 14).

Establishment of consent on part of audiences regarding a particular representation of reality can generate a collective illusion, resulting in homogeneity in terms of in-group beliefs and practices. These beliefs and practices often generate categories "through which we routinely, albeit largely unconsciously, observe and classify events and experiences" (Sarangi and Candlin, 2003, 117). Categorization introduces purpose into our experiences, becoming "representations of who we are, what we stand for, what our values are and what our relationships with others are ... a self-serving schema for the representation of *us* and *them* as social groups" (Oktar, 2001, 313–314). Thus, once a discursive illusion occurs (i.e. an ideological conceptualization of an issue, event etc. which goes on to become a dominant framework of understanding through collective agreement, reinforced through discourse), it becomes part of our belief system, leading to categories and stereotypes of aspects of the social world.

The Discourse of Illusion (drawing on a combination of the Foucauldian and Faircloughian notion of discourse), which is proposed here as an umbrella term encompassing various forms of public discourses, in particular those associated with politics and media, can be viewed as an attempt by writers or speakers to convince their audiences that the conceptualization of reality that they are putting forward is the objective one. Illusions are invariably created through discourse when writers and speakers, through various modalities (such as speeches, newspaper reports etc.), seek legitimization for what they are arguing and what they believe. The discourse here itself becomes the modality, the means to transform audiences' perceptions of the world, and the evolving narrative meanings of complex constructs (see Bhatia, 2015a for a more comprehensive account of the Discourse of Illusion).

The Discourse of Illusion is an appropriate multidimensional framework to adopt in the investigation of Hong Kong's Civic Square because it is concerned with efforts on the part of writers or speakers to gain collective consent for their subjective conceptualizations in order to objectify them. This invariably draws discursive illusions away from basic text to larger areas of context and social reality. The analytical framework employed will explore discursive illusions through three interrelated components – history, linguistic and semiotic action, and social impact – analysed through a combination of three methods (structured immediacy, critical metaphor analysis, and categorization). The integration of these models distinguishes this approach by allowing for a deeper and richer multi-perspective analysis of dynamic discursive processes at both textual and contextual levels.

Methodological framework

In order to more closely explore how discursive illusions are realized, the chapter will draw on a combined analysis incorporating dimensions of historicity, linguistic and semiotic action, linked to an account of some of the social effects of these actions:

1   Historicity – an individual or group's habitus is fundamental to the Discourse of Illusion as it involves recontextualization of past experience into present day action, to analyse which the framework draws on the concept of *structured immediacy* (Leudar and Nekvapil, 2011), focusing on "how participants enrich the here-and-now of action by connecting it to the past" (66), and which we can define as "the unconscious or conscious reconceptualization of historical antecedents in an attempt to situate and present specific instances of current reality, often in relation to the future" (Bhatia, 2015a, 52). In doing so, I also extend Bourdieu's notion of habitus beyond individual practice to include collective practices of dynamic discursive entities (e.g. newspapers, political parties, government, community groups etc.) with evolving repositories of sociocultural understanding and ideologies. Analysis at this level involves looking at temporal references, invocation of past events or sociocultural/ political history, and recontextualization of present occurrences in terms of these past events. In doing so, we discover how situating current activities in history through reference to the past "'thicken' the descriptions of people and activities – providing them with meanings they would not have had otherwise" (Leudar and Nekvapil, 2011, 80).

2   Linguistic and semiotic action – subjective conceptualizations of the world give rise to an individual or group's linguistic and semiotic actions, to analyse which the framework borrows elements of critical discourse analysis (CDA), focusing in particular on *critical metaphor analysis* (Charteris-Black, 2004; 2005), which "aims to identify the intentions and ideologies underlying language use" (Charteris-Black, 2005, 26). The emphasis here is on the speaker or writer's intention in the creation and diffusion of metaphor by blending both cognitive and pragmatic perspectives, recognising that

metaphor is not just a linguistic phenomenon but also a persuasive tool. Analysis at this level involves looking at various metaphors/metaphorical representations which can "bring to a discourse event traces of previous uses and of previous discourse events" (Cameron, 2003, 27). Furthermore, different components of a metaphor (focus/frame and topic/vehicle) enable subjective representations of reality to become more acceptable and feasible, while also creating new ways to conceptualize complex issues.

3   Social impact – the language and actions of an individual or group engender many categories and stereotypes, which can be analysed through Jayyusi's (1984) concept of *categorization* that explicates how people "organize their moral positions and commitments round certain category identities" (183). Analysis at this level involves identifying three classes of membership categories: self-organised groups (united by common beliefs, interests and commitments); type categorisation (predicting actions believed to be "embedded in the features of that categorisation" (Jayyusi, 1984, 24)); and individual descriptor designators (assigning labels with both an ascriptive and descriptive function to "types" of people in those groups). Put together, analysis of categorization at these levels reveals the ideologies behind the positive or negative representation of self and other groups in the context of complex issues.

Data

The data for this study have been taken from English-language online news-papers (of various political leanings) in Hong Kong, including *South China Morning Post* (SCMP), the *Ejinsight* (the English language subsidiary of the *Hong Kong Economic Journal*) and *Hong Kong Free Press* (HKFP). The first two are regarded as the most credible newspapers in Hong Kong (based on a 2016 public survey conducted by the Chinese University of Hong Kong of perceived "credibility" on a scale of ten[4]), though in recent years, there has been a slight change in SCMP's ideological trajectory, marking "the beginning of a shift towards a 'corporate face' and away from … community service" (Partridge, 2012). And especially after its buyout in 2015 by the Alibaba Group (a Chinese mul-tinational e-company), SCMP has adopted a relatively less critical stance towards the government. *Ejinsight* adopts a comparatively more critical stance towards both local and Mainland governments, particularly in the editorials. The third is a free and independent news source, hosting journalists concerned about declining press freedom, with a much more critical lean towards international and national affairs (compared to the previous two papers).

The primary data set consists of e-articles taken from the *News* and *Opinion* webpages of the newspapers, during the month of April 2017 when the debate surrounding the Square resurfaced with the formal appointment of Carrie Lam Cheng Yuet-ngor early in the month. The debate was revisited as a result of curiosity on the part of democracy protestors who hoped the new CE would take a different line on the Square from her predecessor, in appealing to the new CE to reopen the grounds and grant permission for the annual Handover Day rally on 1 July 2017. In addition, I draw on *User Comments* posted on the articles either on the official news websites or on social media re-posts to assess the degree to which dominant narratives are absorbed into informal public discourse. The paper also draws on a secondary data set comprising news and views expressed in a variety of new media and academic English-language sources in order to better inform understanding of the socio-political issue (e.g. notion of public square, urban space, Hong Kong politics etc.) and its analysis.

Although it is entirely possible to identify the slant of newspapers/periodicals based on the editorials for example, the focus of this study is not on the allegiance of the newspapers from which articles are analysed but rather the narrative construction of the Civic Square in society. It is for this reason that the study, given the context, regards the newspapers as a conduit of information reflecting the arguments of different discourse clans. As such, the study, in its analysis, identified two primary discourse clans that tended to adhere to two distinct narratives about the Square: first, C. Y. Leung and his then exiting government who conceptualized the Square in terms of fear and threat; and second, freedom protestors (including non- or demonstrating activists/party representatives) who conceptualized the Square in terms of freedom to assembly and free speech.

The square as a symbol of fear and threat

On 17 July 2014, after a series of protests by the public on various issues, including the introduction of national education in the local school curriculum, the Hong Kong government issued a press release announcing the temporary closure (till August 2014) of the Easy Wing Forecourt of the CGO for construction works. The government saw this as a necessary decision, arising from the need "to enhance the overall capacity of the CGO to withstand potential security threats to the building."[5] Subsequently, a three-metre high fence was installed around the 1000 sq. metre forecourt, colloquially known as the Civic Square, and it has remained there to continued public safety concerns of the government. The following extracts illustrate how the outgoing CE, C. Y. Leung, reconceptualizes the Square as a site of violence and fear in defence of his government's decision to indefinitely cordon it off.

> (Extract 1) However, incumbent Chief Executive Leung Chung-ying said on an RTHK programme on Saturday that the government maintains a "clear position" that it is not yet time to reopen the forecourt. He also corrected the talk show host, who referred the area using its colloquial name. "It is the government headquarters," he said. He said there may be a public safety risk as there are glass doors and windows on the ground floor facing the forecourt. He added that the need to conduct a risk evaluation is "not unique to Hong Kong – cities big and small also does it given the political climate we face today."
>
> (Ng, HKFP, 25/4/17)

(Extract 2) "This is Lam's decision. I believe she will do an assessment before she makes any decision," [CY] Leung said. "But we have to consider the safety of civil servants working at the headquarters.... Considering the situation in Hong Kong and recent attacks around the globe, it is not appropriate to reopen the complex.... Over the years, some have lit fires outside, while some have smashed the glass door of the Legislative Council complex," he said. "The [doors] of the headquarters are made of glass, with traffic outside. The design is different from other buildings."

(Leung, SCMP, 25/4/17)

(Extract 3) But Leung said on Tuesday that it should not be reopened, claiming the government has conducted risk assessments and considered attacks in foreign countries. "In the past few years, you have seen arson of a rubbish bin outside a government building, [and] some tried to break open and crash though a glass door of the Legislative Council," he said. The Legislative Council still has a demonstration area, but not directly outside the government headquarters. Leung said: "There are a lot of demonstration areas around the government headquarters."

(Cheng, HKFP, 26/4/17)

(Extract 4) On Tuesday, Leung said the administration decided against it after a security assessment in light of what he called "local and overseas attacks." He said that while the government should make sure people can demonstrate outside government headquarters, it also has to ensure the safety of civil servants who work there and visitors to the building. Leung also cited past cases of protesters setting a rubbish bin on fire and forcibly pushing glass doors of the adjacent Legislative Council complex.

(Yeung, *Ejinsight*, 26/4/17)

We see in these extracts repetition of the importance of 'risk assessment' in relation to the 'headquarters' which are deemed vulnerable because they 'are made of glass', the term assessment implying not an arbitrary fear of threat, but rather a calculated and measured 'evaluation' of circumstances and potential risks. Fear is evoked through the topos of external threat (Wodak et al., 1999) when the headquarters are conceptualized as a possible target vulnerable to "local and overseas attacks" given the "political climate we face today." Use of the all-inclusive "we" generalizing the threat against all members of the public, and not just members of the government.

Local demonstrations by members of the public are correlated with 'attacks in foreign countries' and 'recent attacks around the globe', thus intentions and actions of protesting groups are interpreted through the recontextualization of the protests against the backdrop of various terror "attacks around the globe" (which have taken place variously on the scale of intensity, for example, 2013 attack on Westgate Mall in Nairobi, 2014 attack on Jewish Museum in Brussels; 2015 Charlie Hebdo attacks in Paris etc.), the emotions of fear and danger associated with these attacks correlated with the fear for safety of the CGO compound. Leung indicates that Hong Kong is not "unique" from other countries, thus insinuating it is just as susceptible to attacks. He further reiterates previous incidences in conjunction with use of temporal references ("over the years," "past few years," "past cases") where "some" have "lit fires" and "smashed glass" to reiterate the aggression that the "headquarters" can incite, in order to strengthen the parallel between terror "attacks around the globe" and local threats; words and phrases that fall into the semantic category of attack and threat ("lit fire," "smashed the glass door," "attacks," "arson," "break open," "crash through," "setting on fire," "forcibly pushing") illustrated with a general lack of agency, strengthening his rhetoric of fear.

Such recontextualization can be seen to illustrate how different discourse clans creatively render the meaning of events and issues, thus making "accountable connections between something in the present and something in the past, uniting the two in a figure-ground relationship" (Leudar and Nekvapil, 2011, 72). This has the repercussion of transforming history into a tool that discourse clans can use to un/knowingly, dis/associate the here-and-now with the past to justify the present or future. In this instance, use of the word 'attack' works to arouse fear of an impending threat, framing the future in terms of the past, and in doing so discursively constructing the Civic Square as a symbol of fear and threat, something to be defended against. As Smith (1997) explains, "when individuals perceive some phenomenon as highly threatening but also perceive themselves as capable of defending themselves against the threat (or as efficacious), they are motivated to protect themselves against the threat" (273). The evocation of fear helps create illusions, which sustain power asymmetries and create dangerous categorizations, within which activists can be turned into terrorists and acts of protest into violence (see Bhatia, 2015b).

Leung further grounds his fear through the topos of threat (Wodak et al., 1999) that opening up the Square would pose, by specifying that the fear for safety is not directed at politicians who have lost much goodwill but rather for 'civil servants who work there' and 'visitors to the building', ordinary members of the public who can potentially become victims of attacks. In this instance, the topos helps his audience in surmising the correct frame of experience in order to interpret this particular version of reality, as Bednarek (2005, 703–704) points out "certain topoi would lead the hearer to infer the correct interpretative frame even if s/he came to the text without prior knowledge or expectations." We see here the efficacy of the Discourse of Illusion if it is seen as a response to the emotion of fear, as audiences are more likely to be convinced by a particular representation of reality if it appears as a solution to their fears and worries. In identifying potential threats and possible solutions to them, Leung casts himself in the role of a protector, as being responsible for the well-being of those not only under his employ but also under the guardianship of his government. In further positive self-presentation of his government, he does not deny members of the public the space for assembly since he believes the "government should make sure people can demonstrate outside government headquarters" but points them to "demonstration areas around the headquarters" and in doing so denies protestors the symbolism of space. This is also evident in his use of the formal designation of the Square as opposed to its "colloquial name," use of which would dilute legal control and right over the space. In this regard, the government's control over the creation of that space also confers a certain power over the processes of social reproduction. Hierarchical structures of authority or privilege can be communicated directly through forms of spatial organization and symbolism. Control over spatial organization and authority over the use of space become crucial means for the reproduction of social power relations (Harvey, 1989, 186–187).

But true to the nature of discursive illusions, groups and individuals can have "double contrastive identity" (Leudar et al., 2004), owning multiple, often contrasting identities, including the role the group perceives itself to be playing and that which others perceive the group to be playing. In this case, while Leung depicts his government as a responsible one, concerned about the public's welfare, contesting discourse clans portray him to the contrary:

> (Extract 5) Considering both pivotal events were the worst political crises Leung had to face as chief executive, perhaps he has developed a psychological attachment to the fence, a kind of post-traumatic response. But let me play Sigmund Freud here. Face down your fear. Take down the fence, CY. Show the people you are magnanimous. Don't wait till Lam does it, as surely she will. Do it as one of your last political acts, as a symbol of peace and reconciliation.
>
> (Lo, SCMP, 27/4/17)

Here we see Leung's 'risk evaluation' is reconceptualized through a mental health metaphor as 'a kind of post-traumatic response' to previous protests against his attempts to introduce contested policies, which are adjudged 'the worst political crises'. Use of the word 'psychological' to describe his state of mind, in conjunction with the superlative 'worst' creating a nightmare scenario by which Leung is scarred and rendered irrational, thus discrediting his version of reality through the strategy of delegitimization (Wodak et al., 1999). In this case, the writer takes on the role of noted psychoanalyst "Freud," instructing Leung to "face down your fear" by taking down the fence, insinuating that Leung is a coward for choosing to erect that barrier in the first place. His support of the fence surrounding the Square is further depicted as mean-spirited and he is advised to be "magnanimous," reconceptualizing the Square "as a symbol of peace and reconciliation." In asking for the Square to be returned, it is discursively transformed from a government building into a civil right, a public space where citizens can air private voices. It is a physical symbol of the political possibility in which public opinion can be voiced by the ruled and heard by those with the power to do something more than chant. The emergence of such illusive spaces in cities, thus, becomes a "physical pause in the urban landscape … creating a space where people can come together, by design or happenstance. City squares are planned absences … [they are] an extension of urban life … with a function that alters through history" (Packer, 2016). The tangible, physical space that any Square offers can source numerous intangible and interdiscursive possibilities to its users, including as a space for intransigency, for threat, for peaceful protest, etc.

User comments (anonymized)

A bunch of thugs and criminals not willing to abide by the rules and laws!

Just don't allow them to break the law without severe punishment and hold the majority hostage to their foolish and disruptive ways.

Violent criminal behaviour from street protesters is what got civic square closed in the first place. These thugs never learn.

HK government must take tough action against these destructive hooligans. Protect the 7 million plus HK residents against these 1,000+ fools and traitors.

Western infiltrated thugs just keep showing they are frauds and liars. Giving in to the vile beasts only emboldens them. Their only aim is to openly violates the Basic Law and the international treaty under which it exists. Those lying dogs, bark incessantly and keep braying about lost sovereignty where there is none in the first place. China holds the sovereignty over Hong Kong. These mad dogs getting more and more rabid as they know their game is up. They reinforce daily their plan to ignore their obligations to honor the Basic Laws and China's sovereignty.

Genuine re-open the square? For him to storm and damage public property again and attack officials? For his information, the closing of the square in the first place was because of him and the bunch of radicals, who obstruct the law and cause chaos. He his beyond of any right and position to make any demands. Put him back to jail!

We see in these user comments an echoing of the representation of reality put forward by the former CE and his government. Protesting in the Square is equated with violating the Basic Law, reiterating the government's standing on the legal status of the Square – not as public space but as government property. Freedom activists are categorized as criminals breaking the law ("thugs," "criminals," "hooligans," "liars and frauds"), their actions falling into the semantic category denoting criminal violence ("attack, hold hostage," "break the law," "destructive," "lying," "violate," "damage," "obstruct," "cause chaos") and thus entitled to severe punishment. This form of outcasting gives legitimate power to one side, the more moral side, over the other, implying they are on the side of the law. Furthermore, criminalization allows any measures taken (in this case by the local government) to be seen as punishment, as deserved, further giving the moral side legal superiority, since "[c]rime and punishment is fundamental to the moral accounting metaphor and ethical legitimization because '[w]hen you disobey a legitimate authority, it is moral for you to be punished'" (Charteris-Black, 2005: 188). Protestors are further hyperbolized in a severe negative other presentation through an animal metaphor as "mad dogs" and "vile beasts," the use of animal imagery implying the less than civilized actions of the protestors, attributing non-human qualities to them, and as a result an inhuman moral code of conduct, serving to delegitimize their agenda.

The square as a symbol of right to assembly and free speech

A second narrative that emerges in the telling of this issue is one that reconceptualizes the Square as a symbol of democracy and right to assembly and expression. Generated largely by freedom activists, this representation of reality depicts the Square as rightfully belonging to the public for the freedom of assembly. In this narrative, the city Square assumes "a collective character and confer[s] a public identity on private individuals. They possess a theatrical quality, as if the square is a stage and everyone in it a performer ... [becoming] instruments for autocratic control or democratic change" (Packer, 2016).

(Extract 6) But security for whom? If there is any justification for building a humongous block of government buildings in a prime location, it's to provide easy access to the public. Well, that's the on-record rationale. We all know the real reason was, of course, to provide a "commanding height" for glorified civil servants and ministers to look down on the rest of us.... But protection for the government honchos means inconvenience for the public.

(Lo, SCMP, 27/4/17)

(Extract 7) Instead of occupying government space Hong Kong people are justly entitled to have access to, protesters end up taking up the surrounding streets. But, if people want to protest and rally, why shouldn't they be able to do it to the extreme inconvenience of over-privileged people on the public payroll, on government ground? Ministers, like it or not, are paid to take the heat.

(Lo, SCMP, 27/4/17)

(Extract 8) ...unsightly barrier that makes a mockery of the "Open Door" design of the CGO complex, which is meant to represent openness and transparency in government. Yes, that symbolism has seemed more a bad joke than a sincere promise during these years of Leung's hardline politics of confrontation."

(Ewing, HKFP, 26/4/17)

(Extract 9) If Leung's successor, Carrie Lam Cheng Yuet-ngor, were to begin her administration in July by tearing down the three-metre-high fence that has been erected there – giving the square ... back to the people for whom it was originally designed – she would be making a grand gesture of reconciliation after five long years of division and polarisation under Leung.... Remember, this is the site where tens of thousands of protesters, led by the then 15-year-old Joshua Wong Chi-fung, staged a 10-day rally in August and September of 2012 that eventually forced Leung to shelve his plan for a mandatory patriotic national education curriculum that critics branded as "brainwashing." This is where the Umbrella Movement was born when group of students, with Wong again in the vanguard, clambered over the recently erected fence in September of 2014, declaring their intent to "take back" the square ... the Occupy campaign, whose repercussions continue to haunt the city today.

(Ewing, HKFP, 26/4/17)

Contrary to Leung's concern that the fence is a solution to 'public safety risk', and quite typical of discursive illusions which give rise to contested versions of reality, the extracts here contradict Leung's show of concern by questioning "security for whom?," raising doubts about Leung's agenda. The extracts create a hierarchal demarcation through the strategy of emphasizing difference (Wodak et al., 1999) engendering an Us vs. Them demarcation between the "glorified civil servants and minister" and "Hong Kong people." This version of reality negatively represents Leung and members of his administration ("glorified," "honchos," "over-privileged") to emphasize their untrustworthiness and delegitimize their "on record rationale" and "justification." The "unsightly barrier" is personified into a being that "makes a mockery" and a "bad joke" of the CGO"s "Open-Door" design, further delegitimizing the actions and explanations of the government, "establishing a sense of negative, morally reprehensible or otherwise unacceptable action or overall state of affairs" (Vaara, 2014, 503).

The power play on the hierarchal demarcation of Us vs. Them is manipulated in the repetition of the term "inconvenience" for the "public" and for "over-privileged people," when the latter is justified because "Minsters" are reminded that they are "paid to take the heat," now placing the public higher up in the hierarchy because it is on the "public payroll" that Ministers are hired. The superlative adjective "extreme" reiterating the unjust annoyance on the part of the government in having to hear public opinion. In this instance, the "over-privileged" become disadvantaged because of their social standing, their conceptualization of reality deemed a lie because "we all know the real reason." The use of the all-inclusive pronoun "we" unites the public against the government in a castle metaphor which places the elite at an abusive and protected "commanding height" in order to "look down on the rest of us."

The same power hierarchy is manipulated, again, in a series of parallelisms and rhetorical questions which illustrate the privilege of the elite and the disadvantage of the ruled in the creation of a victim-abuser scenario, which invokes sympathy for a powerless populace ("is there any justification," "protection of the government honchos means inconvenience for the public," "if people want to rally, why shouldn't they be able to do it to the extreme inconvenience," "more a bad joke than a sincere promise"). Placed at either end of the power hierarchy, within this narrative that reconceptualizes the Square as a symbol of "openness and transparency," Leung and his associates emerge as the antagonists, since the validity of the public's claims is based on "juxtaposition of the 'establishment' against the interests of ordinary people" (Vaara 2014, 507).

While a negative other presentation of the "over-privileged" Ministers is encouraged, this narrative positively represents, and in doing so unites, ordinary members of the public, and the "tens of thousands of protestors" who have been robbed of their claims to the Square "they are justly entitled to have access to," and which they are justified to "take back." Positive presentation of the Us side in this regard influences "the myriad of opinions and attitudes We have about Them in more specific social domains" (Van Dijk, 1998, 25). The conceptualization of the square as a possession is extended as the new CE is advised to 'give the square back to the people for whom it was originally designed', again, bestowing the public with legal, rightful ownership of the Square, but also further reifying the Square into a 'grand gesture of reconciliation' waiting to be offered.

The protesting public is further given the face of "15-year-old Joshua Wong Chi-fung," this metonymy transferring onto the public the innocence and optimism of a young boy, which when juxtaposed with the term "vanguard," can be seen to insinuate youthful courageousness. These qualities carry with them an ascriptive function, thereby becoming "explanations and justifications for actions and ... give clues to possible future actions of the individuals" (Jayyusi, 1984, 28). In this case, the '10 day rally', 'the Umbrella movement', and when the "group of students" "clambered over the erected fence" are seen as a result of their bravery and fight for rights against "government honchos" who try to implement policies that are "branded as brainwashing."

Audiences are emotionally pleaded with to "remember," invoking a collective memory, and a reminder of the scar left on the collective psyche of Hong Kong's population, of the Square as the site where young protestors succeed in forcing "Leung to shelve his plan." The memory of the Umbrella movement is roused, personified as an entity that came into existence when "born," and which even after its demise continues to "haunt" the city, the reference to a past event reiterating the sanctity and history of the Square, and the public's entitlement to it. Specific temporal references ("rally in August and September of 2012, "September 2014") connect the past to the present, justifying the demand for a specific future course of events, drawing on the strategy of unification (Wodak et al., 1999), emphasizing shared struggle. The memory of past events in this instance recontextualizes the meaning of the current one, and in doing so, demonstrates how "the meaning of socio-political events and

issues can be creatively rendered through ideologically solid connections between the past and present (through either denial of a historical connection or
historical conditioning of the present with it) (Leudar and Nekvapil 2011)"
(Bhatia 2016, 559).

User comments (anonymized)

> The issue is one of erosion of the rule of law, destruction of freedom of
> thought, association, expression and movement. These are critical issues not
> just for HK but also for China.

> It is admirable that many of us who believe in Hong Kong's Rule of Law
> tradition came out in its defense. It is wonderful that Hongkongers have the
> courage to do what is right even when the promise of success is remote.

> How dare the people of Hong Kong exercise their rights to free speech and
> to petition their government that is nominally theirs, although the main
> persons are appointed by the communist thugs who do not want anyone to
> think they have rights other than the right to obey the communists' every
> order, as the sheep in the mainland do. Perish the thought that we should
> have any rights to be on public property that we pay for. My goodness, what
> next? We are to expect our government to work for us? How silly. The
> pro-tyranny parties work for the communists. Carrie Number 2 and her
> minions are appointed by Beijing and work for them. How dare we seek to
> exercise the rights that have been accorded to us under our laws. It's
> an outrage.

> It belongs to us. We have the right to petition our government and to free
> speech. Sorry you don't like it.

> The square is paid for by the tax dollars of HK people and HK citizens
> should have a said what to do with it. CF's living room belongs to himself or
> his parents and his family can do whatever he wishes to and really none of
> your business

Again, user comments here reflect consent to this second narrative by arguing
Hong Kong people have the legal rights to protest in the square because it
"belongs to them," as it is "paid for by the tax dollars of the HK people." The
square is conceptualized as property that has legal owners ("nominally theirs,"
"public property that we pay for," "belongs to us," "paid for by tax dollars"),
this metaphor emphasized in the comparison of the square to C. Y. Leung"s
personal home ("living room") which he owns so he can "do whatever he wishes
to." Quite in contrast with the earlier narrative which correlated protesting in the
square with violent criminal behaviour punishable by law, in this narrative denial
of access to the square is equated with "erosion of rule of law, freedom of

thought." Further as part of double contrastive identity, a typical feature of the discourse of illusion, the same people who labelled protestors as thugs and animals are now deemed "thugs" and "sheep" themselves, their opposition to this narrative correlated with support for tyranny and communism. In asking for the Square to be returned, it is discursively transformed from a government building into a civil right, a public space where citizens can air private voices ("rule of law," "rights to free speech," "rights to be on public property," "rights that have been accorded to us under our laws," "right to petition our government and to free speech"). It is a physical symbol of the political possibility in which public opinion can be voiced by the ruled and heard by those with the power to do something about issues of concern. The tangible, physical space that any Square offers can source numerous intangible and interdiscursive possibilities to its users, including as a space for intransigency, for threat, for peaceful protest etc.

In this version of reality, the Civic Square is seen to both "shelter and nurture the expression of the people's civil rights ... [reconciling] a heritage overloaded with strong notions of identity and particularity with a modernity that is essential for contemporary life" (Rabbat, 2012, 208). The Square represents a gesture of reconciliation, personified as the public's voice, and treatment of the Square is treatment of "public opinion." In this representation of the issue, the Square is conceived as the physical voice of "the people," a voice that echoes their sentiments, a voice that has been taken from them and muted; voices which when allowed to echo "may not change the status quo position or result in fundamental policy reform, [but] contesting public spaces [can] give the powerless 'rhetorical and operational openings' (Sassen, 2011)" (Lubin, 2012).

Conclusion

In this chapter, I have made an attempt to explore the complexity of the discursive construction of Hong Kong's Civic Square, proliferated through local media, by employing the *Discourse of Illusion* framework, which could be simply defined as a product of one's subjective representation of reality, emerging from a historical repository of experiences, embodying various linguistic and semiotic actions, and often leading to intended socio-political consequences (Bhatia, 2015a). The analysis of the (re)conceptualization of the Civic Square revealed the emergence of two competing narratives, which contradictorily transformed the Square into both the symbolic representation of a) fear and threat and b) the right to assembly and free speech. To persuade audiences of the objectivity of their narratives, the competing discourse clans drew on various linguistic and rhetorical tools, including insinuation, temporal referencing, metaphor, topoi, recontextualization, framing, positive and negative presentation, creating, as a result, conflicting versions of reality. The juxtaposition of these two different versions of reality, generating powerful discursive illusions in the attempts to attribute meaning and value to present day issues, created evidence that such contested discourses cannot be treated as "neutral or innocuous signifiers" (Dunn, 2006, 371) but rather as ideological reasoning that encourage social beings to act on them, with concrete socio-cultural and political implications (cf. Bhatia, 2016). As a result of these contested and illusive representations then, the Square ceased to be a plot of cemented land becoming instead the vehicle of civil right to public assembly, a channel of communication, the cure to civic polarization, a violent threat to public security, a flag of compromise, and the pursuit of democracy.

The framework of the Discourse of Illusion proved to be especially useful to this study as it worked to deconstruct how discursively shaped social issues can be reflective of the ideological conceptualizations of various discourse clans, in support of their respective socio-political agendas. Such discursive constructions come to mean different things depending on a range of variables, especially the macro- and micro-contexts, leaving one to believe that our engagement with the world is based on interpretation – we make sense of the world around us through the social construction of the meanings, characteristics, and "truth" that make reality "knowable." There is no way to step outside interpretation. There is no objective Truth to discover; only competing interpretations to navigate (Dunn, 2006, 377).

What the Discourse of Illusion attempts then to bring to light is the struggle between competing narratives offered by various discourse clans in society in an attempt to generate a single hegemonic discourse that becomes associated with the understanding of certain socio-political constructs and issues, in an effort to maintain or reform economic, social, or political status quo. The framework can be further applied to the investigation of various other socio-political and cultural constructs, in addition to study of Public Square movements, including, democracy, tyranny, fundamentalism, fake news, diversity, and globalization, as each of these issues becomes the embodiment of ideological tensions of competing discourse clans. Such issues come to *mean* different things in different contexts and by different voices, often playing a significant hand in societal understanding.

The analysis further reveals the value of Public Squares in densely packed cities of countries with convoluted political systems (in the case of Hong Kong's Basic Law, its conceptualization as part of One Country Two Systems), whereby disunited factions, or where a disengaged or apathetic populace can come together as a collective entity in the pursuit of socio-political change, or at the very least as a channel for self-expression, where private concern can become public discussion, heard by those with the power to implement change. The Public Square, as such, becomes a "dignified space" (Parkinson, 2012, 112) which sends "cues that 'this matters'. If certain voices and perspectives are never heard in that dignified space, then … they are not seen to matter, and thus have less impact on the political agenda or the outcome of public deliberation" (ibid.). Regardless of the system of governance then, it would seem that social change requires social *place*, but certainly discursive performance can transform physical space into a social cause.

Notes

1 www.yearbook.gov.hk/2011/en/pdf/Photos.pdf.
2 www.news.gov.hk/en/categories/admin/html/2014/10/20141022_130715. shtml?pickList=topstories.
3 Discourse clans here refer to groups of various sizes that could form minorities or majorities in any given social context, governed by similar ideological systems, and therefore adhering to a mutual narrative regarding particular conceptualizations of reality (adapted from Hajer's (1993) notion of 'discourse coalition', but without the necessary emphasis on discourse structuration and institutionalization).
4 www.com.cuhk.edu.hk/ccpos/en/research/Credibility_Survey%20Results_ 2016_ENG.pdf.
5 www.info.gov.hk/gia/general/201407/17/P201407170201.htm.

References

Bednarek, Monika A. 2005. "Frames revisited – the coherence-inducing function of frames." *Journal of Pragmatics* 37(5): 685–705.
Berger, Peter L. and Luckmann, Thomas. 1966. *The Social Construction of Reality*. London: Penguin Books.
Bhatia, Aditi. 2015a. *Discursive Illusions in Public Discourse: Theory and Practice*. London, New York: Routledge.
Bhatia, Aditi. 2015b. "Construction of discursive illusions in the Umbrella Movement." *Discourse & Society* 26(4): 407–427.
Bhatia, Aditi. 2016. "Discursive construction of the 'key' moment in the Umbrella Movement." *Journal of Language and Politics* 15(5): 551–568.
Bourdieu, Pierre. 1990. *The Logic of Practice*. Cambridge: Polity Press.
Cameron, Lynn. 1999. "Operationalising 'metaphor' for applied linguistics research." In Cameron, Lynn and Low, Graham (eds), *Researching and Applying Metaphor*, 3–28. Cambridge: Cambridge University Press.
Cameron, Lynn. 2003. *Metaphor in Educational Discourse*. London: Continuum.
Carfantan, Serge. 2003. Philosophy and spirituality. http://perso.club-internet.fr/ serecar/english/cours/traduction7.htm (accessed 3/3/05).
Charteris-Black, Jonathan. 2004. *Corpus Approaches to Critical Metaphor Analysis*. Hampshire: Palgrave Macmillan.
Charteris-Black, Jonathan. 2005. *Politicians and Rhetoric: The Persuasive Power of Metaphor*. New York: Palgrave Macmillan.
Cheng, Kris. 26 April 2017. "C. Y. Leung 'uses every opportunity to create conflict' in refusing to reopen protest site, rights group says." Hong Kong Free Press www. hongkongfp.com/2017/04/26/cy-leung-uses-every-opportunity-create-conflict-refusing-reopen-protest-site-rights-group-says/ (accessed 18/5/17).
Chu, Koel. 27 December 2017. "'Political show': Civic Square to reopen Thurs, but protests allowed only on Sundays and holidays." Hong Kong Free Press www. hongkongfp.com/2017/12/27/activist-joshua-wong-slams-govt-political-show-as-civic-sq-to-reopen-with-protest-allowed-only-on-sundays/ (accessed 10/1/18).
Cialdini, Robert B. 1997. "Interpersonal influence." In Shavitt, Sharon and Brock, Timothy C. (eds), *Persuasion: Psychological Insights and Perspectives*, 195–217. Boston: Allyn & Bacon.

Dunn, Kevin C. 2006. "Examining historical representations." *International Studies Review* 8(2): 37–381.

Ejinsight. 20 April 2017. "Civic Square seen likely to reopen after Carrie Lam takes office." Economic Journal Insight www.ejinsight.com/20170420-civic-square-seen-likely-to-reopen-after-carrie-lam-takes-office/ (accessed 18/5/17).

Ewing, Kent. 26 April 2017. "Carrie Lam, tear down this fence and reopen Civic Square." *Hong Kong Free Press* www.hongkongfp.com/2017/04/26/carrie-lam-tear-fence-reopen-civic-square/ (accessed 19/5/17).

Hajer, Maarten. 1993. "Discourse coalitions and the institutionalization of practice." In Fischer, Frank and Forester, John (eds), *The Argumentative Turn in Policy Analysis and Planning*, 43–76. Durham, NC: Duke University Press.

Hart, Joseph K. 1929. "Mind and matter." In Sommer, Daniel Robinson (ed.), *An Anthology of Recent Philosophy: Selections for Beginners from the Writings of the Greatest 20th Century Philosophers*, 492–500. USA: Thomas Y. Crowell Company.

Harvey, David. 1989. *The Urban Experience*. Baltimore: John Hopkins University Press.

Hume, David. 1970. "The self is a bundle of perceptions." In Kuykendall, Eleanor (ed.), *Philosophy in the Age of Crisis*, 277–278. New York: Harper & Row.

Jayyusi, Lena. 1984. *Categorization and the Moral Order*. Boston: Routledge & Kegan Paul.

Kant, Immanuel. 1970. "The active mind: The judgements of experience." In Kuykendall, Eleanor (ed.), *Philosophy in the Age of Crisis*, 346–355. New York: Harper & Row.

Leudar, Ivan, Marsland, Victoria and Nekvapil, Jiri. 2004. "On membership categorization: 'Us', 'them' and 'doing violence' in political discourse." *Discourse & Society* 15(2–3): 243–266.

Leudar, Ivan and Nekvapil, Jiri. 2011. "Practical historians and adversaries: 9/11 revisited." *Discourse & Society* 22(1): 66–85.

Leung, Christy. 25 April 2017. "Protest area known as Civic Square outside Hong Kong government HQ will not reopen, leader C. Y. Leung says." *South China Morning Post* www.scmp.com/print/news/hong-kong/politics/article/2090380/hong-kong-leader-cy-leung-says-he-will-not-reopen-civic (accessed 20/5/17).

Li, Yi. 23 July, 2014. "Fencing Off Civic Square Enrages Hong Kongers." *Epoch Times* www.theepochtimes.com/n3/811619-fencing-off-civic-square-enrages-hong-kongers/ (accessed 19/5/17).

Lo, Alex. 27 April 2017. "Hey CY, tear down that fence." *South China Morning Post* www.scmp.com/comment/insightopinion/article/2090936/heycyteardownfence (accessed 19/5/17).

Lubin, Judy. 2012. "The 'Occupy' Movement: Emerging protest forms and contested urban spaces." *Berkley Planning Journal* http://ced.berkeley.edu/bpj/2012/09/the-occupy-movement-emerging-protest-forms-and-contested-urban-spaces/ (accessed 18/5/17).

Ng, Ellie. 23 April 2017. "Pro-gov't lawmakers suggest reopening former protest site 'Civic Square'." *Hong Kong Free Press* www.hongkongfp.com/2017/04/23/pro-govt-lawmakers-suggest-reopening-former-protest-site-civic-square/ (accessed 19/5/17).

Ng, Ellie. 23 April 25 April 2017. "Chief Exec.-elect Carrie Lam considers reopening former protest site 'Civic Square'." *Hong Kong Free Press* www.hongkongfp.com/

2017/04/25/chief-exec-elect-carrie-lam-considers-reopening-former-protest-site-civic-square/ (accessed 17/5/17).

Oktar, Lütfiye. 2001. 'The ideological organization of representational processes in the presentation of us and them'. *Discourse & Society* 12(3): 313–346.

Packer, George. 2016. "How public squares disrupt city life and why that's a good thing." *The Daily Beast* www.thedailybeast.com/articles/2016/05/12/how-public-squares-disrupt-city-life-and-why-that-s-a-good-thing?via=twitter_page (accessed 18/5/17).

Parkinson, John. 2012. *Democracy and Public Space: The Physical Sites of Democratic Performance.* Oxford: Oxford University Press.

Partridge, Samuel. 2012. "The end of the South China Morning Post and legitimate investigative journalism in South Asia." www.freedomobservatory.org/access-to-truth-surfeit-of-inquiry/ (accessed 19/5/17).

Perloff, Richard M. 1993. *The Dynamics of Persuasion.* New Jersey: Lawrence Erlbaum.

Rabbat, Nasser. 2012. "The Arab Revolution takes back the public space." *Critical Inquiry* 39(1): 198–208.

Sacks, Harvey. 1992. *Lectures on Conversation Volume I & II.* Oxford: Blackwell.

Simon, Roger. 1999. *Gramsci's Political Thought: An Introduction.* London: The Electric Book Company.

Smith, Susan L. 1997. "The effective use of fear appeals in persuasive immunization: An analysis of national immunization intervention messages." *Journal of Applied Communication Research* 25: 264–292.

Sarangi, Srikant and Candlin, Christopher N. 2003. "Categorization and explanation of risk: A discourse analytical perspective." *Health, Risk & Society* 5(2): 115–124.

Vaara, Eero. 2014. 'Struggles over legitimacy in the Eurozone crisis: Discursive legitimation strategies and their ideological underpinnings." *Discourse & Society* 25(4): 500–518.

Van Dijk, Teun A. 1998. "Opinions and Ideologies in the Press." In Bell, Allan and Garrett, Peter (eds), *Approaches to Media Discourse.* 21–63 Oxford: Blackwell.

Varsity, Chinese University of Hong Kong. April 2015. "The politics of public space." http://varsity.com.cuhk.edu.hk/index.php/2015/04/politics-of-public-space/2/ (accessed 19/5/17).

Wodak, Ruth, De Cillia, Rudolf, Reisigl, Martin and Liebhart, Karin. 1999. *The Discursive Construction of National Identity.* Edinburgh: Edinburgh University Press.

Yeung, S.C. 26 April 2017. "Is Civic Square a place of shame for C. Y. Leung?" *Ejinsight* www.ejinsight.com/20170526-is-civic-square-a-place-of-shame-for-cy-leung/ (accessed 19/5/17).

Zhao, Shirley. 1 January 2018. "Showdown as police surround Hong Kong protesters at 'Civic Square' after New Year's Day march." *South China Morning Post* www.scmp.com/news/hong-kong/politics/article/2126414/scuffle-police-surround-hong-kong-protesters-civic-square (accessed 11/1/18).

8 Finding a way forward

A discourse analysis of the online popularization of restorative justice in the United Kingdom

Antonella Napolitano

Introduction and background

Restorative justice

In recent years, the efficacy of retributive justice for victims' satisfaction and offenders' social rehabilitation have come to be questioned. Apart from administering punishments proportional to the offenses, a legal system should also be aimed at healing the victims' wounds and rehabilitating offenders. Nevertheless, punitive approaches often prove unresponsive to victims' needs and do not encourage a recovery process in the offended party and in the affected community. Moreover, they do not guarantee the offenders' redemption and reintegration into society; on the contrary, high rates of recidivism are sadly recorded. In order to respond to a need to build a safer and healthier society, alternative paths to criminal prosecution and conventional sentencing have thus been developed to address conflicts and harms, promoting the application of procedures such as mediation and restorative practice (see Abbamonte and Cavaliere 2012; Van Ness and Heetderks Strong 2015). Restorative justice, in particular, has radically transformed traditional principles of jurisprudence such as incapacitation, deterrence, rehabilitation, and crime prevention. It can be defined as:

> a process whereby all the parties with a stake in a particular offence come together to resolve collectively how to deal with the aftermath of the offence and its implications for the future.
>
> (Marshall 1996: 37)

Restorative justice is based on the key concepts of harm, needs, obligation and engagement. While ordinary criminal justice centres on laws and punishment, restorative justice views crime as harm caused to people and communities. For this reason, it is concerned with victims and their needs and seeks to repair the damage they suffered. Moreover, it holds offenders to account for the wrongs they committed and helps them understand the impact of their actions, take responsibility and make amends. The process of restorative justice engages not only offenders but also all of the stakeholders affected by a crime – i.e., victims, offenders, family and members of the community – in a search for solutions (Zehr and Gohar 2003: 21–23). Restorative justice entails the transformation of people, relationships and communities. It views criminal offence as more than an act of breaking the law, examining instead also its impact on society, as it is based on the belief that the origins of crime lie in social conditions and relationships. The role of communities in conjunction with governmental action is, therefore, crucial to prevent crime and recidivism, by (re-)establishing relationships and (re-)integrating individuals into societal groups (see Abbamonte and Cavaliere 2013: 123).

In fact, restorative justice reintroduced some of the views already in use in some legal systems of the past, which, for instance, expected offenders and their families to make amends to victims and their families.

Some of the first practical examples of restorative justice in modern Western justice systems are represented by family group conferencing programmes run from 1989 in New Zealand and Australia as an alternative to charging young offenders with juvenile offences. Restorative justice is today practised mainly in Australia, New Zealand, the United States, as well as in Austria, Norway, England, Wales and other European States (Abbamonte and Cavaliere 2013; Van Ness and Heetderks Strong 2015).

Previous studies have investigated restorative justice from a discourse perspective. Abbamonte and Cavaliere reflected on the values and orientation of conferencing and on the mediator's skills (2012) and carried out an appraisal and contrastive analysis comparing linguistic exchanges in the USA and Italy, focusing on mediator's values and interdiscursive skills (2013). Multiple studies have centred on youth Justice Conferencing in Australia. In particular, Martin (2009) investigated how young offenders use semiotic resources to state their teenage identity. Martin et al. (2013) performed a multimodal discourse analysis of the language and body language used by offenders to enact their young (especially 'angry boy') identity. Martin et al. (2014) mapped the personas embodied by young offenders in youth justice conferencing. Zappavigna and Martin (2014) focused on the supportive role of parents (in particular of the 'crying mum'), prompting the young person to express remorse. In 2018, Zappavigna and Martin also published a comprehensive study on youth justice conferencing, with an overview of the genre, exchange structure, expression of emotions, body language, and identity performance.

The (em)power(ment) of law through the power of narrative

Victims often feel like the crime has taken away the control they had over their property, bodies, emotions, and dreams (Zehr and Gohar 2003: 13). Being involved in their own case as it goes through a justice process, victims can recover the power they had lost. The discourse of restorative justice actually involves empowerment of the injured party, who takes an active part and attempts at moving beyond the role of victim, in order to be restored to the community. From a social constructivist perspective, what is constructed as 'society' or 'community' is constituted through communicative acts of participants in a territory (Blundo and

Greene 2009: 327). Communication, which is at the basis of human interaction, plays a crucial role in restorative practice. The restorative process is developed through dialogistic exchanges that take place with the support of mediators who discuss the issues with victims, offenders and supporters, first separately and then collectively. All those affected by an offence are given voice, having the opportunity to express their feelings and needs, to tell their story in order to find ways forward (Abbamonte and Cavaliere 2013: 122–124). Victims are encouraged to produce narratives about the incident to explain the real impact that the offence had on their life, express the desired solutions and, potentially, receive an explanation and an apology. It also provides offenders with a possibility to express regret, take responsibility and make amends. Narratives are crucial in relieving emotions and achieving empathy between the parts. Telling the story of what happened is an essential element in healing, since "part of the trauma of crime is the way it upsets our views of ourselves and our world, our life-stories" (Zehr and Gohar 2003: 13). The therapeutic function of narratives of disruptive life events, of personal troubles that alter expected biographies, is fulfilled within a community of hearers (Riessman 2001b: 74). Storytelling is a relational activity, a collaborative practice which involves tellers and listeners and encourages sharing, understanding and empathising. It assumes the presence of tellers and listeners/questioners who interact in particular cultural contexts which are essential to the interpretation of a story (Riessman 2001a: 697).

Narratives are "'innate' ways of understanding and structuring human experience" (Rideout 2008: 55), which makes them inherently persuasive. Since they describe a particular fact from a specific point of view, personal "narratives have no need to justify the accuracy of their claims" (Dahlstrom 2014: 13616). They are subjective rather than objective accounts and, as such, they have "integrity both to the speaker and to the listener" (Centre for Justice and Reconciliation 2018). The narrator is the agent, the real expert, whose "positioning aligns the listener with the narrator in a moral stance" as the 'I' knows better than the 'other'" (Riessman 2001b: 78). The structure of the narrative links its events into a cause-and-effect relationship so that the consequences and the conclusion seem inevitable to the reader (Dahlstrom 2014: 13616).

Restorative justice in the United Kingdom

The present study investigates the issue of restorative justice with a specific focus on the British context. In the United Kingdom, the practice was introduced in the 1980s and then implemented in the 1990s, profoundly changing the youth justice system and increasingly influencing the treatment of adults. In 1996, the Audit Commission produced a national report entitled *Misspent Youth: Young People and Crime*, which exposed the inadequacies of the youth justice system. The document laid the foundation for the 1998 *Crime and Disorder Act* and the *Youth Justice and the Criminal Evidence Act* of 1999, built on the principles of restorative justice. In 2003, the UK enacted the *Criminal Justice Act* that introduced the *Conditional Caution*, a diversionary disposal applied to both young and adult offenders: if the offender admits the offence and complies with the condition(s) – such as reparation or rehabilitative treatment – the case is finalized and no prosecution is initiated. Alongside these normative references, the UK Parliament encouraged the use of Restorative Justice through the *Action Plans* of 2012, 2013 and 2014. The *Revised Victims Code* and the *Crime and Courts Act* of 2013 included restorative justice for the first time, with the intention of raising awareness amongst victims and courts (see CPS 2018).

The UK Restorative Justice Council (RJC) represents the independent third sector membership body for the field of restorative practice. It champions clear standards for restorative practice and provides a national voice advocating the widespread use of all forms of restorative justice. The RJC website[1] collects resources for victims and practitioners, publishing guidance materials and offering dedicated support.

Aims and purposes

Restorative justice, mediation and conferencing may not be familiar concepts to victims and offenders. Facilitators and mediators have to introduce the idea of a restorative process to potential participants, acquire informed consent from each participant and then to arrange a meeting or an exchange of information. Popularization through simplified and user-friendly materials is also of particular usefulness. Considering these premises, the present study aims at analysing how the Restorative Justice Council website popularizes and promotes restorative practice online.

Methods and data

The Restorative Justice Council website collects a vast amount of information for ordinary citizens and practitioners. The study analyses texts collected from a selection of sections, focusing in particular on:

- six Fields of Application (1640 tokens, 554 types);
- nine Frequently Asked Questions (808 tokens, 285 types);
- 36 Case studies, i.e. testimonials in the form of personal narratives by people involved in restorative justice programmes (overall 50,954 tokens, 3,562 types), including 28 stories told by victims (41,868, 3,257 types), 5 by offenders (5,303 tokens, 999 types), 1 by a facilitator (1,086 tokens, 370 types), and 2 by both an offender and a victim (2,697 tokens, 563 types);
- 60 Twitter messages published by the Restorative Justice Council account @ RJCouncil between November and April 2018 (1,181 tokens, 447 types).

The research combines multiple perspectives of investigation. It considers the popularization techniques (see e.g. Gotti 2005; Garzone 2006) enacted by the RJC to inform potential participants about restorative justice practices. Narratives are examined from a corpus and discourse perspective in order to investigate the positive role they play in enhancing victims' empowerment (see the paragraph *The (em)power(ment) of law through the power of narrative* in the present chapter), with the aim of persuading readers to voluntarily undergo restorative practice. In recent years, public bodies and organizations have been increasingly multiplying their online presence, exploiting the communicative potential of social media. In particular, the RJC makes use of the microblogging service Twitter to spread its official messages. Tendencies and patterns recurring in the informative pages, FAQs, stories and *tweet* messages published by the Council are identified through the aid of the corpus linguistics suite Antconc 3.4 (Anthony 2014), to be subsequently interpreted and contextualized (see e.g. Baker 2006).

Analysis

Homepage

The homepage of the website links to the main informative and promotional contents provided.

To ensure that the user stays on the site, it is crucial for a website to strike a balance between presenting news that promotes the service but also seems relevant to the web user (see Askehave and Ellerup Nielsen 2005).

Figure 8.1 shows the Restorative Justice Council homepage, which appears to be mainly addressing two categories of readers: victims and operators working in the sector. The website actually provides information tailored specifically for those wishing to resort to restorative practice (see section *What is restorative justice*, and the paragraph *Informative sections* in the present chapter). Moreover, the website offers the possibility for practitioners, service providers and trainers to be registered in the RJC lists of experts (*Find a service*), to participate in meetings and seminars (*Events*) and to gain a RSQM, i.e. a Restorative Service Quality Mark, an external recognition of quality restorative practice (*Standards and quality*). The *Resources* section contains written and audio-visual materials (case studies, publications, videos, policy and research) addressing a diversified audience. The website homepage also reports the most recent news and posts from the RJC blog and the latest tweets from @RJCouncil Twitter account.

Informative sections

The page titled *What is restorative justice* provides general information about the practice. The subsections about the fields of application explain how restorative justice can be applicable to multiple areas, mainly:

- *Criminal justice*, favouring the meeting between victims and offenders of a crime;
- *Early intervention*, i.e. with youth offenders;
- *Community*, for conflicts in local communities and neighbourhoods;

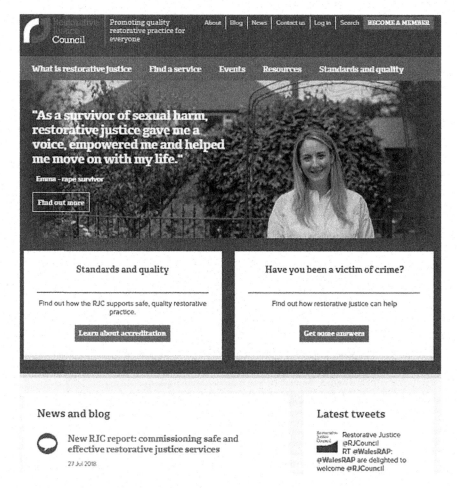

Figure 8.1 The Restorative Justice Council homepage.

- *Housing*, especially for neighbour disputes;
- *Schools*, in issues such as disputes, bullying, truancy;
- *Workplace*, for instance in cases of mobbing or disrespectful behaviour.

Considering the frequencies in the subcorpus collecting the *Fields of application* pages, it appears interesting to notice the recurring use of the modal verb *can* (20 hits, 1.22%). The verb substitutes here all forms of legal phrasings, preferring instead a simpler and more effective language. The modal collocates with expressions suggesting the improvement possibilities offered by restorative justice, as in (1):

(1) Restorative practice can be used to build strong communities.

As in (1), it is worth noting the extended use of metaphors of 'building': *build**
(six instances in the *Fields of application* subcorpus, 0.37%), *repair* (four, 0.24%)
create* (two, 0.12%), *constructive, constructively, rebuild* (all present in 1 instance, 0.6% each):

> (2) restorative principles can be effective at repairing damage done by long-
> term historic conflicts.

In line with the definition of the process as 'restorative,' these expressions are
used to constantly convey the idea of the possibility to restore the harm suffered/
caused. The metaphor supports therefore a persuasive popularization of the
process.

Texts use an impersonal tone, avoiding the use of personal or possessive
pronouns such as *you/your* and *we/our. Victim/s* (nine instances, 0.54%) and
offender/s (nine instances, 0.54%) tend to appear in correlation, thus stressing
the idea of restorative justice as a two-way process (see also example (4)):

> (3) Restorative justice is about victims and offenders communicating within
> a controlled environment to talk about the harm that has been caused and
> finding a way to repair that harm.

The choice of impersonality may also be due to the delicate matter, dealing with
criminal actions that may have left a painful mark, especially on the victims. An
impersonal tone may help to avoid reopening painful wounds in victims who may
still feel guilt or shame. The tone may also avoid making offenders feel accused,
inviting them to access the programme, as an alternative to the legal system.

The use of deontic modal *must* (four occurrences, 0.24%) in the pages indicates the fundamental conditions necessary to carry out a restorative practice:

> (4) the offender must have admitted to the crime, and both victim and
> offender must be willing to participate.

The modal auxiliary *must* enacts therefore the role of simplifying and popularising the more archaic legal form *shall*, as it combines two fundamental functions
of legal language, compulsoriness and reference to the future (Williams
2007: 252)

Restorative justice can represent an alternative path or a diversionary process to
the traditional justice system, as stated in the informative sections:

> (5) Restorative processes have also been used to deal with regulatory
> breaches [...] where people want to find a positive outcome and avoid
> using the legal system.

The pages appear to popularize and promote restorative practice without explicitly mentioning any legislative references or legal terminology which may be

useful to citizens wishing to access the service. For instance, no reference is made to the *Criminal Justice Act* of 2003, which establishes the conditions necessary to obtain *conditional cautions*. This may be due to the fact that, since restorative process still represents a voluntary choice, the RJC aims more at persuading citizens to participate in a restorative process than at simplifying legal knowledge.

Frequently asked questions

The informative sections of the website also include a page named *Do you need restorative justice?*, which offers clarifications about the practice, especially for victims who would like to take part in the process. The information is provided through a list of nine Frequently Asked Questions and answers, namely:

1   What is restorative justice?
2   Why would I take part?
3   Which offences can restorative justice be used for?
4   How will I know what to do?
5   Can I stop the process at any time?
6   Is restorative justice safe?
7   When does restorative justice happen?
8   How can I access restorative justice?
9   How can I hear from other people who have been through restorative justice?

FAQs are employed to establish an ongoing conversation between the Restorative Justice Council and the victim (often signalled by the *I* employed in questions, 5 occurrences, 0.6% of the FAQs corpus). As Fairclough states "conversational discourse practices which traditionally belong to the private sphere are being systematically simulated within organizations" (1992: 8). The question/answer mechanism, exploited as a 'conversational device,' is fully developed, in that the victims state their concerns in an open-question form, and receive an answer which assuages their concerns by describing what restorative justice is and how it works. The implied reader/victim goes on to ask further questions which refer directly to the content of previous answer.

A close look at the nine sections shows that the RJC FAQs are interrelated by non-genuine adjacency pairs, i.e., pairs in which the answer is both formally and semantically independent from the question. The interrelation thus lies on the thematic development realized in the adjacency pair. The answers are not dependent on the questions for the primary meaning interpretation, nor would they sound inappropriate if isolated. It is worth noting that the institution's answer is in two cases not directly addressed to the single victim. The one-to-one is turned into a one-to-all type of interaction. The individual question is used by the institution as a starting point in order to widen the issue and illustrate how RJ can help and protect victims.

The conversational device is also fully developed in that the answers abundantly use the pronoun *you*, which is the fifth most frequent word in the FAQs (24 instances, 3% of the *FAQs* corpus). Direct speech is used here as an "inclusive device" through which the reader is positioned as the "universal I" or "ideal subject" (Fairclough 2001: 41) and thereby feels that the law can cater for his/ her specific needs and concerns. This FAQ device thus functions as a "simulated face-to-face dialogue" (Fairclough 1992: 98; see also Hughes and Napolitano 2013) which entails a division between an individual producer or a relatively small production team and a body of receivers that is undetermined in size (Chouliaraki and Fairclough 1999: 43).

(6) Why would I take part?

Many victims feel that the criminal justice system does not give them a chance to get involved […].

A further linguistic strategy which aims at balancing the independence of the pairs is the use of *Yes* on two occasions. I posit the direct response beginning with an assertion is both conversational and immediately reassuring, then to be followed by a more complete explanation:

(7) Can I stop the process at any time?

Yes. Restorative justice is entirely voluntary and you can pull out at any time, including on the day of a conference or even while the meeting is going on. The facilitator will support you and try to make sure that there are no surprises as you go through the process, but whether you go through with it is entirely up to you.

(8) Is restorative justice safe?

Yes. Facilitators are trained in assessing risks and making sure that the process is safe for everybody involved. They would never let a restorative justice conference go ahead if they were not confident that it could be done safely. You would never be left alone with the offender and the facilitator would support you every step of the way.

The following elaboration in support of the initial affirmative response is a short text which assuages the victim's concerns by empathetically reassuring the interlocutor. The second person pronoun *you* is constantly repeated in the quoted answers describing how restorative justice and its mediators will assist and support the victims throughout the process.

The answer to the ninth FAQ redirects the reader to narrations of real stories, thus consolidating the promotional and informative function of the previous answers, further reassuring and persuading victims to undergo restorative practice.

Case studies

Narratives by people who have successfully used restorative practice play a pivotal role both in the popularization project and in the promotion of restorative justice. The stories analysed involve disruptive life events, told in first person, in which the speaker represents an expert whose positioning aligns the reader with the narrator. The speaker reassures users about the success of the mediation and expresses his/her satisfaction and gratefulness. Stories are available in different formats: video, text on webpage, text on a downloadable publication. The present study considers the narratives in form of written case studies. The stories available are told from different perspectives (see also the section *Methods and data* in this chapter), but the most space is devoted to narratives telling the victims' experience.

As evident from Figure 8.1, the homepage itself attracts the users' attention to the importance of first-hand testimonies, by showing a picture occupying the central part of the page representing a smiling witness and accompanied by a significant quotation from his/her story. Due to the sensitive nature of the situation, real names of witnesses may be replaced by invented names and pictures may not portray the actual victim or offender. The use of prototypical first-hand testimonials by victims of crimes recalls a typical device employed mainly in promotional genres. For instance, in advertisements, celebrity or typical user endorsement are often exploited to lend credence to a given product (Bhatia 2004: 65). In the case of the RJC website, the endorsement comes from a typical and credible beneficiary of the outcome of the desired action (see Bhatia 2004: 99). Endorsement and testimonials are used to empower and support individuals, making them feel part of a community of people who have faced similar issues (see also Hughes and Napolitano 2013).

Considering the structure of the narrations, some typographical features distinguish the story into a set of sections, namely: the RJC introduction and summary, the personal story and the highlighted quotes. One of the most visually striking features is actually the intrusion of quotes into the main text: some of the most relevant parts of the narratives are repeated in bold and alternated with the story sequences to attract the reader's attention. Such sentences also summarize the issue and allow readers to immediately notice a change, e.g. repentance and relief, in the life of the people involved. For instance, the site presents the story told by an offender, Alex, who had vandalized an elderly man's car. The following quotations may summarize his tale:

(9) "The police could see that I wanted to put things right."

"When he walked in the room it was very awkward and there was quite a lot of tension in the air."

"It was hard for me, but I needed to hear how my actions had consequences for those around me."

"I'd say to anyone thinking about going through restorative justice to do it, as it really helped me." (Alex's story)

The popularization and promotional purposes are thus enacted not only by telling a story but also by highlighting significant declarations from the account.

Such distinctive quotes were even repurposed over the RJC publications and posters, as in Figure 8.2.

Emotional language

One of the most frequent terms in the *Case Studies* corpus is represented by the verb *feel*, a lexical term which conveys the subjective experiential constituent of emotions. In particular, in the victims' corpus, the most frequent forms of the verb were *felt* (140 occurrences, 0.33% of the *Victim*'s subcorpus), *feel* (77 occurrences, 0.18%) and *feeling* (20 occurrences, 0.05%). Considering the concordance lines, the verb appears to play an instrumental role in the narratives under investigation. It serves the purpose of communicating both the experience as well as the process of relief and performance. Its usage helps the sharing of past as well as current feelings, usually on a path of recovery towards well-being, stating prospective emotional aspirations (i.e., the desired feelings for the future). The verb is exploited to describe the

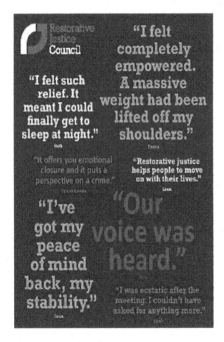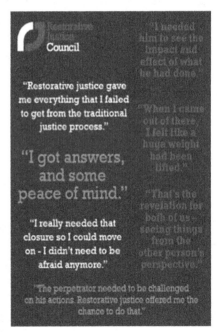

Figure 8.2 Restorative Justice Council publication reusing phrases by victims' and offenders' stories.

result of the restorative justice meeting, which represents a first step in overcoming the *weight* of the victims' past and recovering their control. Metaphorical expressions representing empowerment and relief are thus commonly exploited by participants:

(10) When I walked out of that meeting, I felt as if I could knock out Mike Tyson – I could have taken on anything or anyone. In the days and weeks afterwards, it was as if a massive weight had been lifted off my shoulders. [...] I felt completely empowered (Emma's story).

(11) The meeting was done in a very respectful, considerate way for both of us and I actually gave Anneka a hug before I left. Afterwards, it felt like a weight had been lifted off of my shoulder. I felt a lot lighter (Celine's story).

The verb phrases *felt like* (23 occurrences, 0.1%) and *feel like* (15 occurrences, 0.04%) are also used in the narratives not as a linguistic hedging but to describe the way the victims/offenders *felt* or *feel* before and after the restorative process, also expressing their insecurities and worries about meeting the offender:

(12) I didn't feel like the flat was home anymore (Ed and Rumbie's story).

(13) I just didn't feel like I could face Brian, so everything was put on hold for several years (Laura's story).

The word *feel* followed by positive adjectives emerges as a tool to express catharsis and success of the restorative process, while framing the subject's positions within a discourse of emotional disclosure. In particular, *feel* is followed by *better* (11 occurrences, 0.02% of the *Victims'* subcorpus), *empowered* (six occurrences, 0.01% as in example (10)), *strong/er* (five occurrences, 0.01%), *comfortable* (three occurrences, 0.01%).

(14) It made me feel better, and I felt I'd got through to those girls (Eileen's story).

(15) You feel empowered by being able to say what you feel (Susan's story).

Being able to offer sincere apologies and provide an effective account represents one of the most relevant parts of the mediated dialogue. The verb *feel* is also present in the offenders' stories in the present corpus, especially in the forms *felt* (15 occurrences, 0.3% of the *Offenders'* subcorpus) and *feel* (four occurrences, 0.1%), which together account for 0.3% of the whole offenders' subcorpus, compared with the higher normalized frequency of 0.6% in the *Victims'* corpus.

Through the usage of the verb *feel*, offenders' narratives also offer an insight into the experience of the repenting subjects:

> (16) The first meeting came. I remember it was a couple. When they first walked in, I literally felt like cracking in half and disappearing (Kelvin's story).

> (17) It felt good to get things off my chest (Alex's story).

Intensifiers appear to have a particular relevance in the victims' stories, since extreme language helps the website construct an opposition between a bad past and a good present. The most frequent are *really* (132 occurrences, 0.32% of the *Victims'* corpus) and *very* (131 occurrences, 0.32%). Utterances containing the adverb *really* represent indirect speech acts of evaluation rendering implicit information (see e.g. Volkova 2013), thus making the utterance an invaluable tool for influencing the hearer in the process of speech interaction.

> (18) It really damaged my sense of safety in my own house and I considered moving (Ruth's story).

> (19) I became very depressed, and my health deteriorated even further (Waseem's story).

Similar considerations may be applied to the offenders' corpus. The use of *really* is also particularly relevant here (18 occurrences in the subcorpus, 0.34%), while *very* is present in just one instance (one occurrence, 0.02%). The intensifier *really* appears therefore to be preferred by offenders, supposedly as it implies a sense of truthfulness and sincerity:

> (20) I didn't go into the conference expecting forgiveness and that was the part that really brought me to tears (Jason's story).

> (21) It felt really good that I'd taken a bit of the weight off their shoulders and that I'd done something right (Kelvin's story).

Tweets

The present study also considered the Twitter messages published by the Restorative Justice Council. Twitter is an online social networking service that enables users to send and read short messages of up to 280-characters, the *tweets*. The limited amount of characters available makes language direct and essential. Users can share, or *retweet*, other users' posts and publicly exchange messages (see also Zappavigna 2012). Twitter use has grown exponentially within many communities and the RJC itself manages an institutional Twitter page.

Twitter has considerable potential as an information dissemination tool and as a means to create affiliation for an organization. It is employed for professional communication and as a marketing and promotional tool to increase the RJC's popularity. As is evident from Figure 8.1, RJC's tweets can be accessed from the site's homepage, as well as directly from the RJC Twitter page. The RJC Twitter account signals events and campaigns through hashtags and invites further readings through links and retweeting.

RJC posts messages it authored or retweets posts by other users, who may be workers in the field or people who have taken part in RJ. The addressees are mainly operators in the field and ordinary people potentially interested in restorative justice. These include freelance consultants, practitioners, independent charities, commissioned services, trainers in the field, but also the public at large, especially victims, offenders and supporting parents.

The messages analysed appeared to be mainly exploited to share: constant updates on the organization of events and meetings; information about the results of the meetings; intervention of experts, consultants at meetings and seminars; services offered by credited practitioners and associations; news about developments and evolution of the service; comments on news coverage on restorative justice; thanks and congratulations by users (in the form of retweets).

Present tenses prevail in the tweets, especially when referring to events and meetings that are taking place at the moment, 'live' as in (22). Tweets make use of both impersonal forms and first-person plural references. In particular, the possessive adjective *our* (15 occurrences, 1.27% of the Tweets) represents the most frequent personal reference.

(22) All set for our Newcastle #RestorativeJustice workshop today @NUFC with @NorthumbriaPCC @DurhamPCC @northyorkspcc and more #RJCNewcastle18y (26/03/2018).

(23) Great meeting @rocrestore staff and volunteers today to celebrate 5 years delivering #restorativejustice with communities in Greater #Manchester with our patron HRH The Princess Royal (17/01/2018).

The noun *quality* (12 occurrences, 1.02%) also appears to recur in the tweets, used to inform the public about the reliability of the service offered and in the selection and instruction of the practitioners. The term quality is also repeated in the texts in the acronym *RSQM* (eight instances, 0.7%).

(24) Congratulations to Conexus Conflict Consultancy @tjbevington on achieving the TPQM for delivering high quality #restorative training (31/01/2018).

(25) Lunch almost finished, we are all lined up for our RSQM award ceremony later this aft recognising high quality (21/11/2017).

The RJC account is thus exploited not only to promote restorative justice services among ordinary citizens but also to offer its paid services and qualifications to experts and organizations, especially the RJC's Restorative Service Quality Mark (RSQM) practitioner accreditation and the Training Provider Quality Mark (TPQM). The RJC account thus comes to represent an authoritative voice in the field of RJ in the UK which is also publicly recognized and appreciated by external subjects (see e.g. example (23)).

Discussion and conclusions

Restorative practice is a voluntary and still largely unknown process which may promote the development of a safer and more peaceful society. In particular, restorative justice benefits all the main actors in a crime or dispute. It saves the state time and resources, as it diverts cases away from an overloaded criminal justice system. It gives offenders a chance of rehabilitation, by accepting responsibility for the harm committed. Moreover, and most importantly, it empowers victims, helping them overcome the psychological consequence of a crime and to regain control of their lives (see e.g. Garkawe 1999).

In the United Kingdom, the Restorative Justice Council represents one of the main authorities promoting restorative practice and offering professional training. The present study focused on the dissemination and persuasion techniques exploited on the RJC website. The analysis revealed that the website appeared to efficiently popularize and champion the service online through different media and genres. The informative sections popularize and promote restorative practice without explicitly mentioning any legislative references or legal terminology. They suggest the multiple areas of human relationships which may benefit from restorative practice, as a way to repair past harms and shape a better future. Moreover, through the direct question and answer structure, FAQs provide general information about the practice and reassure potential users through a fictional dialogue.

The website also offers multiple resources and testimonies of successful outcomes, both in written and audio-visual formats. In particular, the study analysed the first-person narratives of positive experiences. Such stories represent one of the most powerful tools exploited by the website to endorse restorative practice. Narratives make use of emotional verbs, extreme language and metaphors to convey the sense of psychological distress experienced at the time of the crime, then contrasted with the sense of relief and empowerment reached after restorative encounters. Stories generate empathy in the reader and concretely show the positive impact of the process in real people's lives.

Finally, the Restorative Justice Council Twitter channel provides constant updates about events organized by the body and about the advancement of the practice. Testimonies of appreciation by other users and operators are also exploited to endorse the quality of the service provided. Tweets are generally used to raise awareness about the possibilities offered by the RJC and by restorative practice in general, attracting and maintaining attention and inviting participation.

Nevertheless, the potentiality of the RJC website informative sections and of Twitter as dissemination tools are not exploited to the full. These online services are generally not used to convey legal knowledge or specific information about the restorative process to ordinary citizens, who would therefore need to further enquire about the programme requirements and itinerary.

Note

1 Restorative Justice Council. https://restorativejustice.org.uk/.

References

Abbamonte, Lucia and Cavaliere, Flavia. 2012. Restorative justice and mediation: The healing power of language. *Explorations in Language and Law. Approaches and Perspectives 1*: 110–123.

Abbamonte, Lucia and Cavaliere, Flavia. 2013. Restorative justice, a comparative analysis of discursive practices: Dialogistic exchanges in the USA and Italy. In Williams, Christopher and Tessuto, Girolamo (eds). *Language in the Negotiation of Justice: Contexts, Issues and Applications.* Farnham: Ashgate (121–144).

Anthony, Laurence. 2014. *Antconc 3.4.*

Askehave, Inger and Ellerup Nielsen, Anne. 2005. Digital genres: A challenge to traditional genre theory. *Information Technology & People 18(2)*: 120–141.

Audit Commission. 1996. *Misspent Youth: Young People and Crime.* London: Audit Commission.

Baker, Paul. 2006. *Using Corpora in Discourse Analysis.* London and New York: Continuum.

Bhatia, Vijay K. 2004. *Words of Written Discourse: A Genre-Based View.* London: Continuum.

Blundo, Robert and Greene, Roberta Rubin. 2009. Social Construction. In Greene, Roberta Rubin (ed.). *Human Behavior Theory and Social Work Practice*, 2nd edition. New Brunswick, NJ, and London: Aldine Transaction, a division of Transaction Publishers (309–340).

Centre for Justice and Reconciliation (A Program of Prison and Fellowship International). 2018. Lesson 1: What is Restorative Justice? Encounter. *Restorative Justice.* http://restorativejustice.org/restorative-justice/about-restorative-justice/tutorial-intro-to-restorative-justice/lesson-1-what-is-restorative-justice/encounter/#sthash.PoktnLI2.dpbs

Chouliaraki, Lilie and Fairclough, Norman. 1999. *Discourse in Late Modernity: Rethinking Critical Discourse Analysis.* Edinburgh University Press.

CPS (Crown Prosecution Service). 2018. www.cps.gov.uk/

Criminal Justice Act. 2003. *Chapter 44.* Parliament of the United Kingdom.

Dahlstrom, Michael F. 2014. Using narratives and storytelling to communicate science with nonexpert audiences. *Proceedings of the National Academy of Sciences of the United States of America 111(4)*: 13614–13620.

Fairclough, Norman. 1992. *Discourse and Social Change*. Cambridge: Polity Press.

Fairclough, Norman. 2001. *Language and Power*, 2nd edition. Essex: Pearson Education.

Garkawe, Sam. 1999. Restorative justice from the perspective of crime victims. *QUT Law Review 15*: 40–56.

Garzone, Giuliana. 2006. *Perspectives on ESP and Popularization*. Milan: CUEM.

Gotti, Maurizio. 2005. *Investigating Specialized Discourse*. Bern: Peter Lang.

Hughes, Bronwen and Napolitano, Antonella. 2013. From primary legislation to public presence: The language of gay rights: From legislation to lobbying. In William, Christopher and Tessuto, Girolamo (eds). *Language in the Negotiation of Justice: Contexts, Issues and Applications*. Farnham: Ashgate (207–231).

Marshall, Tony F. 1996. The evolution of restorative justice in Britain. *European Journal on Criminal Policy and Research 4*(4): 31–43.

Martin, J.R. 2009. Realisation, instantiation and individuation: Some thoughts on identity in Youth Justice Conferencing. *DELTA-Documentação de Estudos em Linguistica Teorica e Aplicada 25*: 549–583.

Martin, J.R., Zappavigna, Michele, Dwyer, Paul and Cléirigh Chris. 2013. Users in uses of language: Embodied identity in Youth Justice Conferencing. *Text and Talk 33*(4–5): 467–496.

Martin, J.R. and Zappavigna, Michele and Dwyer, Paul. 2014. Beyond redemption: Choice and consequence in Youth Justice Conferencing. In Fang, Yan and Webster, Jonathan J. (eds). *Developing Systemic Functional Linguistics: Theory and Application*. London: Equinox (18–47).

Restorative Justice Council. 2014. *Restorative Justice and Policing. Information Pack*. Restorative Justice Council.

Rideout, J. Christopher. 2008. Storytelling, narrative rationality, and legal persuasion. *Journal of Legal Writing 14*: 53–86.

Riessman, Catherine Kohler. 2001a. Analysis of personal narratives. In Gubrium, Jaber F. and Holstein, James A. (eds). *Handbook of Interview Research: Context and Method*. Thousand Oaks, CA: Sage (695–710).

Riessman, Catherine Kohler. 2001b. Personal troubles as social issues: A narrative of infertility in context. In Shaw, Ian and Gould, Nick (eds), *Quality Research in Social Work*. London, Thousand Oaks, CA, and New Delhi: Sage Publications (73–82).

Rossner, Meredith. 2011. Emotions and interaction ritual: A micro analysis of restorative justice. *The British Journal of Criminology 51*(1): 95–119.

Van Ness, Daniel W. and Heetderks Strong, Karen. 2015. *Restoring Justice: An Introduction to Restorative Justice*, 5th edition. Waltham, MA: Anderson Publishing, an imprint of Elsevier.

Volkova, Lidiya M. 2013. Illocutionary potential of the discourse marker 'really.' *Messenger of Kyiv National Linguistic University, Philology 16*(2): 35–40.

Williams, Christopher. 2007. *Tradition and Change in Legal English. Verbal Constructions in Prescriptive Texts*. Bern: Peter Lang.

Zappavigna, Michele. 2012. *Discourse of Twitter and Social Media: How We Use Language to Create Affiliation on the Web*. London: Bloomsbury.

Zappavigna, Michele and Martin, J.R. 2014. Mater dolorosa: Negotiating support in NSW Youth Justice Conferencing. *International Journal for the Semiotics of Law 27*: 263–275.

Zappavigna, Michele and Martin, J.R. 2018. *Discourse and Diversionary Justice: An Analysis of Youth Justice Conferencing.* Sidney: Palgrave Macmillan.

Zehr, Howard and Gohar, Ali. 2003. *The Little Book of Restorative Justice.* Intercourse, PA: Good Books.

Zehr, Howard and Mika, Harry. 2017. Fundamental concepts of restorative justice. In Roche, Declan (ed.). *Restorative Justice.* London and New York: Routledge (73–81).

9 Helping Aussie women online

A discourse analysis of the Australian eSafety Commissioner website

Carmina Meola

Introduction and background

Cyber-security and e-safety

The growth in the use of the Internet over the past several years has produced a corresponding growth in the number and types of illegitimate practices undertaken over the Internet. From the annoying, but relatively innocuous, invasion of spam emails to more insidious practices such as identity theft, online fraud, sales of counterfeit and/or unauthorized trademark misuse. The Internet has also provided numerous opportunities for enterprising fraudsters and adult users to access children, young people and women for the purposes of sexual abuse. According to Davidson and Martellozzo (2008), Internet sex offender behaviour includes the construction of sites to be used for the exchange of information, experiences, and indecent images of children; the organization of criminal activities that seek to use children for prostitution purposes and that produce indecent images of children at a professional level, and the organization of criminal activities that promote sexual tourism. However although the Internet has been ascribed a negative reputation, for the reasons mentioned, and for its potentially damaging influence on its users, as addiction, depression, and loneliness, it also provides a rich environment which may include significantly positive aspects, hence when used appropriately, it can improve the quality of life for its users.

Cyber-security is, in fact, the protection of Internet-connected systems, including hardware, software and data, from cyber attacks. According to the TechTarget global network of technology specific websites (2016), cyber-security requires the coordination of efforts throughout an information system which includes:

- Application security;
- Information security;
- Network security
- Disaster recovery/business continuity planning;
- Operational security;
- End-user education.

E-safety, short for Internet safety or online safety, differently from cyber-security, does not only apply to the Internet but to other ways in which people, especially young people, communicate by using electronic media, e.g. mobile phones. According to Jecinta Morgan (2018) the difference between Safety and Security is:

> Security refers to the protection of individuals, organizations, and properties against external threats that are likely to cause harm. It focuses on ensuring that external factors do not cause trouble or unwelcome situation to the organization, individuals, and the properties within the premises. On the other hand, safety is the feeling of being protected from the factors that causes harm... feeling of being safe is an emotional aspect while security has to do with physical aspects.
>
> (www.differencebetween.net.language March 9, 2018)

E-safety therefore, means ensuring that users are protected from harm and supported to achieve the maximum benefit from new and developing technologies without risk to themselves or others. The aim of promoting e-safety is to protect young people from the adverse consequences of access or use of electronic media, from bullying to inappropriate sexualized behaviour or exploitation. Appropriate use of electronic media by service provider staff and professionals is covered by other protocols and procedures with individual services and organizations. Nowadays most agencies already have an appropriate use policy in place, and all are encouraged to develop one.

In Australia, a very efficient initiative as regards online safety came out in 2011 with the so-called Office of The eSafety Commissioner, on behalf of the Australian Government. The Office of the eSafety Commissioner is Australia's leader in online safety and is responsible for promoting online safety for all Australians. The Commissioner is assisted by the eSafety Staff of the Australian Communications and Media Authority to perform functions and exercise its powers.

The eSafety Commissioner

This chapter will focus on the affirmative aspects of the Internet, the Office of The eSafety Commissioner website,[1] in particular on eSafety Women, and on ways in which the Internet may be used to enhance and increase surfers' well-being, both collectively and individually. That is to say, how a website is at the disposal of people who are needy of help to protect them from online, technological or domestic abuse. The Commissioner is aimed at helping all Australians to have safer, positive experiences online – just as they would offline (The eSafety Commissioner, 2017). The eSafety Commissioner Office co-ordinates and leads the online safety efforts of government, industry and the not-for profit community. It has a broad remit which includes:

- providing a complaints service for young Australians who experience serious cyberbullying

- identifying and removing illegal online content
- tackling image-based abuse.

It has offices in Sydney, Melbourne and Canberra, and eight sections that are supported by the eSafety Commissioner's Corporate Team (see Figure 9.1).

As for online safety for women, in 2012 Australia released the "National plan to reduce violence against women and their children" and in support of it, it launched the "Women's Safety Package to Stop Violence," consisting of a $100 million budget to help keep women safe. The Plan also issued a project to enhance virtual safety for women, hence, *eSafety Women*. The initiative run by the Office of the eSafety Commissioner was established in 2015 through "The Enhancing Online Safety Act" with a mandate to coordinate and lead online safety efforts within the country.

When the Office was established, the eSafety Commissioner's functions and powers primarily related to enhancing online safety for Australian children. Later, in 2017, the Act was amended to expand the Commissioner's remit to promoting and enhancing online safety for all Australians, focusing attention on cyber bullying complaints and administering an image-based abuse portal.

The Government's Office of the eSafety Commissioner is helping to ensure that women, children and elderly Australians are well supported and can take advantage of the social, cultural, health and economic benefits that enhanced connectivity can bring. There are issues, apps, games and social networks that shape the online world. The esafety issues are concerned with what it is, how to deal with it and where to go for help for all online issues facing youth today.

The big issues are:

- Cyber abuse
- Cyberbullying
- Image-based abuse
- Offensive or illegal content
- Sexting information for young people
- Social engineering
- Social networking
- Unwanted contact

Whereas other online issues are:

- Balancing online time
- Digital reputation
- Online gaming
- Protecting online information.

The opening website page of the Office of the eSafety Commissioner (see Figure 9.2) displays several options: *eSafety issues* (types of threats); *get help*,

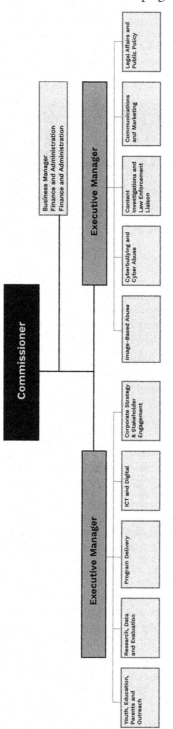

Figure 9.1 The structure of the eSafety Commissioner.[2]

Figure 9.2 The eSafety Commissioner website opening page (since updated).

addressed to all those who need immediate help for being cyberbullied and would like to report it or have a confidential chat with someone who can really help; *iParent*, which provides online safety resources targeted to the specific needs of parents and carers; *eSafety Women*, addressed to all Australian women who are empowered to take control online; *Games, apps and social networking sites*, popular among children and adults, to provide appropriate strategies for all users to interact without encountering risks. There are also *Helpful Websites* provided for further assistance, and finally, at the bottom of the page, there is the locution "follow us" that allows users to connect to three social channels: Facebook, Twitter and YouTube. However, these social media are not for violence reports as they do not keep anonymity. They are merely advertising and sponsoring pages.

All of these options provide Australians with information and resources for safe and positive online experiences, and how they may interact directly with the Office by writing messages or leaving comments on published posts.

It should be imperative at this point as Calder (2004) argues, that it is essential to encourage appropriate and safe use of the Internet by assisting children, young people and women at risk to feel comfortable and supported in navigating the information highway. If the use of technology is combined with education and awareness among children, parents and teachers, and effective inter-agency partnership working, it would be easier to maximize the few available resources and move closer to making cyberspace a safe place for all users. Thus, the net experience can (1) help socially inhibited people and those with a negative social stigma; (2) give social support systems; (3) improve intergroup relationships; (4) help solve the conflict between individuality and belonging to a group. It is suggested that understanding the positive aspects of the net will promote its potential to improve the psychological well-being of surfers (Amichai-Hamburger and Furnham, 2007).

Victims of violence

Reporting stories of violence suffered by victims is a way to make them feel less isolated and encouraged to take control. The use of narrations encourages identification with women, who look normal, but in many circumstances, hide many weaknesses. Victims report how technology is being used to abuse, control and humiliate them. They also inform of how they are tracked by a GPS track finder application and receive threatening and intimidating messages from the perpetrator. Threats may be indirect or phrased in a way that may avoid "breaching" an apprehended violence order, yet the woman knows it has a threatening intention. Logan, Walker, Cole and Shannon (2006) argue that a violent partner often knows how to specifically torment their victim, using their intimate knowledge to threaten her in ways that may not seem obvious to others, but cause enormous fear for the victim, especially anxiety, and depression. El Moez et al. (2004) report that domestic violence against women is prevalent in every country, cutting across boundaries of culture, class, education, income, ethnicity, and age. Domestic violence against women results in far-reaching physically and psychological consequences. Although the impact of physical abuse may be more visible, psychological scarring is harder to define and claim. Usually the perpetrators are men who are, or have been, in positions of trust and intimacy and power such as husbands, fathers, fathers-in-law, stepfathers, brothers, uncles, sons, or other relatives. Domestic violence is, in most cases, violence perpetrated by men against women. Women can also be violent, but this generally accounts for a small percentage of domestic violence.

From a survey[3] carried out in Australia in 2016, two out of five females from the age of 18 onwards had experienced violence since the age of 15 (see Figure 9.3). The data show that two out of five people (39% or 7.2 million) aged 18 years and over experienced an incident of physical or sexual violence since the age of 15, including 42% of men (3.8 million) and 37% of women (3.4 million). Four out of ten men (41% or 3.7 million) and three out of ten women (31% or 2.9 million) experienced physical violence. One in five women (18% or 1.7 million) and one in twenty men (4.7% or 428,800) experienced sexual violence. Women experienced sexual assault mostly by a male they knew and mostly in the respondent's home or in the perpetrator's home. However, the majority of these women, about 87%, did not contact the police (ABS, 2016 Personal Safety Survey). *ESafety Women* was rightly issued to help women report and stop violence. In most cases abuse and violence includes the use of technology to control and stalk women, therefore the overall aim of e*Safety Women* is to empower in Australia to take control of online interaction. The website will shortly also include targeted resources for Indigenous women, women from culturally and linguistically diverse communities, and women with disabilities.

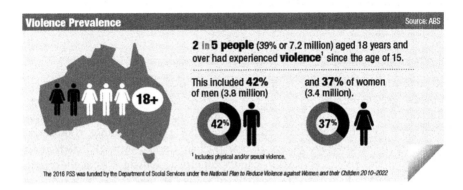

Figure 9.3 Prevalence of violence since the age of 15.

The eSafety Women website homepage

Websites, according to Weideman (2013):

> have a number of attributes, some more easily measurable than others. Usability comes to mind, as well as a large number of usage metrics including hits, bounce rate, page views and pages per visit. Website visibility is another metric which describes the ease (or lack thereof) with which a search engine crawler can index a given Web page, once found. This degree of visibility to a crawler is a combination of a large number of factors, as opposed to a single value on a linear scale. Some of these factors which could improve the visibility of a Website include the quality and quantity of inlinks, keyword usage in Web page body text and the use of metatags.
>
> (18–4 paper 599)

It is claimed in a 2006 study that hyperlinks provide the most common structure on which Web studies are based (Heimeriks and Van den Besselaar, 2006).

The *eSafety Women* website (see Figure 9.4) provides easy accessibility and navigability, employs an easy-to-read language to enact a series of linguistic and explanatory devices (Garzone, 2006; Barron, 2012). It presents three different macro-areas: *Lifestyle, Being social* and *Take control*. The *Lifestyle* section explains how to approach new devices, apps, phones and computers in a safe way, by following some easy steps, e.g. increase privacy, never leave them unattended, turn off location services, save passwords and backup e-data. Furthermore, there is also particular space dedicated to online shopping and banking, and procedures to avoid scams.

Being social describes how to use blogs and social apps appropriately in order to communicate and share information from politics, sport, to online dating and gambling without encountering risks.

Take control is the most important section, as far as women online safety is concerned, and is divided in five sub paragraphs:

Figure 9.4 The eSafety Women homepage.

a   *Online abuse* covers a range of behaviours that people use to control, frighten and humiliate other people through technology with negative comments, sexual unwanted requests or by being trolls and haters. The site explains how to recognize risky and abusing behaviours, the so-called "red flags" (frequent and unwanted texts or messages, abusive or silent calls, post defamatory comments and malicious rumours, intimate pictures without consent). All of these can influence women's feelings and lead them to anxiety, fear, shame and self-blaming. To help women face this problem the site offers a free phone assistance, especially for IBA (image-based abuse).

b   *Cyber stalking* is addressed to women who want to report cases of harassment and stalking. Unfortunately, these victims feel depressed, anxious, and in many cases, isolated.

c   *eSafety planning* consists of a summary of the practical help and advice supplied to avoid online problems and abuses, as already mentioned.

d   *Keeping children safe* is dedicated to children who are victims of domestic violence or online abuse. A list of safety rules and support are supplied to keep children safe. Children, even younger ones, are encouraged to expose their problems without having to be frightened, either for online abuse or domestic.

e   *Women's stories* is the "autobiographic" section, with real stories of ordinary women. Each story is written in third person using fictional names and characters, followed by a video where the case is reported.

Facebook, Twitter and YouTube are also available to provide Australians with information and resources for safe and positive online experiences, and how they may interact directly with the Office by writing messages or leaving comments on published posts.

Aims and purposes

The present study explores the resources offered by the Australian government to support women who are object of online abuse. For the purpose, the materials published on the *eSafety Women* platform were collected, considering both written and audio-visual texts. The research will analyse how legal issues are popularized by the Australian Government through web-mediated communications and how the victims and abusers are constructed through textual and multimodal representations.

Methods and data

The study considers the website architecture of *eSafety Women* and the Internet environment supplied to help women manage technology risks and abuse by giving them the tools they need to be confident when they are online. Women are guided to take control of inappropriate behaviours in particular, of malevolent subjects who may exploit their vulnerabilities by making use of technology to harass them, making unwanted contact, sharing private pictures or videos, accessing private information or online profiles, posting humiliating or intimidating comments on social media, and monitoring their movements.

Australia is considered a country of women, in that, they detain the world's Guinness Record of institutional roles in key positions, both in terms of politics and social concerns. An online article released in Italy in 2013, (ilgiornale.it/news/2013/01/13/benvenuti-in-australia-il-paese-delle-donne/874293/) reported that in Australia there is a greater consideration and openness towards the opinions of women. It is not a rare attitude towards the tenacity of Australian women, it incorporates the spirit of the pioneers who had to face many adverse conditions and pay with first-rate achievements to obtain their rights. Although Australian women have basic social and political roles they are equally exposed to danger and harm, both physically and virtually, as already seen.

The corpus for this study consists of a short selection of case study stories of women who have reported to *eSafety Women*. The stories have been investigated both as written and as audio-visual texts.

The study analyses the *eSafety Women* real life stories, and, in particular it considers the discursive construction of women victims and how their abusers are presented. The texts have also been studied from a multimodal perspective, as Multimodality (Kress, 2010) serves for the merging of various sources of information, of multiple channels of communication, auditory (words, prosody, dialogue acts, rhetorical structure) and visual (gesture, posture, graphics). In fact, in human-computer interface design, a multimodal interface is the natural

Table 9.1 Corpus data

Texts	Tokens	Types
6 Women life stories texts	3,445	817
6 Videos	3,445	817

extension of spoken dialogue systems where the user can communicate with speech and gesture and, in return, get multimodal output. Annotation of multimodal dialogue on audiovisual media (video) is crucial for case-studies, training (machine learning), testing and evaluation (Kipp, 2001).

The work is supported by the corpus analysis software AntCon 3.5.7 for Windows (Anthony, 2018) to obtain statistical data and signal tendencies.

Table 9.1 shows the number of texts analysed, the tokens and word types calculated with AntConc.

In particular this study takes into consideration the grammatical features of pronouns, verbs, nouns, adjectives, and adverbs used by the participants, and which of these have more occurrences. Attention is given to the 'structure' or 'patterns' of the discourse, but also focuses on the more 'dynamic' aspects of discourse organization, such as the mental, interactional or social strategies in which they are engaged in. Finally, especially in a more psychological perspective, the analysis focuses on structures or strategies and processes of the production and comprehension of discourse, that is the way discourse or its meanings are represented in memory, or how mental models of events are formed or activated during production or comprehension.

Results

The new world of the Internet poses new challenges for law application. Users deliberately or inadvertently spread their personal information on the web, often holding the illusion that a monitor may grant them privacy, anonymity, distance from their interlocutors. Yet, as mentioned the Internet has actually also created an environment which may encourage inappropriate behaviours. Apps offer abusers a terrifying new toolbox to control their partners and exes. Phone software allows abusers to follow their partners' or exes' movements, monitor their calls, texts and emails–and even watch them (Williams, 2015). The case studies in *eSafety Women* are stories of women who have reported being threatened through the use of technology, especially smartphones. Their ex partners have all used cyber stalking apps to enable continuous and secret tracking through their mobile phone to check intimate conversations, appointments, online banking activity, intellectual musings and minute-to-minute movements. The stories analysed have titles and have been given a number from 1 to 6 for research reasons, as follows:

1 Alison's story
2 Lin's story
3 Bella's story

4   Sam's story
5   Alicia's story
6   Rose's story

Discourse analysis is to look at the patterns of language across texts and considers the relationship between language and the social and cultural contexts in which it is used (Paltridge, 2006). All of the stories analysed start with a narrative presentation, following a regular scheme. Then a video is shown where the victims are played by fictional characters, in order to keep anonymity. The individual case studies of stalking victims document their pervasiveness of fear, anger, and distress at not being able to control their privacy. For example:

Alison's story: (1)

> Alison is worried about her granddaughter Jess because her boyfriend seems to control her and her behaviours. Alison offers support to Jess. (www. esafety.gov.au/women/take-control/case-studies/Alison's story)

The narrator then intervenes to give advice by using the second-person, as point of view (POV) to cast the reader/viewer as the protagonist. By speaking in the second person, the author/narrator can hold a mirror to society, revealing emotions, actions and particular nuances of the times (Valante, 2015). That means that if a woman connects to the webpage to be assisted, she is almost "forced" to act and think in ways that might not be authentic for her, but will make her feel involved and empowered to leave her report. In fact, in the following statements the word *you* has the effect of directly addressing the reader/viewer.

- let them know *you* are there to help when they are ready to tell;
- tell them *you* are worried about them and why;
- keep in touch;
- tell them it is not their fault;
- ask how *you* can help, don't tell them what to do
- respect their decisions and support them
- collect evidence on a safe device
     (www.esafety.gov.au/women/take-control/case-studies/Alison's story)

Another case study, Alicia's story (5), is presented as follows:

> She left her violent partner and has a violence order in place. The video looks at the online harassment that occurred after she left her partner and how she avoided online abuse to keep her daughter safe. (www.esafety.gov.au/ women/take-control/case-studies/Alicia's story)

The advice given is:

- being stalked can be traumatic so seek support

- never wait more than two weeks to report it
- in case, contact police and ask what evidence they need
- make a safety plan
- report every incident to the police
     (www.esafety.gov.au/women/take-control/case-studies/Alicia's story)

The language appears assertive as it presents the information in a powerfully worded way, giving the text an authoritative edge and making it sound indisputable: *seek support, never wait, contact police, report.*

Lin's story (2) is about a woman who is trying to start a new relationship after her divorce. Online she gets advice on how to start dating again.

The advice given is:

- do homework about the different sites
- take your time to get to know each other before meeting in person
- meet in a public place
- have a backup plan, if you're not feeling comfortable
- trust your instincts
     (www.esafety.gov.au/women/take-control/case-studies/Lin's story)

The voice used is rather informal to help engage the addressee in a more familiar and relaxed way, and it helps form a clear picture of what steps women may take to obtain help. This strategy can create a friendly tone and make the reader/viewer feel more involved. It may cause a friendly, inviting, and even confiding situation for the person involved. Although it can also feel forceful and persuasive at times, the participant is however sharing a feeling that is not just personal but something many other women will have experienced, and are experiencing, thus, they share the same emotional response. The research results show that the most used pronoun in all the stories is the first person singular, which is used most times as subjective referring to the speaker as a person hurt, worried. According to Rude, Gortner and Pennebaker (2004), this suggests a higher index of psychological and emotional distress in stages where abuse has been somewhat internalized.

I appears with a frequency of 5% and refers to the victim's point of view. It is connected to verbs that indicate safety and protection in the online area such as "checked," "developed and safety plan" and "installed." It appears mostly in stories 1 and 5.

The pronoun *he*, undoubtedly one of the most common mechanisms to refer to the perpetrator, is less central in the users' discourse to convey a situation which has almost been overcome, the *he* who has brought so much pain and anger to the woman's life. The *he* accounts for 1.30% and is connected to verbs that refer to the action of controlling women such as "became controlling" and "sent me abusive texts." It appears mostly in stories 1 and 5.

She appears with a frequency of 1% and it refers to the victim's mood.

It is connected to verbs that refer to a women's state of closure such as "became anxious," "felt stupid" and "broke down." It appears exclusively in the first story, because it is the only one which is not narrated by the victim but by her grandmother.

The most recurrent verb is *was*. It appears in every story, with a frequency of 1.40% to express women's past experiences, their feelings but also their abuser's behaviours. It is followed by adjectives and adverbs that indicate the victim's mood such as *scared, afraid, hysterical* and *confused*, as well as the abuser's reactions such as *controlling* and *abusive*.

The three nouns which are mainly used in the stories are *online, safety* and *abuse*, to refer to the means of protection in order to be safe online (privacy setting accounts).

"Safety" is used related to the nouns "plan" and "help," referring to the sort of advice granted to women to prevent violence.

"Abuse" is used mostly related to the nouns "control" and "violence," referring to behaviours that can humiliate women.

The adjectives which mainly occur are "scared," "afraid," "worried" and "abusive."

"Scared" and "afraid" are used as synonymous to indicate the psychological mood of the victims and the fear of abusers' reactions. They appear mostly in stories 1 and 5 in expressions as "scared of him" and "afraid of making him angrier."

"Worried" is used to refer to friends and family, to ask for help and to refer to the abusers' reaction, and appears mostly in story 1 in expressions as "worried about her," "worried he might get angry."

"Abusive" is used to refer to men's behaviours and their offensive means. It appears mostly in stories 5 and 6 in expressions as "abusive texts" and "psychologically abusive."

The most recurrent adverbs are "really," "very" and "always."

"Really" and "very" are used to emphasize the veracity of the systematic occurrence of abusive facts. They appear mostly in stories 5 and 6 in expressions such as "really stupid," "very stressful."

"Always" is used with the same aim and it appears mostly in story 5 in expressions as "he seemed to always know where I was."

The following tables summarize the results obtained from the research.

Discussion and conclusions

Domestic violence in Australia is a long standing, complex social issue. However, there has been a profound transformation in public awareness about this problem in the last decades. The Government has been particularly sensitive and has supplied its citizens with reporting facilities and instructive materials. As part of the Government services, The Office of the eSafety Commissioner, that is, a statutory office-holder, was created by the Enhancing Online Safety Act, in 2015. In the same year the Office of the Commissioner was established with a mandate to coordinate and lead online safety efforts across government, industry and the not-for profit community. The *eSafety Women* initiative is part of the Office's project and is designed to

Table 9.2 Relevant lexico-grammar items used by the victims

Pronouns	Frequency %	Person	Stories	Times Occurs
I	5,00%	Victims' point of view	1,2,3,4,5,6	164
He	1,30%	The abuser	1,2,3,4,5,6	45
She	1,00%	Victim	1	39

Verbs	Frequency %	Aim	Stories	Occurs
Was	1,40%	To express women's past experiences, their feelings and abusers behaviours	1,2,3,4,5,6	48

Adjectives	Aim	Stories	Occurs
Scared/Afraid	Use of that synonymous indicate the psychological mood of the victims and the fear of abuser's reaction.	1,5,6	5
Worried	For friend and familyabout asking helpabout abuser's reaction	1,3,5,6	7
Abusive	It refers to men's behaviours and offensive means	1,5,6	5

Adverbs	Aim	Stories	Occurs
Really/Very	Used to emphasize the veracity, the systematic occurrence of abusive facts.	1,5,6.	12
Always	To highlight the frequency of act.	1,5,6.	6

Table 9.3 Occurrences of nouns used by experts

Nouns	Reference	Occurs
Online	Means of protection to be safe online (privacy settings accounts)	16
Safety	Advice given to women to prevent violence	7
Abuse	Behaviours that can humiliate women	3

empower all Australian women to take control of their online experiences thus forming part of the Australian Government's Women's Safety Package to Stop the Violence.

The present research focused on the Office of The eSafety Commissioner website, and in particular on eSafety Women. A great amount of information is available on the website which seems to provide easy tools for surfing and interaction. The language is user-friendly, and the information is easily accessible.

The eSafety Commissioner platform exploits many web features which grant self-help, guides, educational material, public messages and all sorts of resources to help people be safe when using technological devices. Furthermore, the website also offers access training courses for frontline support services, face-to-face workshops and online training programs for domestic and family violence frontline workers.

The texts analysed in the *eSafety women* section showed that most of the victim-participants used the same tone and register of language: simple and straightforward. The word types were similar in all the stories, and the occurrences of pronouns, nouns, verbs, adjectives and adverbs were mainly the same in all the stories.

As a conclusion, the study shows that the Australian Government is very concerned and committed with online safety matters for its citizens and in particular with all measures that may somehow help and prevent children and women abuse. The Office of The eSafety Commissioner website is very detailed and offers many more resources and updated materials for further research and outcomes as regards to online safety for all Australians.

Notes

1 Australian Government, Office of the eSafety Commissioner. www.esafety.gov.au.
2 www.esafety.gov.au.
3 The Australian Bureau of Statistics' (ABS) 2016 Personal Safety Survey PSS. cat. no. 4906.0.55.003.

References

Amichai-Hamburger, Yehuda and Furnham, Adrian. 2007. The positive net. *Computers in Human Behavior 23*, 2: 1033–1045.
Barron, Anne. 2012. *Public Information Messages. A Contrastive Genre Analysis of State-Citizen Communication*. Amsterdam and Philadelphia: John Benjamins Publishing Company.
Calder, Martin C. 2004. The internet: Potential, problems and pathways to hands-on sexual offending, in Calder, Martin C. (ed.) *Child Sexual Abuse and the Internet: Tackling the New Frontier*, pp. 1–24. Lyme Regis, UK: Russell House.
Davidson, Julia C. and Martellozzo, Elena. 2008. Protecting vulnerable young people in cyberspace from sexual abuse: Raising awareness and responding globally. *Police Practice and Research, 9*, 4: 277–289.
El Moez, Khaled Abd, Mona Elsyed, Ismail, Youse, Amany Waheed Eldeen and Wafa, Ellithy. 2014. Psychosocial characteristic of female victims of domestic violence. *Egyptian Journal of Psychiatry 35*, 2: 105–113.
Garzone, Giuliana. 2006. *Perspectives on ESP and Popularization*. Milan: CUEM.
Heimeriks, Gaston and Van den Besselaar, Peter. 2006. Analysing hyperlinks networks: The meaning of hyperlinks based indicators of knowledge production. *International Journal of Scientometrics, Informetrics and Bibliometrics 10, 1*.
Morgan, Jecinta. 2018. Difference between safety and security. *Difference Between.net.language*. March 6.
Kipp, Michael. 2001. *A generic annotation tool for multimodal dialogue*. Eurospeech Scandinavia 7th European Conference on Speech Communication and Technology, Aalborg, Denmark.

Kress, Gunther. 2010. *Multimodality: A Social Semiotic Approach to Contemporary Communication*. London: Routledge.

Logan, T.K., Walker, Robert, Cole, Jennifer and Shannon, Lisa. 2006. The impact of differential patterns of physical violence and stalking on mental health and help-seeking among women with protective orders. *Sage Journals*, Lexington, USA.

Paltridge, Brian. 2006. *Discourse Analysis: An Introduction*. London and New York: Continuum.

Rude, Stephanie, Gortner, Eva Maria and Pennebaker, James. 2004. Language use of depressed and depression-vulnerable college students. *Cognition & Emotion 18*, 8: 1121–1133.

Valante, Tal. 2015. The second-person point of view: Give your story a new perspective. *thewritelife.com*. April 22.

Weideman, Mellius. 2013. Comparative analysis of homepage website visibility and academic rankings for UK universities. *Information Research 18*, 4, paper 599.

Williams, Rachel. 2015. Spyware and smartphones: How abusive men track their partners. *The Guardian* online, 25 January.

Webliography

From the Office of The eSafety Commissioner website:
www.legislation.gov.au/Details/C2017C00187
www.esafety.gov.au/women
www.esafety.gov.au/
www.facebook.com/esafetyoffice
www.twitter.com/esafetyoffice
www.youtube.com/c/esafetyoffice
www.esafety.gov.au/women/take-control/case-studies/alisons-story
www.esafety.gov.au/women/take-control/case-studies/lins-story
www.esafety.gov.au/women/take-control/case-studies/bellas-story
www.esafety.gov.au/women/take-control/case-studies/sams-story
www.esafety.gov.au/women/take-control/case-studies/alicias-story
www.esafety.gov.au/women/take-control/case-studies/roses-story
TechTarget global network of technology specific websites (2016):
www.techtarget.com.network
www.theguardian.com www.theguardian.com/lifeandstyle/2015/jan/25/spyware-smartphone-abusive-men-track-partners-domestic-violence.

Programs

AntConc (Windows, Macintosh OSX, and Linux) Build 3.5.7 (April 23, 2018) Laurence Anthony, Ph.D. Center for English Language

10 Discursive illusions and manipulations in legal blogs on medically assisted procreation

Parrillo v. Italy Case

Jekaterina Nikitina

Introduction

The topic of medically assisted procreation ("MAP") continues to elicit strong reactions as these methods and techniques manipulate the beginning of human life, either under the form of reproductive cells or interventions on an embryo or foetus, and this inevitably gives rise to a number of ethical and legal questions. Paradoxically, not all issues concerning MAP are regulated in the same way in the common European legal space, often leading to disputable phenomena, such as reproductive tourism, for instance.

This study took inspiration from one of the most controversial recent rulings on MAP by the European Court of Human Rights (ECtHR), which generated strong media attention and elicited criticism both in legal and bioethical circles, paving the way for a heated discussion. For the first time in its history, in the case of *Parrillo v. Italy* (application 46470/11) the ECtHR had to rule on donation of embryos for scientific research purposes. The circumstances of the case, as expressed in the judgment based on the original application by Parrillo, date back to 2002, when Adelina Parrillo and her partner underwent in vitro fertilization treatment, as a result of which five embryos were created and stored for cryo-preservation. In November 2003 Parrillo's partner died under tragic circumstances and in February 2004 Italy passed a new law prohibiting experimentation on human embryos. After some time Parrillo requested the specialized clinic where her embryos were stored to release them as she took a decision not to proceed with a pregnancy – in any case impossible for widows under the new regulation – but to donate embryos to scientific research, rather than see them stored for an indeterminate period of time. The clinic however allegedly declined her verbal requests on the grounds that such an act would have been illicit in view of the new law. In 2011 Parrillo made a written request with the same negative result. Then she applied to the European Court of Human Rights claiming that her right to respect for private life (Art. 8) and to the peaceful enjoyment of her possessions (Art. 1 Prot. 1) had been violated by the blanket ban introduced by the new Italian law. The Grand Chamber of the ECtHR heard the case in June 2014 and delivered a final judgment in August 2015. The judgment declined the application under Article 1 of Protocol 1 ("property rights") and confirmed the applicability of Article 8 in the part concerning "respect for private life" on the grounds that

> the embryos contain the genetic material of the person in question and accordingly represent a constituent part of that person's genetic material and biological identity.
>
> (*Parrillo v. Italy*, no. 46470/11 §158; 2015 ECHR)

However, the Court found no violation as Italy enjoyed considerable room for manoeuvre ("wide margin of appreciation") on this sensitive question, and there was no European or international consensus on this subject.

Popularization through blogs

This work builds upon the notion of popularization, understood here as

> a vast class of various types of communicative events or genres that involve the transformation of specialized knowledge into "everyday" or "lay" knowledge, as well as a recontextualization of scientific discourse.
>
> (Calsamiglia and van Dijk 2004: 370)

The popularization paradigm is highly applicable to the transfer of information from an institutionalized context of the ECtHR, represented by the final judgment, to the less regulated web-domain of legal blogs.

The judgment is situated in a conventionalized communicative setting and represents a rather crystallized genre, with clearly defined communicative purposes and participants; it also has stable structural parts (the procedure, the facts – circumstances of the case and relevant domestic law and practice, the law – alleged violation and submissions by the parties, the dispositive part and, if any, separate and dissenting opinions, see White 2009 for details). In terms of its function, a judgment is a combination of expository and operative elements (Tiersma 1999), meaning that its goal is to assess a legal situation and to implement a dispositive part through the neutral operation of legal reasoning. As concerns the drafters or legal authors, the judgment belongs to the language of judges (Mattila 2006).

While literature on court judgments is extensive and consolidated, legal blogs entered the focus of linguists not so long ago. Relevant sources on blogging (Myers 2010a, 2010b; Mauranen 2013), and specifically legal blogging or blawging, have been growing, offering both analyses by legal practitioners (Caron 2006; Cornett 2009; Romig 2015) and by linguists (Garzone 2014a; Tessuto 2015). Romig (2015: 29) defines it as a type of "public legal writing" in that legal professionals who engage in blogging do it "not for any specific client but for dissemination to the public." Legal blogs serve as a means of legal professional communication exchange (Garzone 2014a: 167). It can be said that blogging involves the linguistic, textual and discursive re-elaboration of specialized knowledge, which is often accompanied by an increased level of subjectivity, evaluation and stance (Myers 2010b) since blogs act as vehicles for expressing the position of bloggers (Tessuto 2015: 85).

Popularization researchers have uncovered important insights into the nature of this knowledge dissemination process and have listed a number of linguistic phenomena association with this process: denominations, definitions, explanations, reformulations, generalizations, cognitive analogies and recontextualizations (Calsamiglia and van Dijk 2004; Garzone 2014b). It has been also posited that popularization involves a certain ideological slant as operations of deletion, simplification and reconstruction of knowledge structures give room for manipulation (Garzone 2014b: 100). This aspect of popularization acquires particular relevance when the popularization vehicle is a genre (a macro-genre to be exact, see Garzone 2015: 39), which is admittedly prone to the formation or expression of stance and opinions (Myers 2010b).

Methodological and analytical framework

This study adopts a multi-perspective approach to analyse the phenomena of knowledge alteration in blogs. I draw on van Dijk's (2001; 2006) triangulation approach (including social, cognitive and discursive dimensions) in the field of Critical Discourse Analysis to the study of discursive manipulations in legal blogs covering the delicate – and highly opinionated – issue of embryo donation. Van Dijk (2006: 360) defines manipulation as follows,

> Manipulation not only involves power, but specifically *abuse* of power, that is, *domination*. That is, manipulation implies the exercise of a form of *illegitimate* influence by means of discourse: manipulators make others believe or do things that are in the interest of the manipulator, and against the best interests of the manipulated.
>
> (van Dijk 2006: 360, original emphasis)

It is felt that by increasing the salience of particular aspects of an issue – through various strategies that are typical of blogging and popularization as such – blogs could activate corresponding beliefs and influence the formation of either positive or negative attitudes, often leading to cognitive illusions (Pohl 2005). An interesting conceptualization of such illusions can be found in Bhatia (2015) under the label of *(inter)discursive illusions*, or *discourse of illusions*, standing for a subjective reconceptualization of our perceptions of objective realities (Bhatia 2015: 11). Drawing on Fairclough's concept of "naturalised ideologies" (1995: 35), Bhatia (2015: 10) claims

> Our subjective representations of realities in themselves do not create an illusion; it is when we mistake this subjectivity for the actual physical and true reality without the applied consideration of an alternate, more objective reality (cf. Russel 2002, 2003) that we create illusions. In mistaking our subjective

conceptualizations of reality as objective, we are prone to *acting* on them, taking decisions, laying ground for future actions, categorizing and structurising society on the basis of them.

(Bhatia 2015: 10, original emphasis)

As the global reach of blogs allows these texts to cover a vast readership, any dominant subjective representations of reality lay the groundwork for collective illusions. If done intentionally, these could amount to manipulative discourse, or discursive power abuse (van Dijk 2006: 359). Since manipulation is often hard to distinguish from argumentation, I also tap into argumentation theory (van Emereen and Grootendorst 1992; van Emereen 2013) during the analysis (see the Fallacious and logically forced argumentation section below). I particularly draw on the argumentation *adequacy condition* (Woods and Walton 1989: 17) and on the theory of fallacious argumentation adopting van Emereen's (2013) pragma-dialectical approach to argumentative fallacies.

The aim of this study is to identify more precisely the complex mechanisms that shape the discursive illusion and that could lead to readership manipulation in the popularized context of blogs as compared to the institutional settings of judgments.

Materials

The materials used for this study pertain to the case of *Parrillo v. Italy* and include: the final judgment (19,872 words) accompanied by six judicial opinions (20,094 words) rendered by 11 judges out of 17 (two concurring opinions – by Judge Pinto de Albuquerque and Judge Dedov, one joint partially concurring opinion, one joint partially dissenting opinion, one partially dissenting opinion and one dissenting opinion of Judge Sajó, who voted against the majority judgment) and ten blog posts (12,375 words) from such websites as Lexis Nexis Blogs, Bioethics Observatory, BioNews, UK Human Rights Blog, Turtle Bay and Beyond, etc. In addition to the main texts, I also use for consultative purposes two texts produced by the ECtHR Registry for dissemination purposes – the legal summary of the judgment (1,441 words) and the press release (1,669 words), as these texts are more similar to the average length of blog posts analysed (1,237 words).

Analysis and findings

It is somehow believed that the language of manipulation is notoriously ill-formed (Maillat 2013: 190). However, deviations and slight informational shifts discovered in blogs were quite skilful and ranged from early cognitive prepping of the reader's perceptions at the paratextual level of an image and a title to the content level of careful selection of facts. In terms of language use, blogs engaged in evaluative vocabulary and dexterous use of selected quotes and attributions. On a more discursive level, they presented instances of biased interpretation and fallacious arguments.

Paratexts as pre-selected reading keys

Genette (2001 [1997]) in his book *Paratexts. Thresholds of interpretation* artfully compares a paratext to an "'undefined zone' between the inside and the outside, [...] an edge, or, as Philippe Lejeune put it, 'a fringe of the printed text which in reality controls one's whole reading of the text'" (Genette 2001 [1997]: 2). Paratexts, including titles and images accompanying texts, should not be underestimated in their influence on the reader's perceptions.

Traditionally, legal texts are not accompanied by images and have inexpressive titles. In fact, neither judgments, nor press releases, nor legal summaries feature an image. As for the title, the judgment and the legal summary have a numerical reference to the initial application by Parrillo and a simple title "Parrillo v. Italy." The press release – following the popularization goals of engaging a greater audience – opens with a more elaborate title: *Banning a woman from donating embryos obtained from in vitro fertilisation to scientific research was not contrary to respect for her private life.* In essence, this title represents a synopsis of the ECtHR ruling.

The paratextual presentation of blogs is undoubtedly more picturesque. All blog posts have evocative titles, and in 8/10 cases these are accompanied by an eloquent image, guiding the reader towards a certain interpretation by cognitively prepping our framing of the event. Remarkably, there is an interesting variation observable. Only one blog post starts with a photograph of the ECtHR, three posts open with images of embryonic cells, two blog posts lead in with images of foetuses, one post features a picture of a plump baby and a cell, and one blog post offers as a starting point a stylized "torn" picture of a baby in mother's hands. The dichotomy between the representation of embryos as more baby-like or more cell-like is further underlined by the choice of a title.

1   Embryos, mere pieces of property or are they more?
2   Woman's wish to donate unwanted embryos to scientific research rejected by Strasbourg Court.
3   Dignity of the human embryo from fecundation is recognised by the European Court of Human Rights.

For instance, in example (1) the question-like title was accompanied by the picture of a formed foetus, thus implicitly supplying the reader with an answer: embryos are unborn babies. In contrast, title (2) went together with an image of a cell and a needle, underlining the scientific framing of embryos as cells, not yet babies. In example (3) the blogger went even further by effectively misreporting (Bell 1991: 216) the ECtHR's findings, as the Court did not deal with the aspect of embryo dignity. Quite logically, the latter example was accompanied by an image of a formed foetus, misleading the reader into equalling an embryo to a more baby-like foetus.

In general, different embryo conceptualization served as a roadmap throughout the whole texts and can be recapped as follows.

Table 10.1 Conceptualisation of embryos across blogs

Conceptualisation	No. of blogs	Appraisal of Parrillo's claim
Embryo is an unborn baby with dignity and rights	5	Negative
Embryo is a potential human being, but decisions about it are in the primary control of the mother	3	Positive
Not mentioned	2	–

Half of the blogs "weaponised" the representation of embryos as unborn babies to trigger a negative appraisal of Parrillo's claim: no normal mother should wish to destroy her unborn babies and give them to research. Two posts did not frame embryos in any way, and three blog posts achieved a more complex conceptualization in line with the dissenting opinion by Judge Sajó. They agreed with the fact that an embryo is a potential human being, however, on account of the proportionality of rights represented Parrillo in a positive light as it was her right to take the deeply moral decision concerning donation of her surplus embryos to research.

Selective factualization

Most blogs presented to a lesser or greater degree the facts and circumstances of the case, which were not modified in *per se* and remained thus legitimate pieces of information. However, different posts selected and omitted different factual details, thus creating a discursive illusion and leading to a different perception of the event, and different appraisal of the actors.

Table 10.2 gathers four factual details originally present in the judgment and their use in blog posts. The judgment indicates simply Parrillo's year of birth (1954) and the place of residence (Rome) as well as the fact and date of IVF

Table 10.2 Selective factualisation in blogs as compared to the judgment

Judgment	Blog posts
Personal details (date of birth) + Fact and time of the IVF treatment	Not mentioning or explicitly mentioning her age (48y at the time of IVF)
Circumstances of her partner's death	1 – absent; 4 – "died"/"deceased"; 4 – tragic circumstances; 1 – "loss"
Desire to donate embryos to scientific research to promote advances in treatment for diseases that are difficult to cure	2 – absent; 3 – scientific research and cures (+); 5 – negative (mention just "destruction")
Unsuccessful requests to release her embryos before applying to Strasbourg	5 – omitting; 3 – reiterating her lack of control; 2 – absent facts at all.

treatment. However, this information is presented differently in blogs, which either do not mention it or, vice versa, do the math for the reader and calculate the exact age of the Applicant at the moment of IVF treatment (48 years), which can be interpreted as being unfavourable to Parrillo, playing on ageism bias.

As to the death of her partner, the judgment indicates that he died "in a bomb attack in Nasiriya (Iraq) while he was reporting on the war" (*Parrillo v. Italy*, no. 46470/11 §13; 2015 ECHR). At the same time, the blogs opt for a variety of ways to present this detail: four posts use simply the statement that Parrillo's partner "died" or was "deceased," four posts report also the tragic circumstances of his death using such words as "war," "Iraq," "bomb attack," one blog post does not overview the facts of the case and one post goes for an understatement "lost her husband."

Next, the judgment indicates the applicant's decision to donate embryos to scientific research "and thus contribute to promoting advances in treatment for diseases that are difficult to cure" (*Parrillo v. Italy*, no. 46470/11 §14; 2015 ECHR). Remarkably, only three posts mention this information and even extend on the issue of finding cures for incurable conditions. At the same time, two posts do not overview this fact and five blog posts use the word "destruction" instead of "donation," without mentioning any noble goals and representing the action as somewhat abominable.

Finally, the judgment, making reference to the Applicant's pleadings states that she made "a number of unsuccessful verbal requests for release of the embryos at the centre where they were being stored" (*Parrillo v. Italy*, no. 46470/ 11 §15; 2015 ECHR). This detail is omitted in five posts, stressing the applicant's straightforward application to Strasbourg, not covered in two posts and mentioned in three posts.

The handling of these facts resembles the art of origami, as these legitimate details – true and originating from the same sheet of paper – are skilfully folded in different ways to evoke a different image. The combinations focusing on age, omission or understatement of the partner's death and omission of her attempts to resolve the issue at the national level portrayed the applicant in a markedly negative light (see example (1)).

> (1) [A] woman who in 2002, *at the age of 48*, decided together with her husband to have children by means of medically assisted procreation. In 2003, *the applicant lost her husband* and *gave up the idea* of having one of the embryos implanted. Eight years later, in 2011, *dissatisfied* that Article 13 of the Italian Act 40/2004 (Act 40) *forbids the destruction of human embryos* (including through scientific research), the applicant *applied directly* to the ECtHR, *without exhaustion of national remedies*.[1]

Another pattern of negative portrayal revolves around the variant, where donation is not mentioned and where the reasons for the application are misreported. In example (2), for instance, the blogger mentions only the "juicy" aspect of property rights overlooking the applicant's claim for respect for private life.

(2) Adelina lost her dream of becoming a mother and *requested that the embryos be destroyed.* Right at the end of 2003, Italy approved a law prohibiting experimentation with embryos and their destruction. In 2011, Adelina *decided to sue the Italian state before the Strasbourg court for violating her property rights over the frozen embryos.*

On the other hand, blogs that concentrated on donation to research, her partner's tragic death and curing diseases, omitting potentially negative mentions of Parrillo's age, portrayed her in a positive light.

(3) The Grand Chamber of the Strasbourg Court has ruled that the Italian ban on the donation of embryos obtained by IVF procedures to scientific research was within Italy's margin of appreciation and therefore not in breach of the applicant's right of private life and autonomy, *even though she was willing to give the embryos to scientific research, since she no longer wanted to proceed with pregnancy after her partner was killed covering the war in Iraq.* By donating these cryopreserved embryos to research she would, she argued, *make an important contribution to research into medical therapies and cures.*

Selective use of quotes

In addition to selective factualization, blogs made recourse to carefully chosen quotes, both under the form of direct citations and indirect reported speech to achieve what Sinclair calls "attribution" (Sinclair 1986) or "projection" in Halliday's terms (1994: 250ff). The extensive use of quotes in popularized texts is widely documented elsewhere (see, e.g. Garzone 2014b: 96–97) and is generally a widespread journalistic device. In online writing using verbatim quotes of legal sources is very effective as it bestows authoritativeness and an appearance of credibility at a time when

> the vast quantity of and accessibility to information online has prompted concerns about credibility because the origin of information, its quality, and its veracity are less clear than ever before.
>
> (Metzger and Flanagin 2013: 210)

It also allows bloggers to use the existing materials verbatim, reducing the time necessary for writing a blog entry.

Most blogs chose not to quote the judgment but to rely on the legal summary/press release. Quoting from the legal summary and press-release is admittedly easier as these documents already present pre-packed and concise information, and these sources are reliable as they have been filtered by professional gatekeepers. Only one blog post with a clearly legal orientation used references to the judgment; however, it did not feature any full quotations.

Curiously enough, most quotes stemmed from the separate judicial opinions attached to the judgment, which were quoted extensively, representing the so-called arguments from authorities (van Eemeren and Grootendorst 1992: 136–137). Since the judgment was accompanied by six opinions, the choice was rather wide; yet only three opinions were cited repeatedly: the two concurring opinions by Judge Pinto de Albuquerque and Judge Dedov and the only truly dissenting opinion by Judge Sajó. The opinions represented two opposite tendencies. Judges who wrote the concurring opinions, in essence, would have preferred a more determined formulation of the judgment, whereas Judge Sajó argued the incorrectness of the majority ruling. The quotes were generally used in a consistent way throughout the blogs; however, they tended to depict only one side of the coin.

(4) Judge Sajo *correctly* pointed out, "The embryo would have the potential to develop into a human being, but this remains merely a potential as it cannot happen without the consent of the donor(s)"

(5) Judge Dedov *regretted that the Court did not go the whole way:* "In my view, the embryo's right to life is a key criterion [...]"

(6) He [Judge Sajó] *is completely taken aback* at his colleague's refusal to uphold the applicant's right under Article 8 to make autonomous decisions regarding her own and her partner's genetic material.

The peculiarity of using quotes concerned also the fringes of those quotes, where bloggers evaluated the statement (see (4)) or even attributed a certain reaction to the concurring or dissenting judges (see (5) and (6)). Apart from clear attributions, the very fact of choosing only those quotes that serve the blogger's intentions can be construed as potentially deluding because it is slanted towards one subjective point of view and does not present the alternate version of reality.

Fallacious and logically forced argumentation

Another manipulative pattern in the use of quotes concerns the alternation of legitimate quotes (or facts) and their immediate biased interpretation either for rebuttal or expansion, which could amount to a discursive manipulation as the quotes are cut and pasted almost in bad faith.

(7) It also stated that conceived embryos "contain the genetic material of the person in question and accordingly represent a constituent part of that person's genetic material and biological identity." *This is equivalent to saying that a human embryo is not fundamentally distinct from its parents and has no claim to personhood.*

The first adequacy condition for the argument from authority formulated by Woods and Walton (1989: 17) stated that "the authority must be interpreted correctly." In blog posts quoting the ECtHR judgment (as in (7)), this condition was violated, as the bloggers tried to force their own biased interpretation of the quote on the reader.

Such attempts at argumentation may be defined fallacious, not only on the grounds of logical unsoundness (the so-called logical *Standard Treatment* (Hamblin 1970)), but also in that they are

> in some way or other prejudicial or harmful to the realization of the general aim of resolving a difference of opinion on the merits.
>
> (van Emereen 2013: 148)

While the general approach to argumentative fallacies concerns their invalid character from the critical point of view (van Emereen 2013: 146), van Emereen (2013) argues for a more comprehensive pragma-dialectical approach to argumentative fallacies. He observes that sound and fallacious argumentative moves represent a continuum, and it is not always easy to distinguish between the two categories of strategic manoeuvring (van Emereen 2013: 148). It appears that when such questionable argumentative moves are placed in close proximity to the legitimate sources of information, such as quotes or facts, they are prone to creating discursive illusions and thus may mislead the potential reader, without contributing to the critical discussion.

There are also several attempts by bloggers to convince their audience and achieve a sort of social legitimation of their conceptualization of reality as "objective." They usually start with legitimising or presenting as "factual" a certain aspect (X), and then proceed with a logical chain of a kind: if X is true, then Y is true, and Z is a part of Y, so it is also true (see example (8), letters are added).

> (8) There certainly is *scientific consensus* that the human embryo is a human being that, having a unique and distinct genetic identity, cannot be considered a part of its mother. (X) But if it is a human being, there should be no room for doubt that it also is a bearer of human rights, (Y) including the most fundamental of all human rights, which is the right to life. (Z)

As the argument is presented as logically sound, and the other point of view as unacceptable, such a discursive move may also be considered to be manipulative and fallacious.

Evaluative language

From the production point of view, it is certainly challenging to distinguish between persuasion and manipulation techniques. Consequently, it seems relevant to look pragmatically at the receiver's reaction elicited as a result of such argumentation or manipulation. The cognitive evaluation of an attitude towards a situation can trigger either positive or negative reactions (White 2015: 2).

Table 10.3 Evaluation of different actors or actions

Evaluated action/actor	positive	negative	neutral	absent
Donation of embryos to research	3	5	–	2
The applicant	4	4	1	1
The Italian law	2	4	1	3
Court's ruling/operation	2	8	–	–
External agents	1	2	–	7

Table 10.3 shows the data concerning the evaluation of the main actors and actions involved in the case, obtained through the analysis of factualization (see Selective factualization, above) and the evaluative language used.

Positive and negative appraisals (Martin and White 2005; White 2015) of different actors are arranged in a number of patterns in different blogs, represented below with pluses and minuses respectively, with the number of blogs using the pattern indicated in brackets:

- Parrillo +, donation +, law –, Court –, Judicial opinion + (3)
- Parrillo –, donation –, law +, Court – (1)
- Parrillo –, donation –, law +, Court +, external agent – (1)
- Parrillo –, donation –, law –, Court –, external agent – (1)
- Parrillo –, donation –, Court +, external agent + (1)
- Parrillo –, donation –, Court – (2)
- Court – (1)

It emerges that in every pattern there is at least one actor that is negatively appraised. The blogs shift between positive and negative representations to attribute some blame, where possible, and probably to elicit anger in the potential readership by representing the blamed actor as a responsible party in control of the situation, as attributions of responsibility influence which emotions are elicited (Kühne 2014: 3). Some blogs just use the case to address national problems (see example (9) below), which are not directly linked to the case at hand. In these cases, it is the external agent – most frequently the State – who is an object of criticism.

(9) The seriousness and firmness of the protection of the embryo in these European court judicial decisions contrasts with *the treatment given to the embryo in Spain*, both legislatively and judicially by some sectors of our highest authorities.

[Blogs]

Apart from some deviations to address connected issues on the national level, the blogs follow a recurrent pattern of negative representation of the Court, activated in 80% of texts. The critique ranges from overviewing inconsistencies and deficiencies in the ECtHR legal reasoning and ruling to explicit attacks on the Court as such, by extension.

One blog post is particularly rich in strong negative lexis referred to the Court, such as "long-standing failure," "absurd," "moronic," "unreliable," "travesty," "using pretexts" and "backdoors," "wretched," "should be dissolved," "inflicts further damage on the human rights idea." While it could be unpleasant, the intensity of evaluative lexis reduces possibilities that the post be perceived as objective; consequently, reducing its illusional potential.

Apart from the above post, other blog entries use negative vocabulary less expressly and less frequently, which makes it possible to masquerade eventual appraisals among other elements of the post. In those blogs the Court is portrayed as unpredictable and lacking legal certainty through the use of such seemingly neutral adjectives as "surprising" and "alarming" and similar expressions belonging to the same semantic field of absence of stability. The judgment and the legal reasoning behind it are described as incomplete ("avoiding," "missed opportunity," "not all the way," "lacking proportionality test," "did not go the whole way"). In general, the Court is portrayed as incoherent ("unclear," "incoherencies," "inconsistencies") and somewhat abnormal ("strange," "bizarre") as well as insecure, taking "relativistic standpoint," being "afraid" and proceeding "warily."

All the evaluations are masked by the close proximity to real facts and actions of the ECtHR. As a result, the court is skilfully represented in control but doing little, which, according to appraisal theories, could lead to eliciting anger. Consequently, such negative – bordering on manipulative – representations of the Court in the blogs are potentially damaging the reception of its judgments, disrupting trust towards the ECtHR within the lay and legal community, which is already facing challenges in some countries. In this regard, it is laudable that the Court undertakes its own efforts at knowledge dissemination by preparing neutral reviews (press release and legal summary) with a popularising function, which could contrast discursive illusions permeating the press.

Conclusions

Dissemination of specialized knowledge is an arduous task as it involves working with varying levels of expertise and other textual and discursive constraints. Bloggers and human rights observers undoubtedly make bioethical and legal knowledge more accessible and palatable to vast audiences; however, blog entries need to be read with caution. This study has focused on the distinction between the legitimate use of information as a dissemination process and its distortion through careful selection of convenient facts or authoritative sources, omissions and evaluations. These together trigger specific emotions by activating selective appraisal patterns and, consequently, manipulating information processing and opinion formation.

In particular, the distortions – or points of view? – are present at different levels, starting from paratextual elements that lead towards a certain interpretation, involving different object definition and problematization, to different responsibility attribution through a combination of facts, discursive illusions, biased interpretations and evaluations. The challenge of reading behind the ideological lines lies in the close proximity between the manipulated elements and the legitimate elements. Skilful folding of reality, interspersed with strategic evaluative language, makes the manipulation hard to trace in most cases and creates an illusion of truthful representation. Consequently, blogs are to be positioned primarily as subjective texts, even though they claim to report and overview the judgment. The issue of combination between facts and illusions invites further research on a larger corpus.

Acknowledgement

This study contributes to the national research programme "Knowledge dissemination across media in English: Continuity and change in discourse strategies, ideologies, and epistemologies", financed by the Italian Ministry of Education, University and Research for 2017–2019 (nr. 2015TJ8ZAS).

Note

1 Emphasis is added in all examples.

References

Bell, Allan. 1991. *The Language of News Media*. Oxford: Polity.

Bhatia, Aditi. 2015. *Discursive Illusions in Public Discourse: Theory and Practice.* London – New York: Routledge.

Calsamiglia, Helena and van Dijk, Teun. 2004. Popularization discourse and knowledge about genome, *Discourse and Society*, 15(4): 369–389.

Caron, Paul L. 2006. Are scholars better bloggers? Bloggership: How blogs are transforming legal scholarship, *Washington University Law Review* 84(5): 1025–1042.

Cornett, Judy. 2009. The ethics of blawging: A genre analysis, *Loyola University Chicago Law Journal 41*: 221–262.

Fairclough, Norman. 1995. *Critical Discourse Analysis: The Critical Study of Language*. London: Longman.

Garzone, Giuliana. 2014a. Investigating blawgs through corpus linguistics: Issues of generic integrity. In Gotti, Maurizio and Giannoni, Davide S. (eds), *Corpus Analysis for Descriptive and Pedagogical Purposes: ESP Perspectives*. Bern: Peter Lang (167–188).

Garzone, Giuliana. 2014b. News production and scientific knowledge: Exploring popularization as a process. In Bongo, Giancarmine and Caliendo, Giuditta (eds), *The Language of Popularization: Die Sprache der Popularisierung*. Bern: Peter Lang (73–107).

Garzone, Giuliana. 2015. The legal blog (blawg): Generic integrity and variation. In Bhatia, Vijay K., Chiavetta, Eleonora and Sciarrino, Silvana (eds), *Variations in Specialized Genres. Standardization and Popularization*. Tübingen: Narr Francke Attempto Verlag (37–62).

Genette, Gerard. 2001 [1997]. *Paratexts. Thresholds of Interpretation*. English trans. Jane E. Levin. Cambridge: Cambridge University Press.

Halliday, Michael A. K. 1994. *An Introduction to Functional Grammar*, 2nd edition. London: Edward Arnold (1985).

Hamblin, Charles L. 1970. *Fallacies*. London: Methuen.

Kühne, Rinaldo. 2014. Political news, emotions, and opinion formation: Toward a model of emotional framing effects, Working Paper No. 68: Challenges to Democracy in the 21st Century, National Centre of Competence in Research (NCCR).

Maillat, Didier. 2013. Constraining context selection: On the pragmatic inevitability of manipulation, *Journal of Pragmatics 59*: 190–199.

Martin, James and White, Peter. 2005. *The Language of Evaluation: Appraisal in English*. Hampshire and New York: Palgrave MacMillan.

Mattila, Heikki. 2006. *Comparative Legal Linguistics*. Aldershot, Hampshire and Burlington VT: Ashgate Publishing.

Mauranen, Anna. 2013. Hybridism, edutainment, and doubt: Science blogging finding its feet. *Nordic Journal of English Studies 13*(1): 7–36.

Metzger, Miriam J. and Flanagin, Andrew. 2013. Credibility and trust of information in online environments: The use of cognitive heuristics, *Journal of Pragmatics 59*: 210–220.

Myers, Greg. 2010a. *The Discourse of Blogs and Wikis*. London: Continuum.

Myers, Greg. 2010b. Stance-taking and public discussion in blogs. *Critical Discourse Studies 7*(4): 263–275.

Parrillo v. Italy, no. 46470/11; 2015 ECHR GC Judgment.

Pohl, Rudiger (ed.) 2005. *Cognitive Illusions: A Handbook on Fallacies and Biases in Thinking, Judgement and Memory*. New York: Psychology Press.

Romig, Jennifer M. 2015. Legal blogging and the rhetorical genre of public legal writing, *Legal Communication and Rhetoric, 12*: 29–81.

Sinclair, John. 1986. Fictional worlds. In Coulthard, Malcolm (ed.) *Talking about Text: Studies Presented to David Brazil on his Retirement. Discourse Analysis Monographs No. 13*. University of Birmingham: English Language Research (43–60).

Tessuto, Girolamo. 2015. Posted by…: Scholarly legal blogs as part of academic discourse and site for stance and engagement, *Textus (2)*: 85–108.

Tiersma, Peter M. 1999. *Legal English*. Chicago and London: Chicago University Press.

van Dijk, Teun. 2001. Multidisciplinary CDA: A plea for diversity. In Wodak, Ruth and Meyer, Michael (eds) *Methods of Critical Discourse Analysis*. London: Sage (95–120).

van Dijk, Teun. 2006. Discourse and manipulation, *Discourse and Society 17*(3): 359–383.

van Emereen, Frans H. 2013. Fallacies as derailments of argumentative discourse: Acceptance based on understanding and critical assessment, *Journal of Pragmatics 59*: 141–152.

van Eemeren, Frans H. and Grootendorst, Rob. 1992. *Argumentation, Communication, and Fallacies: A Pragma-Dialectical Perspective*. Hillsdale: Lawrence Erlbaum.

White, Peter. 2015. Appraisal Theory. In Tracy, Karen, Ilie, Cornelia and Sandel, Todd (eds) *The International Encyclopedia of Language and Social Interaction*, 1st edition. Boston: John Wiley and Sons, Inc.

White, Robin. 2009. Judgments in the Strasbourg Court: Some reflections, July 2009, *SSRN Electronic Journal*. DOI:10.2139/ssrn.1435197.

Woods, John and Walton, Douglas N. 1989. *Fallacies: Selected Papers 1972–1982*. Berlin: De Gruyter.

11 Jag 2.0

Legal advice and dissemination in online military lawyer forums

Roxanne Doerr

Introduction: the influence of military culture and law on online legal discourse

This chapter focuses on a particularly specialized area of legal practice, i.e. American military law, and the manner in which its principles and mechanisms may be conveyed in an online context such as that of Q&A sections. The American armed forces represent the institutionalization of military culture, which encompasses the "military-as-context" and the "military-as-discourse" (Parcell 2015: 8–9). The military, as opposed to other professions, has its own lifestyle and differs from American civilian culture in that it "values collectivism, hierarchy, structure, authority and control to deal with the uncertainty of war" (Maguire 2015: 20):

> Along the way, these forces grew apart from the rest of society: marks of this separation came to include living together in encampments, wearing identifiable uniforms, gaining a monopoly on certain types of weaponry, developing a private vocabulary, and above all, viewing themselves as an identifiable group in some sense distinct from the rest of society. Because success in military operations of any kind requires resources, order, and organization as well as the subordination of individual preferences to a larger set of common objectives, rules of conduct unique to the armed forces were inevitable and there remains a place for them.
>
> (Fidell 2016: 1)

Accordingly, military justice "aims to maintain order and discipline within its boundaries, including adherence to a host of requirements and prohibitions that have no counterpart in civilian society" (Fidell 2016: 2) and connects professional and personal conduct and ethics such as "disobedience, disrespect, or unauthorized absence" (Fidell 2016: 3) with legal provisions and practices.

Military communication is a specialized professional discourse in its own right and seeks to avoid ambiguity and complex sentence structures while incorporating very specific technical language and terminology through abbreviations, references and rules that are based on shared and exclusive knowledge. This is done for opposing reasons, i.e. to communicate accurately within the community and to secure sensitive information from outsiders. Understanding these cultural differences fosters a better understanding of military law, which is decidedly understudied from a linguistic perspective. This legal jargon in fact is simplified compared to other fields, both because of the typical directness of military communication (Parcell and Webb 2015) and the recent dating of some of its fundamental legislative texts.

The increased presence of web-based technologies and social media has affected professional legal discourse and practice and contributed to the rise and popularity of computer-mediated legal counseling and assistance:

> there are now online services that give state-specific explanations of law, prepare various legal documents, and even offer computer-mediated dispute resolution. In addition, lawyers and law firms are using web pages to solicit class-action plaintiffs, to participate in real-time chat forums, and to bid for legal engagements.
>
> (Backer 2002: 2409)

This benefits both experts and non-experts, in that "the most frequent and important of the many functions of the Internet are information seeking and interpersonal communication" (Turnbull 2013: 6). In fact, they guide non-specialized users through complicated legal matters and lighten the load on traditional institutions by providing brief service and advice (Zorza 1999) on whether or not one should pursue face-to-face legal procedures and how to do so.

The fact that "digital technologies shape collaboration, monitoring, and evaluation and the communication of results, both within the scientific community and to wider audiences" (Wyatt, Scharnhorst et al. 2013: 8) has impacted the degree of empowerment of information seekers. There is an increasing gap in affordances and use between "non interactive" (e.g. FAQs) and "interactive" online legal advice (e.g. Q&As) (Backer 2002: 2412; Suler 2004). The former is only occasionally updated and therefore more asymmetrical in terms of power, since this kind of section presents questions and information that are determined by the administrators (and not necessarily the experts or the users) and provide direct, standardized answers. Non-interactive advice is more focused on the facts themselves, conveyed in a neutral and objective register, and represents an initial guide for non-experts who do not know how to proceed. Interactive advice, on the contrary, implicates a dialogical exchange between experts and non-experts and therefore a negotiation of information and power. Among the main purposes of legal Q&A websites, the literature has hitherto underlined providing tailored legal advice, filtering highly specialized legal knowledge (Gotti 2005; Turnbull 2013) and answering preliminary questions that do not require the presence of a lawyer (Zorza 1999).

Q&As are theoretically asynchronous, in that there may be a temporal gap between the question and the related answer. However, there is an increasing tendency for this gap to be shortened due to the increased speed of online communication, especially in forums such as these whose source of pride is often based on the fact that answers arrive very quickly, usually within minutes, thus demonstrating that "a new site [of knowledge production] draws on existing practices while also calling forth expectations that something new will come out of its deployment" (Beaulieu, De Rijcke and Van Heur 2013: 26).

Such a fast pace entails short, spontaneous messages or the lawyer occasionally having to respond simply to keep the client "on hold" (Myers 2010) while reviewing the case and carefully phrasing the response. Interactive mechanisms not only foster spontaneous and direct communication between the expert and non-expert but they also balance the precision and specificity of military legal discourse with popularizing linguistic accommodation to reduce potential misunderstanding and allow the non-expert to achieve specific legal goals or find further assistance.

Aims and scope

This chapter explores the discursive and linguistic tactics, and consequently the different degree of interaction and empowerment, in two specialized websites, *Just Answer. Military Law*[1] and *Justia Ask a Lawyer*,[2] that employ Q&A formats. It adopts a multidimentional and multiperspective methodological framework based on a Corpus Assisted Discourse Studies approach while underlining ongoing changes in legal discourse due to online and military discourse. The study's dataset and methodology are presented in §3. Afterwards, the analysis considers three different but interrelated occasions of knowledge dissemination and exchange, i.e. popularization, empowerment and mitigation, by addressing the following research questions:

> **RQ1.** Which popularization strategies of legal knowledge and terminology are most implemented in online Q&As concerning military law?

> **RQ2.** How can trust in the professional and the client's empowerment be encouraged in online military law Q&As?

> **RQ3.** How can the lawyer protect him or herself against possible liability issues?

The relevance of the present study consists in its observation of the interaction between military law and the idiosyncrasies of virtual knowledge sharing. Such idiosyncratic exchanges are "developed and sustained by both 'expert' and 'non-expert' knowledge creators" and could potentially contribute to the elaboration and improvement of theories "of (infra-structure) and practice and the way they interact" (Wyatt, Scharnhorst et al. 2013: 2). This, in turn, could hint at new insights on online legal knowledge dissemination.

Dataset and methodology

The dataset consists in 50 Q&A complete exchanges between lawyers and non-experts starting from April 30, 2018 posted in a separate section on American military law of two active websites on legal advice. The dataset was divided into two corpora, one for each website, *Just Answer* and *Justia*, which were further divided into "Questions" and "Answers" corpora by eliminating multimodal material, names, repeated boilerplates and contact information.

Just Answer – 21 lawyers (8 active) www.justanswer.com/military-law/
Words: 30366 words
Questions (client and robot): 4501 tokens; 1156 types
Answers (robot): 1265 tokens; 122 types
Questions (client and lawyer): 4929 tokens; 1123 types
Answers (lawyer): 12355 tokens; 1632 types
Justia – 19 lawyers (30 active) https://answers.justia.com/questions/answered/military-law?page=2
Words: 9659Questions: 3933 tokens; 1020 typesAnswers: 3146 tokens; 942 types

The frequency of posting significantly differs: the *Just Answer* website covered 50 interactions between April 24 and April 30, 2018, while the *Justia* website answered the same amount between September 9, 2017 and April 30, 2018. In order to focus on the complete information-seeking and giving processes, exchanges in which the lawyer or client interrupted the "conversation" were excluded.

In the *Just Answer* Q&A, there was a further initial interaction between the information seeker and the "lawyer"s assistant" which was a robot, whose "Questions" and "Answers" were separated in order to focus on the client's interaction with what he or she perceived as two different subjects.

The study adopts a multidimensional methodological framework in view of the fact that discourse and genre analysis are proceeding "in the direction of a more comprehensive and powerful multidimensional and multi-perspective framework to handle not only the text but also the context in a more meaningful manner than had ever been done earlier," thus including "non-traditional semiotic modes, including the visual and the internet" as well as "'mixed, 'embedded' or 'hybrid' genres" (Bhatia and Gotti 2006: 9–10). This is well suited to military law, which combines indispensable features of legal language with the directness and lexicon of military communication. In addition, written text and specialized legal English coexist with interactive expressions and pragmatic markers that are typical of self-presentation and trust building in spoken contexts.

Corpus Assisted Discourse Studies, or CADS (Partington 2004; Garzone and Santulli 2004; Degano 2007; Evangelisti Allori 2011) has led to insightful qualitative and quantitative analyses of specialized professional discourse (Evangelisti Allori 2011). Corpus analysis, and more precisely the AntConc 3.5.6. (Anthony 2018) software, was applied to find relevant occurrences and collocations and extract empirically verifiable data (Garzone and Santulli 2004). Critical Discourse Analysis (Fairclough 1995; Chouliaraki and Fairclough 1999; van Dijk 2003), representing the qualitative part of the CADS approach and characterized by "an explanatory, holistic approach" (Garzone and Santulli 2004: 352), highlights the balance of power between non-expert and expert, as well as the empowerment or disempowerment of the latter through the construction and negotiation of professional identity and interaction. Pragmatics here is focused on conversational strategies based on (un)certainty and hedging (Marmor 2008; Gibbs and Van Orden 2012; Boncea 2013) that may be employed to foster trust or reduce the lawyer's liability for his or her advice.

Popularization and adjustment of legal language

Legal language draws on a very long tradition and complex linguistic structures that must be mastered by professionals but tend to exclude non-experts. Lawyers therefore become mediators and "translate" institutional discourse and abstract concepts to enable clients to make conscious and informed decisions, for information becomes knowledge only when it is transferred into a conceptual framework and applied "purposefully and proactively" in a real context (Turnbull 2013).

The online popularization strategies (Calsamiglia and van Dijk 2004 in Garzone 2006) that emerge in the two Q&As most clearly are "illustration" and "reformulation." The former (Turnbull 2013: 21) resort to discursive concretization by means of exemplification, scenarios and metaphorical language (e.g. analogies, metaphors and comparisons) (Turnbull 2013: 22). Scenarios (Gülich 2003) are useful in clarifying the client's current and hypothetical situations; from a linguistic perspective, they are conveyed through conditional clauses (especially first and second conditional forms) as in Example 1. General statements in the present tense as in Example 2, make secure predictions based on protocol and a range of possibilities along which the client's case could be located.

(1) Yes, you can get kicked out for admitting drug use. If you were doing so to seek help, as part of a rehab situation, then you can't get a punitive discharge, but you still can be separated from the service.

If you admit to lots of other behavior, it will likely only make matters worse. Nothing about "coming clean" makes it unusable against you. (*Just Answer*)

(2) Some bases will handle DUIs of service members thru the chain of command (UCMJ or administrative punishment). Some Air bases have concurrent jurisdiction with the state and those could be handled thru the state – but those are the rarer instances. (*Justia*)

When well known to the general public, metaphors (Hibbitts 1994; Turnbull 2013) endow something unfamiliar with an immediate image. They are more common in the *Justia* Q&A, where there is only one turn of conversation and briefer explanations. This gives the interaction a more informal and conversational tone, thus making the popularization intent and process less obvious:

(3) Getting out of the military soon and concerned about me being in limbo when finding income to continue CS for my son. (*Justia*)

(4) [T]he commander (with the advice of his legal advisor/Judge Advocate) can use the other tools in his tool box for punishment and correction. (*Justia*)

(5) Again, both of these being well in the past is positive … but you have a bit more of a hurdle with two, separate issues. (*Just Answer*)

The most common instances of reformulation (Turnbull 2013: 23) take on the form of a referential expression, followed by a treatment expression with semantic equivalence such as a repetition, paraphrasing or correction to create a direct association, as in Example 6. Reformulation also reaffirms the expert's authority and competence and protects against ambiguity to the extent of redundancy, often found in legal language (Tiersma 1999), as is evident in Example 7:

(6) The military is a "command driven system," in that the commander (with the advice of his legal advisor/Judge Advocate) can use the other tools in his tool box for punishment and correction (non-judicial punishment, counseling, letter of reprimand, administrative separation, etc.). (*Justia*)

(7) After speaking with your attorney in person, it may be that the attorney recommends cooperation. That attorney can accomplish that, by speaking for you without his/her words becoming evidence. That is the purpose of an attorney. When you speak, every word is evidence. (*Just Answer*)

Efficient popularization of legal language may also be accomplished by simplifying complex legal language through the elimination of typical alienating

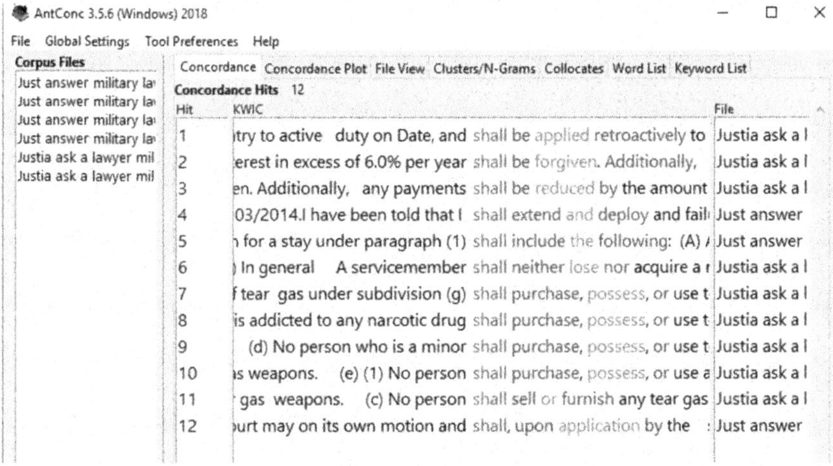

Figure 11.1 Concordances of "shall" (Antconc 3.5.6).

elements such as complex syntactic structure through the previously mentioned strategies. Other, more subtle, omissions are those of "here-" and "there-" words, as well as pronominal constructions like "same" and "aforesaid" (Tiersma 1999; Garzone and Salvi 2007), presumably because they are common neither in everyday conversation nor in military or online language. Modal verbs are always used in their everyday sense and specific legal homonyms are absent so as not to create any misunderstandings (Tiersma 1999; Garzone and Salvi 2007). Moreover, there is no use of performative do or shall as an "enforceable legal obligation" (Tiersma 1999: 207) if not to report laws and their sources, as may be seen in figure 11.1.

Interestingly, one aspect of legal English that is maintained is spelling, which remains that of legal experts except in the third case in which the word "judgement" is written, significantly by the client, according to general spelling rules:

> (8) Lawyer: I am sorry for your loss and your current situation. I would recommend paying the judgment before the sale date. If you don't have the funds, you will need to borrow the money to pay it or risk losing your home. As for the payments not reflected in the judgment amount, I would contact the attorney handling the lawsuit and request a payment history to be sure it matches your records. (*Justia*)

> (9) Lawyer: In Oregon, you can ask for temporary alimony as soon as the divorce action is filed and until you receive your final judgment. (*Just Answer*)

> (10) Client: I am pro se appellee. My ex-husband is appealing the judgement against him to pay what was suppose to be military retirement, but the ex opted for disability pay. Divorce Decree did not allow him to change or stop payment when he was eligible to receive retirement. (*Justia*)

Finally, the frequent switch from colloquial to technical language, as well as the *Justia* pages' hyperlinks to pages explaining specific terms, enable the non-expert to understand and later find and use a new term within professional discourse and context (Gülich 2003) without interrupting the flow of the expert's advice.

Multimodal and linguistic trust building and client empowerment

In interactive online contexts like Q&As, the positioning of the expert and his or her services may be highlighted through evolving affordances that engender trust and confidence in the expert. Significantly, many of these only concern the *Just Answer* website, leading to the conclusion that a difference in affordances can impact the extent and force of online legal knowledge dissemination and empowerment.

The lawyers and "lawyer"s assistant"

The two websites aim at drawing the attention, camaraderie and loyalty of the information-seeker "in a friendly, encouraging manner" (Turnbull 2013: 24). Both websites' lawyer profiles are accompanied by a profile picture, which is generally more "neutral" in *Justia*, while they clearly refer to the military profession in *Just Answer*, where the lawyers "dress the part." *Just Answer* also indicates each lawyer"s years of experience, current or past rank and armed force, or family member in the military if present. *Justia*, on the other hand, divides its experts and cases based on the state in which they are located and leaves space elsewhere for their presentations (e.g. first person, third person, instructions). Accordingly, the *Just Answer* lawyers go more into detail with their answers but the experts of *Justia* often answer questions tagged as "military law" in connection with other legal fields (divorce law, criminal law) and limit themselves (and their client"s empowerment) to recommending where and how to find more fitting assistance.

Another important means of setting the stage in the *Just Answer* website occurs before interacting with a lawyer: the information-seeker is approached by a "lawyer"s assistant" (by means of a pop-up chat box containing a name, picture and brief bio), a robot "who" asks preliminary questions (Hyland 2010) as if she were a secretary in a legal practice, recalling the high power distance that is typical of a military chain of command. This combination of visual presentation and direct chat interaction conveys the impression that "she" is a real person, as many clients seem to assume by the way they treat "her" (thanking, requesting information), except in one case in which someone openly asks if "she" is a bot.

The "assistant" filters information based on: place (and jurisdiction), accompanied by an explanation to reassure the user ("Family/education law varies by state. What state are you in?" or "Are you overseas or stateside?"); involvement of the chain of command, which is significant as the military is "command-centered" (Fidell 2016); past or ongoing legal procedures ("What steps have you taken?"; "Have you filed any papers in family court?"); additional comments (Anything else you want the lawyer to know before I connect you?), an open section that is answered with a conclusive "That is all" answer, a brief explanation of the client's expectations, extra details, or the expression of the hope that someone will help. Interestingly, the robot's questions take on the same format as a direct legal examination (Tiersma 1999: 159–161), i.e. wh- questions, yes/no questions or disjunctive questions that provide limited options ("A or B?"). However, while the client is strategically asked to narrate his or her case at the beginning in court and then asked precise questions to limit oneself to relevant, precise and useful information (Tiersma 1999), the "open" part is positioned at the end in the Q&As, thus giving the client more of a say after being prepared by the previous questions.

A final significant means of assisting the client in the *Just Answer* Q&A consists in the possibility of integrating the online consultation with a phone session in delicate or complicated cases. While this hints at the insufficiency of the current Q&A format, it also gives the consultation activity more solidity and strengthens the bond between expert and non-expert.

Demonstrating professional and discourse community knowledge and competence

Being a tight-knit and communitarian professional community, American military service members prefer their own to help them:

> Soldiers instinctively trust their fellow servicemembers [sic] in ways that they do not trust civilians, however well-intended, primarily because soldiers know that their comrades-in-arms understand their unique problems and will not lead them astray.
>
> (Dunlap 2003: 488; see also Schmitt 2008)

This may be confirmed by the greater balance of power between military information seekers and military lawyers compared to that between a civilian non-expert (e.g. family member, friends) and the expert. For instance, these lawyers prove their knowledge of military language and closeness to the client through military slang, as in the example below with the mirroring of the term "gunny":

> (11) Client: My gunny took my "POV" (motorcycle) and had it sitting out for months and through the weather [...]
>
> Lawyer: You can file a claim under the UCMJ or under federal law. Go see the base legal assistance/claims office. You can also file an 1150 complaint against the gunny. (*Justia*)

Moreover, those with experience in military law point out when they can legitimately provide "insider information" about common practices that are followed by other subjects or institutions (Beaulieu, De Rijcke and Van Heur 2013) that are not known to civilians. This takes on the conversational tone of a confidential exchange that deviates from the theory and textbooks that are known to non-experts and civilians. Such advice is endowed with an exclusive quality and based on personal experience or empathy in some cases, to the point of challenging what authorities have previously told the client:

> (12) Client: NCIS told me that if I tell the truth my career would not be in danger but I do not know how much of that is the truth. I also talked to a former agent and they said to go clean and they shouldn't be so harsh. I took a urine test and then if it comes back negative I heard that they would just take away my clearance.
>
> Military Lawyer: That is what NCIS is trained to tell you, because it makes people feel like they can talk. Then they talk and implicate themselves and give up evidence against themselves for free.

Invoke your right to silence if spoken to again, only cooperate through an attorney. That's the best advice I can give you at this point. (*Just Answer*)

(13) This a complex issue - I have fought it before. You can apply to the Board of Corrections alleging that you should have been, based on your condition, referred to the PEB, and ask them to refer you to the PEB. (*Justia*)

The union of professional lexis, previous testing of alternative "insider" approaches, and professional investment thus create a bond between client and lawyer that resembles the communitarian "brotherhood" value that is dear to the military culture and community.

Hedging and liability reduction

Legal practice itself has had to come to terms with the temporal and spatial fluidity of online communication. As far as the latter is concerned "The extra-territorial nature of the Internet is at odds with the way the legal profession is regulated in the United States" (Backer 2002: 2410). However, online legal advice, with its extra-territorial nature (Beal 2000; Backer 2002) and "place-lessness" (Myers 2010: 9), may actually be particularly helpful in military law, since "military justice also serves to extend national law to personnel serving outside the country and beyond the jurisdiction of civilian courts" (Fidell 2016: 2).

In fact, members of the military community are geographically dislocated and stationed at different military bases for extended periods of time (Parcell and Webb 2015) and are therefore subjected to various jurisdictions (e.g., State laws, Status Of Forces Agreements), legal statuses based on the role of the individual (active duty, civilian, veteran, dependent family member) and the location/context in which the legal dispute takes place (e.g. on or off a military base, during or before/after deployment). Members of the military community may not be aware of their rights and duties in relation to their current time and place because their constant and often unpredictable relocation may confuse them as to who and where to go for legal assistance. Online communities are therefore extremely useful for finding information and advice, as well as solidarity, from people who are or have been in similar circumstances (Maguire 2015).

Professional information provided over the internet has hitherto been considered mere reference but the tendency to make communication between legal experts and clients more direct fuels the unsolved matter on whether providing online advice could constitute an attorney-client relationship (Backer 2002; Lanctot 2002) even though these experts have limited information and power of intervention. Online experts must protect themselves against possible backlashes and negative reviews and their professional liability is enhanced by the fact that the lawyers almost always present their personal and professional details.

From a linguistic standpoint, the issue of defining time and place may be at least partially addressed by indexicality and time/place deixis (Hanks 1999;

Myers 2010), which allow the military lawyer to answer with more precision. Location is directly inquired by the previously mentioned "lawyer"s assistant" in *Just Answer* (Backer 2002: 2413) while questions and answers are preliminarily divided by state (including Puerto Rico) in *Justia*. Moreover, the client is also identified by his or her city and state:

(14) Atlanta, GA asked 2 weeks ago in Family Law and Military Law for Tennessee. (*Justia*)

(15) Client: My girlfriend lives on Fort Knox as a civilian I have passed infractions that were dropped to misdemeanors I have no felonies on my record but Fort Knox is saying that one of them has not been dispositioned in the computers and will not allow me on the army base to visit my girlfriend's home what do I do. (*Justia*)

(16) Client: I know i have to go to court. But am i at risk of getting separated? I'm currently in limbo because I'm on PCS leave so do i tell my unit? (*Just Answer*)

Time deixis and time stamps are also of the utmost importance both for legal purposes and to underline how quickly the online experts answer their questions. While this is only indicated as dates in the case of *Justia*, the *Just Answer* posts specify the amount of time it took for the expert to answer the question in minutes and hours.

More protection for the lawyer is particularly necessary in the field of military law since military justice is very "commander-centric" (Fidell 2016: 9) and often based upon the rules that are in force in the client's military base. Since the degree of certainty of the legal outcome is reduced, illustrating future steps and their consequences resembles the linguistic patterns of financial forecasting that Polly Walsh has observed in economic assessments, where the forecaster is aware of the impossibility of knowing the final result with absolute certainty but nevertheless is anxious not to lose credibility (Walsh 2006). Pragmatics therefore comes into play in relation to certainty and responsibility because "synchronically and ideologically [...] prediction is not always 'innocent'" (Partington 2004: 18).

Boilerplate disclaimers are used to avoid any potential conflict but their validity is contestable since these lawyers provide information on specific cases and not just general information. The only bases for this not being considered legally liable at the moment are the limited means and extent of contact:

(17) The above information is for educational purposes only; if one seeks legal advice please contact the local bar association for a referral to a licensed attorney in your area that is able to review your case in a private, confidential setting and will be able to tailor advise [sic] specific to your situation. (*Just Answer*)

(18) Justia Ask a Lawyer is a forum for consumers to get answers to basic legal questions. Any information sent through Justia Ask a Lawyer is not secure and is done so on a non-confidential basis only:

> The use of this website to ask questions or receive answers <u>does not create an attorney–client relationship</u> between you and Justia, or between you and any attorney who receives your information or responds to your questions, nor is it intended to create such a relationship. Additionally, <u>no responses on this forum constitute legal advice</u>, which must be tailored to the specific circumstances of each case. <u>You should not act upon information provided in Justia Ask a Lawyer without seeking professional counsel</u> from an attorney admitted or authorized to practice in your jurisdiction. Justia <u>assumes no responsibility to any person</u> who relies on information contained on or received through this site and disclaims all liability in respect to such information… (*Justia* at the end of every page)

Hedging is used to mitigate the message and make it polite for trust building and the deflection of aggressiveness or responsibility (through epistemic or evasive hedging) by marking that the information is not completely infallible or reliable so one will have to be careful not to count on it too much. This is common when conversing to not commit excessively in informal contexts, especially those reproposing conversational speech in limited amounts of time like these online Q&As (Markman 2012). Another explicit form of hedging consists in open references to the lawyer's limitations as a mere representative of his or her field:

> (19) Lawyer: This is the part of my job I don't like … when the law is not in favor of my customer. I wish I could tell you that you can still appeal, but I can only provide you information based on the law so that you can act on the best available information to you … I wish I had better news, but can only hope you recognize and understand my predicament and <u>don't shoot the messenger</u>. I'm sorry! (*Just Answer*)

> (20) Lawyer: Please rate me <u>based on my service and not on your satisfaction with the law, which I am not in control of and I am just reporting to you.</u> (*Just Answer*)

In the following example, many hedging expressions are present ("normally," "if," "really," "simply") to limit the force of the answer and redirect the advice, i.e. that the client should refer to her base as the main legal jurisprudence. "Then" indicates an additional factor to take into consideration and the mentioned "services" are limited by the restricting passive "are offered" and the specification "Often they simply provide sample documents" in order to give the client an idea of what to expect in this case, which is not much:

(21) Lawyer: <u>Normally</u> JAG will only assist <u>if a party is in the military.</u> <u>Then</u> the services depend on the particular base where one is stationed (as to what services are offered).

Client: Well I am in the reserves but he is not.

Military Lawyer: <u>It really depends</u> on what base one is associated with. <u>Often</u> <u>they simply provide sample documents.</u> (*Just Answer*)

Other fundamental strategies with the same intent include specifying circumscribed conditions for the realization of the predictions and employing distancing devices such as attribution, agentless passives and if clauses. Such circumstances may regard the status of the client or other involved subjects, as well as the location of the client and the event itself. An example of this may be found below, where the lawyer restricts the validity of the advice to the client's legal place of residence by means of an if-clause:

(22) Lawyer: You could <u>if you are a lawful permanent resident of the United</u> <u>States.</u> (*Justia*)

(23) Lawyer: <u>if paternity has not been established</u> then the mother is the sole legal custodian. (*Just Answer*)

Various studies in legal language have pointed out the presence and role of vagueness (Tiersma 1999; Anesa 2014) and this is found in online Q&As in various instances. It may characterize clients' language because they do not have the expertise to precisely define what is happening:

(24) Client: I called <u>a bunch of</u> places and they said I was only to get a $1000 death benefit. (*Just Answer*)

(25) Client: I have <u>something going on</u> with ncis. (*Just Answer*)

(26) Client: I don't exactly have plans going back home, but I also want to start <u>some form of custody</u> (not sole, but still an option after certain events) so I can finally be a part of my son's growth and life to the fullest. (*Justia*)

Obtaining information enables information seekers to become acquainted with the processes that are currently influencing their life. In other cases, vague language is used by the expert as a technical term that cannot be avoided or referred to in another way. A telling example of this is "reasonable" (Anesa 2014):

(27) Lawyer: To contact the phone company, they [the authorities] would just need a magistrate ordered subpoena based on the <u>reasonable belief</u> that it would give relevant evidence.

The point here is that while there are some legal hurdles they have to jump through, they aren't difficult and none of them relies on any action from you. (*Just Answer*)

The following example is even more interesting in this sense. The legalese of the first sentence's attempt to explain "sufficient proof" is mitigated by a repetition and definition, and the vagueness of the concept is underlined to anticipate the client's doubts. This is followed by a series of potentially confusing explanations and reformulations because the lawyer keeps running into legally vague and contingent terms like "sufficient," "probable," "reasonable," and "evidence":

(28) Proof isn't really mathematically quantifiable. There needs to be sufficient proof, for the commander, to believe there is probable cause.

Probable cause is defined as a reasonable grounds for bringing a charge... Equally loose language.

You also have to understand that there are different burdens of proof for different actions. An administrative action like admin separation, Article 15 or admin reductions only required a preponderance of the evidence ... meaning evidence that makes it more likely than not that something occurred. A court martial (which is pretty uncommon with fraternization/ adultery) required proof beyond a reasonable doubt, which is evidence that leaves a person firmly convinced.

So, in any case, if there are texts, emails, photos, statements by someone that the offense is taking place, etc. that can be sufficient evidence for command to start an investigation to seek more.

That same evidence could be sufficient for a commander to initiate charges. That doesn't mean the charges will stick, but the threshold for starting a claim is much lower than winning a claim. (*Just Answer*)

The only way to evade this chain of vague explanations is to break away from the theoretical explanation with the end of digression signpost "so, in any case" and resort to concretization, i.e. providing a list of concrete elements that may more directly relate to the case at hand.

Final considerations

The present study has yielded a number of interesting findings on emerging genres and professional discourses in an understudied field, i.e. military law, in an evolving online context, i.e. Q&As. The first matter consists in the realization that the same interactive genre may take on different forms based on its affordances and functions. In fact, the *Just Answer* website, with its multiple multimedia channels and increased frequency and extent of interaction, not only disseminates more legal knowledge but also empowers the client more compared to the *Justia* website, which seems to be more of a first stop rather than a comprehensive source of legal assistance. Therefore, enhancing multi-modal tools in knowledge dissemination sources could also increase the extent and benefits of online legal knowledge sharing. The second area introduced here but to be focused on in future research is that of the influence of military culture and communication on military legal language, which is itself a professional legal jargon that presents telling changes and simplifications to legal English in terms of directness and specificity (Bhatia 2010). Such changes are well suited to online communicative contexts and fast-paced messages like those found in Q&As. They could also be connected to the popularization of legal knowledge, which is fundamental in non-expert empowerment and consists not only in discursive practices but also in the very simplification of specialized terminology (Calsamiglia and van Dijk 2004). The final point of interest resides in the use of linguistic strategies such as hedging, mitigating and pragmatic devices not only to empower the client (Turnbull 2013) but also to protect the attorney from a legal perspective, which emphasizes the ongoing and increasingly relevant debate on whether or not these identified legal experts can and should be held accountable for the outcome of the application of their advice even on the basis of the imperfect and incomplete information at their disposal.

Notes

1 https://answers.justia.com/questions/answered/military-law?page=2 (last accessed on May 22, 2018), hereinafter referred to as *Just Answer*.
2 www.justanswer.com/military-law/ (last accessed on May 22, 2018), hereinafter referred to as *Justia*.

References

Anesa, Patrizia. 2014. Defining legal vagueness: A contradiction in terms? *Polemos* 8.1: 193–209.
Anthony, Laurence. 2018. *AntConc* (Version 3.5.6) [Computer Software]. Tokyo, Japan: Waseda University. Available from www.laurenceanthony.net/software.
Backer, Daniel. 2002. Choice of law in online legal ethics: Changing a vague standard for attorney advertising on the internet. *Fordham Law Review 70.6*: 2409–2435.
Beal, Bruce L. 2000. Online mediation: Has its time come? *Ohio State Journal on Dispute Resolution 15.3*: 735–768.
Beaulieu, Anne, De Rijcke, Sarah and van Heur, Bas. 2013. Authority and expertise in new sites of knowledge production. In Wyatt, Sally, Scharnhorst, Andrea, Beaulieu, Anne and Wouters, Paul (eds) *Virtual Knowledge: Experimenting in the Humanities and the Social Sciences*. Cambridge MA: MIT Press (25–56).

Bhatia, Vijay K. 2010. Interdiscursivity in professional communication. *Discourse & Communication 21.1*: 32–50.

Bhatia, Vijay K. and Gotti, Maurizio. 2006. Introduction. In Bhatia, Vijay K. and Gotti, Maurizio (eds). *Explorations in Specialized Genres*, Bern: Peter Lang (9–17).

Boncea, Irina J. 2013. Hedging patterns used as mitigation and politeness strategies. *Annals of the University of Cracovia Series: Philology, English, 19,2*. Cracovia.

Calsamiglia, Helena and Van Dijk, Teun A. 2004. Popularization discourse and knowledge about the genome. *Discourse & Society 15.4*: 369–389.

Chouliaraki, Lia and Fairclough, Norman (eds). 1999. *Discourse in Late Modernity: Rethinking Critical Discourse Analysis*. Edinburgh: Edinburgh University Press.

Degano, Chiara. 2007. Presupposition and dissociation in discourse: A corpus study. *Argumentation 21*: 361–378.

Dunlap Jr., Charles J. 2003. It ain't no TV show: JAGS and modern military operations. *Chicago Journal of International Law 4.2*: 479–491.

Evangelisti Allori, Paola. 2011. Discourse and identity in the professionals. Corporate, legal and institutional citizenships. In Bhatia, Vijay K. and Evangelisti Allori, Paola (eds). *Discourse and Identity in the Professions*. Bern: Peter Lang.

Fairclough, Norman. 1995. *Critical Discourse Analysis: The Critical Study of Language*. New York: Routledge.

Fidell, Eugene R. 2016. *Military Justice: A Very Short Introduction*. Oxford: Oxford University Press.

Garzone, Giuliana. 2006. *Perspectives on ESP and Popularization*. Milan: CUEM.

Garzone, Giuliana and Santulli, Francesca. 2004. What can corpus linguistics do for critical discourse analysis? In Partington, Alan, Morley, John and Haarman, Louann (eds). *Corpora and Discourse*. Bern: Peter Lang (352–368).

Garzone, Giuliana and Salvi, Rita. 2007. *Legal English*, 2nd edition. Milan: Egea.

Gibbs, Raymond W. and Van Orden, Guy. 2012. Pragmatic choice in conversation. *Topics in Cognitive Science 4*: 7–20.

Gotti, Maurizio. 2005. *Investigating Specialized Discourse*. Bern: Peter Lang.

Gülich, Elisabeth. 2003. Conversational techniques used in transferring knowledge between medical experts and non-experts. *Discourse Studies 5.2*: 235–263.

Hanks, William F. 1999. Indessicalità/Indexicality. In Duranti, Alessandro (ed.). *Culture e discorso. Un lessico per le scienze sociali*. Rome: Meltemi (168–172).

Hibbitts, Bernard J. 1994. Making sense of metaphors: Visuality, aurality, and the reconfiguation of American legal discourse. *Cardozo Law Review 16*: 229–356.

Hyland, Ken. 2010. Constructing proximity: Relating to readers in popular and professional science. *Journal of English for Academic Purposes 9*: 116–127.

Kramer, Michael L. and Schmitt, Michael N. 2008. Lawyers on horseback? Thoughts on judge advocates and civil-military relations. *UCLA Law Review 55*: 1407–1436.

Lanctot, Catherine J. 2002. Regulating legal advice in cyberspace. *Journal of Civil Rights and Economic Development 16.3*: 569–585.

Maguire, Katheryn C. 2015. Military family communication: A review and synthesis of the research related to wartime deployment. In Parcell, Erin Sahlstein and Webb, Lynne (eds). *A Communication Perspective on the Military: Interactions, Messages and Discourses*. New York: Peter Lang Publishing (19–37).

Markman, Art. 2012. What do (linguistic) hedges do? www.psychologytoday.com/us/blog/ulterior-motives/201210/what-do-linguistic-hedges-do.

Marmor, Andrei. 2008. The pragmatics of legal language. *Ratio Juris 21.4*: 423–452.

Myers, Greg. 2010. *Discourse of Blogs and Wikis*. London and New York: Continuum.

Parcell, Erin Sahlstein. 2015. Research at the Intersections of the Military and Communication, A Preview and Review. In Parcell, Erin Sahlstein and Webb, Lynne (eds). *A Communication Perspective on the Military: Interactions, Messages and Discourses*. New York: Peter Lang Publishing (1–15).

Parcell, Erin Sahlstein and Webb, Lynne (eds). 2015. *A Communication Perspective on the Military: Interactions, Messages and Discourses*. New York: Peter Lang Publishing.

Partington, Alan. 2004. Corpora and Discourse, a Most Ongrous Beast. In Partington, Alan, Morley, John and Haarman, Louann (eds). *Corpora and Discourse*. Bern: Peter Lang (11–20).

Suler, John. 2004. The online disinhibition effect. *Cyber Psychology & Behavior 7.3*: 321–326.

Tiersma, Peter M. 1999. *Legal Language*. Chicago: The University of Chicago.

Turnbull, Judith. 2013. *A Linguistic Analysis of English Online. Knowledge Dissemination and Empowerment of Citizens*. Rome: Universitalia.

van Dijk, Teun A. 2003. The discourse-knowledge interface. In Weiss, Gilbert and Wodak, Ruth (eds). *Multidisciplinary CDA*. London: Longman (85–109).

Walsh, Polly. 2006. Playing safe? A closer look in hedging, conditions and attribution in economic forecasting. In Bhatia, Vijay K. and Gotti, Maurizio (eds). *Explorations in Specialized Genres*. Bern: Peter Lang (135–152).

Wyatt, Sally, Scharnhorst, Andrea, Beaulieu, Anne and Wouters, Paul (eds). 2013. Introduction to virtual knowledge. In Wyatt, Sally, Scharnhorst, Andrea, Beaulieu, Anne and Wouters, Paul (eds). *Virtual Knowledge: Experimenting in the Humanities and the Social Sciences*. Cambridge MA: MIT Press (1–23).

Zorza, Richard C. 1999. Re-conceptualizing the relationship between legal ethics and technological innovation in legal practice: From threat to opportunity. *Fordham Law Review 67.5*: 2659–2686.

12 The web-mediated construction of interdiscursive truth(s) about the MMR vaccine

A defamation case

Anna Franca Plastina and
Rosita Belinda Maglie[1]

Defamation: language and law

As a communicative act causing damage to a person's reputation, defamation encompasses "injury [...] by libel, the written word, and/or slander, the spoken word" (Neuenschwander 2014: 36). Defamation is therefore couched in language expressing an "accusation," which attributes "responsibility to a specific person for a discreditable or blameworthy act" (Tiersma 2015: 159). Meaning is thus the crucial starting point in any claim for defamation especially as judges are called to determine whether "words in their ordinary and natural meaning are capable of bearing a defamatory meaning" (Keenan 2007: 587) likely to damage/have damaged a claimant's reputation. In deciding what defamatory meanings words could have, judges construct "ordinary and natural meaning" by referring to a hypothetical, reasonable reader/listener. Accordingly, such a person is endowed with reasonable intelligence, an ordinary person's general knowledge, may make implications and inferences and be fair-minded and reasonable, does not read/listen to sensational information with cautious and critical care, goes by broad impression and does not construe words as would a lawyer.[2]

Moreover, "the logic of defamation creates a tangled web" involving at least the plaintiff, the defendant, and a third party interacting "in a wide array of circumstances," and quite often "a far more extensive list of individuals and entities" (Epstein 1986: 785). This implies that potential defamatory language is inevitably mediated at interdiscursive and interdisciplinary levels. From this perspective, propositional content seems to be conceived as an accusation in terms of "community standards"; these, however, vary widely "according to time, geography, and social status," thus making "the definition of defamatory language so elusive" (Tiersma 2015: 161).

Concurrently, while the protection of reputation is central in several legal systems (Tiersma 1987), national defamation laws appear to balance competing interests differently. For instance, English libel law is generally regarded as "the most claimant-friendly in the world" (Hartley 2010: 25), thus having the effect of "silencing authors on important global matters" (Auda 2016: 106). According to the UK Defamation Act 2013 (c. 26), it is, in fact, the defendant who needs to show that: the defamatory statement is *substantially true*; the statement complained of was a *statement of opinion*; the statement complained of was, or formed part of, a statement on a *matter of public interest*.[3] Conversely, US defamation law generally disfavours the plaintiff by invoking the Speech Act 2010, which provides protection against foreign libel judgement.[4] The Speech Act is, in fact, closely tied to the US Constitution which guarantees freedom of speech and thus avoids "chilling the first amendment to the Constitution of the United States interest of the citizenry in receiving information on matters of importance" (Section 2, c. 2).[5] As a result, the plaintiff must prove that the defendant's defamatory statement is false and, in the case of public figures, also show that the defendant acted with actual malice, or "knowledge of falsity of the defamatory statement or reckless disregard for whether it was true" (Johnson 2016: 30). Moreover, US legislation is also "defendant-friendly" in the case of plaintiffs who file a Strategic Lawsuit Against Public Participation (SLAPP) usually under the guise of a defamation claim. Several federal states (e.g. Texas) have anti-SLAPP laws that allow judges the discretion to dismiss defamation claims before reaching jury trials, especially when the direct purpose of seeking legal action is *not* to win a defamation case. Indeed, plaintiffs may tactfully file SLAPPs for the subtle purpose of burdening defendants with the cost of legal defence in order to force them to abandon their criticisms and thus hinder their freedom of speech.

Additionally, judging whether language bears defamatory meaning has become understandably more complex in the current digital age. Online defamation poses new challenges to the fair balance between the rights to reputation and to freedom of speech, especially when there is the need to uncover anonymous tortfeasors and seek justice (Vamialis 2013). On the other hand, overtly authored websites may be appropriated as "mediational means" (Jones and Norris 2005: 49) for the *action of reporting*, for example, medical matters of public interest. This action can be "traced to the interplay of larger Discourses and relations of power in the sociocultural environment" (Jones 2005: 154), and the media texts can be positioned within "multiple, overlapping, and even conflicting discourses" (Scollon 2001: 8). These kinds of websites thus appear to shape new socio-legal media contexts in which defamation is potentially constructed online and then pursued offline in courtrooms as libel suits.

Hence, linguistic analysis seems central to resolving defamation cases as pointed out by Shuy (2010: 37–38), who proposes three main categories of indicators of defamatory language: *malicious language (pejorative terms, sarcasm, exaggeration, rhetorical questions, figures of speech, innuendos); grammatical referencing* (e.g. evaluative adjectives) leading to disputes over intended meanings; and *language cues,* which directly relate to their social context in terms of defamatory intention.

At the interdiscursive level, understanding how defamation acquires meaning presupposes considering the actions taken by individuals with texts and their consequences (Jones and Norris 2005). Gaining insight into the mediated action of defamatory language thus requires accounting for its three interrelated constitutive elements: the *historical body*, or "the aggregation of social practices or repeated experiences of the social actors"; the *interaction order*, or "the roles people take up in social interactions"; the *discourses in place* (Scollon and de Saint-Georges 2012: 71), or the "instances of language use [...] that mark the environment in which the social action takes place" (Pan 2014: 54).

This chapter focuses on the specific defamation case regarding the UK journalist Brian Deer (defendant), who unearthed the fraudulent research claim on MMR vaccine-induced autism made by the discredited former British doctor, Andrew Wakefield (plaintiff). The conflict has been fuelled by Deer's personal website, where the action of reporting truths about the MMR vaccine has been sued by Wakefield as defamatory through libel suits filed in both the UK and US. Through a mediated discourse analysis (MDA) of a corpus of media texts from Deer's website, the chapter makes a contribution to exploring the discursive potential of defaming a person's reputation online. The MDA further considers a corpus of legal texts in the attempt to unfold "discourses in place" springing from Deer's mediated action of reporting, which gives rise to a complex "nexus of practice" (Scollon and Scollon 2004) around the issue of defamation. From an interdisciplinary perspective, the case study contributes to shedding light on the rights to reputation and to freedom of speech in relation to the hotly debated issue of the MMR vaccine.

Materials and method

The materials for the present study were taken from the website, briandeer.com, which is still currently maintained by the investigative journalist, Brian Deer. Part of the website itself represents a "nexus" understood as a "site of engagement," which facilitates free access to an observable "historical body" of socio-legal actions (cf. Scollon and Scollon 2004). These are copiously documented by Deer's journalistic articles on the issue of MMR vaccine-induced autism as the main *social action of inquiry*, as well as by a set of lengthy legal documents reflecting the "interaction order" of the *interdisciplinary action of defamation*. These materials were thus purposely selected to form a corpus composed of a total of 18 texts (132,255 running words). For present research purposes, the corpus was divided into two subcorpora, namely the Defamatory (DEF) subcorpus and the Legal (LEG) subcorpus. The DEF subcorpus is made up of 12 texts (33,159 words) covering a period of five years from 2006 to 2011 and includes one electronic text summarising Brian Deer's investigation, four of Deer's articles published in *The Sunday Times*, four of his articles published in *The British Medical Journal* (BMJ), and four editorials written by the BMJ editor, Fiona Godlee. The LEG subcorpus is made up of six texts (99,096 words) covering a period of nine years from 2005 to 2014 and comprises the approved judgement by the Royal Court of Justice (London) following Wakefield's libel action against Channel 4, 20–20 Production and the reporter Brian Deer; the plaintiff's (Wakefield) original petition at the District Court of Travis County (Texas), the defendants' (BMJ, Deer and Godlee) amended anti-SLAPP motion to dismiss, the Second affidavit by Wakefield vs. BMJ, Deer and

Godlee at the Court of Travis County, Wakefield's SLAPP appeal at the 3rd Court of Appeals (Austin, Texas) and the SLAPP appeal dismissal by the Texas Court of Appeals (3rd District, Austin). While there may seem to be an unbalance between the two subcorpora, the choice of an uneven number of texts was purposely made because the LEG texts are extremely long and complex, and therefore, require a more in-depth analysis than the DEF texts. In this regard, Tiersma (1999: 56) points out, in fact, that "studies show that sentences in legal language are quite a bit longer than in other styles, and also have more embeddings, making them more complex."

The starting point of the analysis springs from the claim made by Deer that "between 31 January 2005 and 25 January 2007, this website, briandeer.com, was in jeopardy, due to a claim for libel, brought by Andrew Wakefield, utilising lawyers made available to him free of charge by the Medical Protection Society."[6] From the UK jurisprudential perspective, the study is thus mainly guided by the Defamation Act 1996 (c. 199), whereby "the defence of truth shall be held to be established if such matter [...] does not materially injure the plaintiff's reputation having regard to any such charges which are proved to be true in whole or in part" (comma 7, par. 2); "in respect of words including or consisting of expression of opinion, a defence of comment [on a matter of public interest] shall not fail [...] provided that such of the assertions as are proved to be true are relevant and afford a foundation therefor" (comma 8, par. 2).

Accordingly, a quantitative-qualitative methodology was adopted to carry out MDA at micro- and macro-discursive levels guided by two main research questions: 1) which features of Deer's discourse as social interaction appear to defame Wakefield's reputation in terms of the three legal elements of malicious language, grammatical referencing and language cues? 2) How is this potential defamatory language mediated at interdiscursive levels in UK and US courtrooms in terms of the three legislative aspects of truth, comment and publication on a matter of public interest?

Raw data was downloaded, transcribed and included in the DEF or LEG subcorpora. Shuy's (2010) indicators of defamatory language (malicious language, grammatical referencing and language cues) were applied to the DEF subcorpus to manually annotate and code potential defamatory tokens at the micro-discursive level. Macro-analysis was then conducted on the LEG subcorpus by first considering the different social actors involved based on their institutional roles (interactional order) and their discourses as social practices (historical body) in order to establish an interdisciplinary mediation as "a nexus of practice" (Scollon and Scollon 2004). At this interdiscursive level, frequency analysis of key words/expressions was performed to identify and code tokens pointing to the three legal criteria of truth, comment and publication on a matter of public interest in accordance with the Defamation Act 1996.

Findings and discussion

Two sets of findings are presented in the following sections. The first dataset reports on the results of the micro-analysis of Deer's use of potential defamatory language, guided by the first research question posed by the study. The second

Table 12.1 Tokens of defamatory language in the DEF subcorpus per indicators

Malicious language	Grammatical referencing	Language cues
867 (44.1%)	528 (26.8%)	573 (29.1%)

Table 12.2 Categorisation of malicious language in the DEF subcorpus

Pejorative term	Exaggeration	Sarcasm	Figure of speech	Rhetorical question	Innuendo
563 (65%)	193 (22.3%)	55 (6.3%)	35 (4%)	14 (1.6%)	7 (0.8%)

dataset refers to findings related to the interdiscursive mediation of defamatory language as socio-legal discourse, guided by the second research question.

The use of potential defamatory language

The micro-analysis of the DEF subcorpus yielded 1,968 tokens of potential defamatory language. All tokens were classified by applying Shuy's (2010) indicators of malicious language, grammatical referencing and language cues, as shown in Table 12.1.

Malicious language

Findings suggest that Deer's language is mainly shaped by linguistic items, which construct meanings of "actual malice" (44.1%) (see Table 12.1). These consist primarily of pejorative terms (65%) and much less of exaggeration devices, sarcasm, figures of speech, rhetorical questions and innuendos (see Table 12.2).

Pejorative expressions of malice were mainly associable with meanings of *dishonesty* (N = 237; 42.1%), linguistically expressed through different combinations of mediated actions + pejorative terms, as illustrated in Table 12.3 for the most recurring structures (listed in alphabetical order).

The word *dishonesty* itself occurs in seven out of 12 texts (DEF 03, 04, 07, 08, 10 and 12). In almost all its occurrences it refers to *the four charges of dishonesty* filed against Wakefield by the UK General Medical Council (GMC) in 2010. Hence, the term is not loaded with defamatory meaning, but rather denotes the action of reporting facts of professional ethics.

When relating on Wakefield's conduct and research, Deer uses verbs which show a consistent negative aura of meaning (Louw 1993: 157), exception given for the verb *found of* denoting a discovery after a thorough study. These verbs contribute to describing the general "habitus" (Bourdieu 1977 in Scollon and de

Table 12.3 Mediated actions of malice: pejoration

Mediated action		Pejorative term
accused of being	+	A Cheat
branded		Dishonest
found to be		Fraudulent
guilty of being		Unethical
labelled		

Table 12.4 Mediated actions of malice: exaggeration

Mediated action		Exaggeration
launched	+	The greatest health **scare** of recent times
triggered		
mounting		The health **scare** of our time
to harvest millions from		Worldwide **scare**
exploited		Public health **scare**
to profit from		A huge **scare**
spread		Vaccine **scare**
caused		MMR **scare**
started		An epidemic of **fear**
		Parents' **fears**
		Panic over the vaccine

Saint Georges 2012) of the social actor in question, Andrew Wakefield, as *dishonest, fraudulent, unethical, a cheat* (Table 12.3). Most of the expressions in Table 12.3 are, in fact, quotes from different sources, and as such, they thus contribute to creating Scollon's so-called "nexus of practice." Indeed, Deer faithfully reports the words of the GMC's verdict, the BMJ editor's question and the accusation brought by Deer and Channel 4 against Wakefield, each of them uttered when the actors involved enacted their respective professional roles.

As for indicators of exaggeration, these mainly conveyed meanings of *fear/scare/panic* ($N = 73$; 39.4%), whereby the pejorative connotation of the MMR vaccine scam was meant to attract people's attention, and raise their *reflective* awareness. Exaggeration was primarily represented through the lexical items *scare, fear* and *panic*, which were combined with nine main mediated actions as shown in Table 12.4.

In particular, the word *scare* occurs in all the 12 texts included in the DEF subcorpus. The set of mediated actions through which Deer provides an account of the MMR case consists of verbs which reinforce the idea of a sudden outbreak of something unpleasant that causes people to experience scare, panic and/or fear. MMR vaccination becomes, in these presumed "exaggerated" reports, a topical issue (*of our time*) gaining ground (*worldwide*) and spreading rapidly (*epidemic*), a problem of great importance (*huge* and *greatest*) involving a very large number of people (*public, parents*) as it affects their *health*.

Grammatical referencing

In the case of grammatical referencing, the study's primary interest was to pinpoint Deer's evaluative language as a potential source of defamation. In this regard, adjectives that were consciously used in an attempt to influence the reader's opinion, attitude and stance, i.e. evaluative adjectives loaded with negative connotation, were the main grammatical category taken into account. This choice was justified by the fact that evaluative adjectives are "one of the most prototypical and canonical exponents of evaluation" (Swales and Burke 2003: 2). The analysis of grammatical referencing was thus conducted according to the four criteria introduced by Swales and Burke (ibid., p. 5), namely *deviance*, which denotes how closely related something is to what one would expect it to be (e.g. *strange); relevance* indicating how closely related something is to the topic or field being discussed (e.g. *important); assessment*, or the more general evaluation of things (e.g. *excellent*), and *size* (e.g. *huge*).

Findings show that of all the 528 occurrences of evaluative adjectives recorded, those predominantly used by Deer pertain to the deviance category (37.5%) followed by those falling under the assessment category (29%), whereas evaluative adjectives belonging to the size and relevance types were used much less frequently, as indicated in Table 12.5.

In detail, the Deviance type of adjectives were all traceable in seven of the nine articles authored by Deer. Their common functional purpose seems to be that of qualifying Wakefield's unscientific conduct as confirmed by 56.6% ($N = 112$) of the tokens found. Except for *gruelling*, the rest of the adjectives are featured by three main prefixes, namely *un-, extra-* and *pre-*, which all generally denote deviance from the expected. However, the use of *un-* for *approved* and *ethical* clearly marks Deer's completely opposite expectation. The primary purpose is to overtly signal Wakefield's lack of deontological ethics in the procedure adopted to carry out *medical research* and his unacceptable way of treating *vulnerable* children who had undergone a *gruelling battery of investigations* and spent *gruelling days of tests* (see Table 12.6). On the other hand, the use of the prefix *extra-* always precedes the *ordinary* to denote how Wakefield deviates from the average income expected from his profession. Hence, his mediated actions always relate to the excessive profit he

Table 12.5 Categorisation of grammatical referencing

I	Assessment	Size	Relevance
198	153	91	86
(37.5%)	(29%)	(17.2%)	(16.3%)

Sources: (based on Swales and Burke 2003: 5)

Table 12.6 Mediated actions of grammatical referencing: deviance

Deviance		Mediated actions
unapproved	+	*medical research*
unethical		*treatment of vulnerable children*
extraordinary		*revenues, gain, rate, business, misconduct*
pre-assembled		*artifacts*
pre-arranged		*"discovery" of features*
gruelling		*days of tests, battery of investigations*

Table 12.7 Mediated actions of grammatical referencing: assessment

Assessment		Mediated actions
Bogus	+	*data*
Deliberate		*fraud*
Undisclosed		*alteration of data*
Hidden		*flaw*
Orchestrated		*referrals*
Unsubstantiated		*"new syndrome"*

made, and to his financial acumen (*revenues, gain, rate, business schemes*),[7] even through the Machiavellian behaviour of taking advantage of *vulnerable children* (*extraordinary misconduct*).

The last set of adjectives with the prefix *pre-* occur in the same article (DEF 8), where Deer makes a comparison between the case of the "Piltdown Man"[8] and that of the MMR vaccine-induced autism, thus alluding to the fact that Wakefield cunningly piloted his actions beforehand to achieve certain desired results: *pre-assembled* and *pre-arranged artifacts* (findings) so as to produce *the "discovery" of features* he wanted.

Further confirmation of the fraudulent link between the MMR vaccine and autism is found in the use of assessment adjectives (Table 12.7).

These types of evaluative adjectives point explicitly to Wakefield's unscientific research in 39.4% of the tokens identified ($N = 76$). As a result, Deer's articles portray Wakefield's study as a *hidden flaw* based on an *undisclosed alteration* of *bogus data* taken from *orchestrated* (children's hospital) *referrals* in order to "create" evidence of a totally *unsubstantiated "new syndrome."* These strong evaluations may appear as a site of potential defamation, which requires a substantial defence of justification on Deer's side.

Language cues

As for language cues, the most significant type of linguistic markers found refer to scientific and legal cues of public interest (68.4%), followed by cues related to

Table 12.8 Categorisation of language cues in the DEF subcorpus

Scientific/legal cues	Public impact cues	Media cues
392	110	71
(68.4%)	(19.2%)	(12.4%)

the public impact of Wakefield's findings (19.2%) and by cues referring to the media interest in MMR vaccine case (12.4%) (see Table 12.8).

When considered in terms of interaction order, findings show that the terms *findings* and *data* (N = 148; 37.8%) consistently create a complex web of statements, or "a nexus of practice" between the UK General Medical Council, other researchers, the GMC panel, Deer, the *Lancet* editor-in-chief and Wakefield himself, each in their own social interactional roles. The statements in Example (1a–f) reformulate and arrange what was found in the DEF subcorpus according to the social actor involved and the corresponding mediated actions taken in order to point out that, although they are taken from different sources, they unanimously voice the belief that Wakefield's research *data* and *findings* were so *false and distorted* that he was eventually struck off the medical register:

(1) a. **Findings** at the UK General Medical Council (GMC) hearing were **examined, discredited, made public** [The UK GMC]

b. Other researchers were unable to **reproduce** Wakefield's **findings** [Medical Research]

c. The GMC panel **ruled** that Wakefield's **findings** were dishonest and his conduct irresponsible [The GMC Panel]

d. **Data** behind claims were exposed by Deer to the medical community as **misreported/faked/"chiselled"/misrepresented/changed** [Deer]

e. **Data** were noted to be utterly **false and distorted** by The Lancet's editor-in-chief Richard Horton [Horton]

f. Wakefield was struck off the UK medical register, with a statement identifying **deliberate falsification** in the **data** published in The Lancet [Wakefield]

In particular, example (f) suggests that the GMC has been legally conferred powers by the UK Parliament following the 1858 Medical Act and the subsequent Medical Act 1983 (c 54), which governs the "General Council's power to advise on conduct, performance or ethics" and thus to rule that medical practitioners' names are erased from the register if the Committee considers that it is fit to do so.[9]

Table 12.9 Mediated actions of language cues: public impact

Mediated actions	Public impact cues
fuelling	**public suspicion** *(of vaccines)*
caused	*(an unprecedented collapse) in* **public**
spread	**confidence** *(in the shot)*
the damage to	**public alarm** *over MMR slumped*
public concern *sent*	**public health** *continues*
Wakefield's words	**vaccination rates** *plummeting*
UK	*were enough to make* **vaccination rates**
After the MMR scare	*plummet*
	vaccination rates *slumped below the level*
	needed to keep measles at bay
	in 1998 **rates** *fell to 80% nationally*

Table 12.10 Classification of socio-legal meanings in the LEG subcorpus

Truth	Fair comment	Publication
563 (64.4%)	113 (12.9 %)	198 (22.6%)

On the other hand, cues referring to the *public impact* of Wakefield's research point to two key topics: the *public* reaction of *suspicion of vaccines* and *alarm over MMR*, and the grave repercussion this *public concern* causes on *public health* and *vaccination rates* ($N = 52$; 47.3%), which inevitably *plummeted, fell* and *slumped* (Table 12.9).

Language cues which directly relate to media interest refer to either the general media coverage of the MMR vaccine issue (e.g. *reports, interviews, articles, blogs, editorials*) or to the media themselves, especially television (e.g. *Dateline NBC TV, Channel 4 Television, BBC*), newspapers (*The Independent, The New York Times*) and magazines (e.g. *Sunday Times, Press Gazette*, etc.), which widely disseminate information about Wakefield's research. Both the print and audio-visual media covered it from the very beginning when the *Lancet* original paper (...) *received so much* **media** *attention* and *the scare was launched at a* **televised press conference** [DEF02] through Deer's *investigation of the MMR issue* [which] *exposed the frauds behind Wakefield's research* [DEF01]; *Wakefield's* attempt *to brazen it out, issuing a further statement to* **media** [DEF03]; *unbalanced* **media** *reporting* [DEF04] to *the extensive* **international media** *response to Deer's first two* **articles** [DEF06] *from New Zealand to Canada* [DEF07].

The interdiscursive mediation of defamatory language

Four main figures, namely Andrew Wakefield (plaintiff), Brian Deer (defendant), David Eady (UK Judge), Amy Clark Meachum (US Judge) were identified as the main social actors involved in the defamation case. Their "Discourses" as "instantiated in the social world as social action" (Scollon 2001: 3) were subjected to frequency analysis of keywords connoted with socio-legal meanings of *truth, (fair) comment* and *publication on a matter of public interest.* Results from the LEG subcorpus yielded a total of 874 tokens as summarized in Table 12.10.

Data findings suggest that interdiscursive mediation of defamatory language takes place primarily through the legal elements of *truth* (64.4%) and *publication* (22.6%), and to a lesser extent through *fair comment* (12.9%). A more in-depth analysis and discussion of the three datasets is provided in the following sections.

Stancetaking in defamation: interdiscursive truth(s)

A total of 563 samples were found to express the social actors' engagement in stancetaking as "a linguistically articulated form of social action" (Du Bois 2007: 139) about the truth(s) of the MMR vaccine. All the tokens are characterized by the key feature of interdiscursive mediation, namely "dialogicality" as "the stancetaker's words derive from, and further engage with, the words of those who have spoken before" (ibid., p. 140). Moreover, the stance acts are grounded in the semantics of evidentiality, justified by the pivotal legal construct of *defamation proof.* The acts can thus be positioned along an evidential scale ranging from *falsehood* and *misrepresentation* to *factuality*, which helps disclose how the actors commit themselves to the issue of proof according to their socio-legal roles, as indicated in Table 12.11.

Results generally show that dialogicality is accomplished across the full range of the evidential scale. Nevertheless, the stance acts clearly reflect how the defendant construes socio-legal meaning predominantly through factuality (54.5%) as do the judges (68.4%) in accordance with their roles; the plaintiff, instead, appears to subvert the conventional practice of defamation proof by relying primarily on misrepresentation (79%) and falsehood (15.6%) and paradoxically, to a lesser extent on factuality (5.4%).

Hence, despite the fact that the burden of proof is on the plaintiff (P), it is the defendant (D) who provides tangible facts as his defence against the accusation of "misrepresentation" (*knowingly misrepresented facts*). These are elaborated dialogically (*just as the Defendant stated*) by the UK Judge (UKJ)

Table 12.11 Mediating truths: interdiscursive stance acts based on evidentiality

Stance acts	Plaintiff (N = 262; 46.5%)	Defendant (N = 222; 39.4%)	Judges (N = 79; 14.1%)
1 falsehood	41 (15.6%)	53 (23.9%)	23 (29.1%)
2 misrepresentation	**207 (79.0%)**	48 (21.6%)	2 (2.5 %)
3 factuality	14 (5.4%)	**121 (54.5%)**	**54 (68.4%)**

with a strong negative connotation (*dishonesty, unprofessionalism*), as illustrated in Example (2):

> (2) P: Defendant Deer knowingly misrepresented facts with the purpose of making false accusations against Dr. Wakefield [LEG01]
>
> D: He altered, manipulated or misrepresented data for the twelve cases in the Lancet paper … he "rigged" the Lancet paper…. Dr. Wakefield hand-picked certain patients for the study [LEG03]
>
> UKJ: The GMC Panel also found that Dr. Wakefield's dishonesty and unprofessionalism continued to the patient participants' diagnosis, the gathering of data, and the reporting of the data, just as the Defendant stated [LEG03]

The plaintiff seems to further take a *subjective* stance towards the falsehood of the defendant's statements (*the defamatory statements were and are false*) on unproved grounds of manipulating information (*omits crucial details*), insinuating "actual malice" (*to achieve the impression of fraud*), as in Example (3):

> (3) P: The Defamatory Statements were and are false … intended to cause damage to Dr. Wakefield's reputation and work…. By the construct of his narrative Deer omits crucial details … in order to achieve the impression of fraud when in fact there was none. [LEG02]
>
> D: *Dr. Wakefield's libel claims fail at the most basic level: He cannot show that any of the challenged statements are false* [LEG03]
>
> UKJ: *The challenged statements are substantially true if, for example, Dr. Wakefield was guilty of anything similar to "fraud," such as "dishonesty," "unethical" conduct, "serious professional misconduct," or providing "misleading" information about his research* [LEG03]

In response, the defendant avails himself of the *truth* defence to the defamation claim by invoking the legal requirement that the plaintiff prove the falsity of the alleged defamatory statement (*he cannot show*). The plaintiff's stancetaking word *fraud* subsequently solicits the judge to seek its "ordinary and natural meaning" in accordance with the legal doctrine of substantial truth (*substantially true*)[10] to determine whether the statement is truthful enough as a defence to the defamation. The synonyms here not only serve the purpose of clarifying the effect of *fraud* on the average recipient's mind, but more importantly, highlight that the GMC had already ruled in this respect, and consequently that the defendant is not liable for any damage caused by the statement.

The defendant's statement *he cannot show* together with the judge's semantic nuances of *fraud* in example (2) trigger further interdiscursive development in terms of *factuality*, which also engages the fourth party, namely the US Judge

(USJ), even though "more remotely along the horizons of [...] prior text[s] as projected by th[is] community of discourse" (Du Bois 2007: 140). Example (4) is a clear case in point:

(4) D: Expressions of opinion, statements of rhetorical hyperbole, and colourful language that cannot objectively be proven true or false do not qualify as assertions of fact and are therefore not actionable in a libel case [LEG05]

UKJ: *It also accepted that the burden lies upon the applicant... to demonstrate, through cogent evidence, that there are sound reasons* [LEG03]

USJ: *the plaintiff must show that the challenged statements by the defendant were more damaging to the plaintiff's reputation in the mind of the average viewer than literally true statements would have been* [LEG06]

In example (4), the defendant semantically expands on the use of *fraud* (*expressions of opinion, statements of rhetorical hyperbole, and colourful language*), claiming that they do not pertain to factuality (*do not qualify as assertions of fact*), and are therefore *not actionable*. The notion of *fact* is then developed by the UK Judge (*burden, demonstrate, cogent evidence, sound reasons*), thus highlighting that "the burden of proof rests on the party who advances a proposition affirmatively ('actori incumbit onus probandi')."[11] Along the same lines, the US judge underlines the importance of factuality (*must show*) in accordance with the construct of the hypothetical, reasonable reader (*average viewer*) and in comparison to the actual truth of statements (*literally true*).

Constructing triad interactions: fair comment

A total of 143 tokens expressing *fair comment* mainly contributed to constructing triad interactions between the plaintiff and the UK and US judges, as shown in Example (5):

(5) UKJ: Using ... libel proceedings ... as a tool for stifling further criticism or debate ... I am not prepared to go along with that [LEG03]

P: *The cases were certainly not filed ... to chill legitimate criticism or comment. They were filed to stop false defamatory statements* [LEG04]

UKJ: *Indeed, it may well be that there is a whiff of tactics in the Claimant's change of stance.... The allegations are very serious indeed and concern matters of considerable legitimate public interest* [LEG03]

USJ: *Wakefield was doing everything he possibly could to delay that hearing ... would offend traditional notions of fair play and substantial justice* [LEG06]

Table 12.12 Interdiscursive mediation of publication on the MMR vaccine as a matter of public interest

Publication	Plaintiff	Defendant	Judges
Website (N = 143)	**115 (80.4%)**	5 (3.5%)	23 (16.1%)
(Hyper)link (N = 55)	**44 (80%)**	2 (3.6%)	9 (16.4%)

The triad interaction in the above example highlights how the two judges appear to create a dyad coalition, whereby both refute the plaintiff's subtle strategies (*a tool for stifling further criticism or debate, a whiff of tactics, doing everything he possibly could to delay that hearing*), and exercise their legal power to warrant the right to free speech (*I am not prepared to go along with that; would offend traditional notions of fair play*), especially as the case of the MMR vaccine is evaluated by the UK judge as a matter of *considerable legitimate public interest* [LEG03]. This then explains the greater attention dedicated to the interdiscursive mediation of defamation in terms of publication.

The web as mediational means: the public matter of the MMR vaccine

The issue of publication (N = 198) was mostly mediated through two keywords, namely *website* (143 instances) and *(hyper)link* (55 instances), which were used by all four social actors involved (Table 12.12).

Findings suggest that the plaintiff considers the defendant's personal website as a powerful public discursive space, where defamatory meanings find their origins, as indicated in Example (6):

(6) P: On his website, the origin of Deer's false assertions is to be found [LEG01]

D: *Nor did he ever seek any correction to my website, where all of my articles and findings were set out* [LEG03]

UKJ: *So far as the website proceedings are concerned, I see no advantage in those continuing in parallel. There is a significant overlap* [with the defamation proceedings] [LEG03]

D: *I published further documents at my website, including, for example, material I obtained under the Freedom of Information Act ... the challenged statements identified in the petition were published on the site well over one year before this case was filed* [LEG03]

USJ: *simply making an alleged article accessible on a website is insufficient to support specific jurisdiction in a defamation suit.... The plaintiff must establish that the non-resident defendant's internet activity was intended to target and focus on the forum* [LEG06]

While potential defamation plaintiffs are quite commonly satisfied with corrections and/or apologies, here the plaintiff does not seem to have made any complaints (*nor did he ever seek any correction to my website*), but rather makes a legal retraction request (*website proceedings*), which according to the UK Judge overlaps with the defamation case itself. Moreover, when the same request is filed in Texas, the defendant avails himself of the legal right to free speech (*material I obtained under the Freedom of Information Act*); he additionally recalls that this state has a one-year statute of limitations for libel claims (*published on the site well over one year before this case was filed*). The US judge elaborates on the issue in terms of jurisdiction as *Wakefield relied heavily on medical records and other documents located in the United Kingdom*, and also of recipients since *the record contains no evidence that the allegedly defamatory articles made available on-line were directed or aimed at Texas* [LEG06].

As for the accusation of defamation due to the use of hyperlinks, the plaintiff files complaints about the links created by the defendant to other websites and also about those linking to the defendant's site, as indicated in Example (7):

(7) P: on the website www.briandeer.com with links to the BMJ article and editorials containing defamatory statements *you* [Mr Owen, Head of Publishing, Immunisation Information, Department of Health] *are now invited to withdraw the Department of Health link to these two websites* [Mr Deer's and the Channel 4 website] *forthwith given that this is an inappropriate use of Governmental weight and authority in such a controversial area* [LEG01]

UKJ: *He* [Mr Owen] *appears to have been made of sterner stuff: "we propose therefore to maintain the links concerned as indeed we propose to maintain the links to websites putting forward views supporting Dr Wakefield"* [LEG03].

The example above clearly shows how the logic of defamation creates an increasingly tangled web, whereby a number of other social actors come into play. The retraction request made by the plaintiff appears to be an empty threat to the Department of Health, referenced by the UK judge who seems to legally accept the position of granting the equal opportunity of free expression to both parties involved in the defamation case. Hence, as Barnett Lidsky and Andersen Jones (2016: 164–165) note:

linking to original sources-which is easy to do in some social-media applications-should often help defendants escape defamation liability. Hyperlinking signals that an author has relied on underlying facts [...] and invites the reader to test the reasonableness of the author's interpretation rather than accept it as gospel.

Concluding remarks

According to MDA "the place to look for struggles of power and ideology" is not in one practice, "but in the way multiple practices converge to influence concrete social actions" (Jones and Norris 2005: 10). Through MDA, the present research findings show, in fact, how, the place to look for Wakefield's struggles of power and 'deviant' ideology is not in his single practice of publishing fraudulent research, but in the way it leads to multiple practices including investigative journalism, website dissemination, libel suits, defences, medical and legal rulings. Together these practices converge to determine at least two opposite concrete social actions, namely fuelling anti-vax campaigns vs. promoting public awareness of the importance of vaccination. Hence, the present study has highlighted how these practices revolve around the Wakefield-Deer defamation case, and more importantly, how defamation is couched in defamatory language and "defamation law operates in the realm of speech" (Ardia 2010: 303).

In detail, MDA findings at the micro-discursive level of the DEF subcorpus show that all three legal elements, namely malicious language, grammatical referencing and language cues potentially concur in construing defamatory meanings although to different degrees as follows:

- Malicious language: the predominant categories of pejoration and exaggeration carry discreditable implications of dishonesty in professional conduct and of Machiavellian scare tactics over MMR vaccination, respectively.
- Grammatical referencing: the prevailing evaluative adjectives of deviance and assessment types indicate that both professional conduct and MMR research diverge markedly from the ethical norm and from established scientific procedure.
- Language cues: the prevalent scientific/legal cues of public interest relate to the deliberate intention of falsifying test results that costs the offender to be erased from the medical register.

At interdiscursive and interdisciplinary levels, the LEG subcorpus first revealed that the logic of defamation involved a complex network of actors – the plaintiff, the defendant, and the UK and the US judges. More importantly, their discourses were embedded with socio-legal meanings reflecting the issue of defamation represented through the legal criteria of truth, (fair) comment and publication on a matter of public interest as follows:

- Interdiscursive Truth(s): the four actors' stance acts grounded in the semantics of evidentiality are elaborated dialogically to determine that groundless accusations are dismissed, the burden of proof rests on the plaintiff, expressions of opinion are not actionable in a libel case, previous conviction by the UK GMC is considered, and eventually that defamatory statements are declared substantially true by the UK and the US courtroom.

- Comment: specific patterns of triad interactions between the plaintiff and the UK and US judges have been observed to uncover how freedom of speech is legally protected both in the UK and the US and how tactical strategies disguised as defamation cases are legally refuted.
- Publication: website and hyperlinks are regarded as new socio-legal contexts where it is possible to avoid defamation liability thanks to the provision of evidence and facts.

On the whole, the study has helped shed light on the fact that language which apparently may be classified as defamatory from the lay perspective turns out to be harmless for reputational damage from the legal viewpoint. The study has further highlighted how in a cross-cultural perspective between the UK and the US, both systems consider the right to freedom of speech as paramount, especially when judges unearth subtle strategies used by plaintiffs to chill legitimate criticism on matters of extremely vital public interest as that of the MMR vaccine.

Notes

1 Although this research was jointly conducted by both authors, Anna Franca Plastina is responsible for the sections on Defamation: Language and law and the interdiscursive mediation of defamatory language and related subsections; Rosita Belinda Maglie for the sections on Materials and methods, The use of potential defamatory language and related subsections, and Concluding remarks.
2 The law of defamation-terminology http://francisdavey.github.io/defamation/pages/staying_protected/i---the-law-of-defamation.html.
3 See www.legislation.gov.uk/ukpga/2013/26/pdfs/ukpga_20130026_en.pdf.
4 This limited the phenomenon of libel tourism, whereby plaintiffs (e.g. public figures) would previously bring their claims for defamation to the more plaintiff-friendly courts in the UK, and then have these judgments enforced by US courts.
5 See www.gpo.gov/fdsys/pkg/PLAW-111publ223/html/PLAW-111publ223.htm
6 https://briandeer.com/wakefield/lawsuit-deer.htm Although a partial retraction of the 1998 Wakefield et al. paper had been made by the *Lancet* in 2004, a full retraction took place only in 2010 after the UK General Medical Council ruled that Wakefield's conduct was irresponsible and dishonest. This allowed Wakefield to file his libel law suits in the meantime.
7 Wakefield was also found guilty of taking money and having conflicts of interest when carrying out the MMR vaccine research (further information at briandeer.com).
8 The Piltdown Man case (1910–1912) has been one of the most elaborate hoaxes of the history of science, according to which "the discovery" of bone fragments were presented as remains of an extinct hominid.
9 Since the enactment of the 1858 Medical act, the UK Parliament has conferred on the GMC powers to grant various legal benefits and responsibilities to registered medical practitioners; The Medical act 1983 (c 54) governs the "general Council's power to advise on conduct, performance or ethics" (Part V, Section 35), whereby "the Committee may, if they think fit, direct- (1) that his name shall be erased from the register" (Part V, Section 36).

10 The legal doctrine affects libel and slander laws in common law jurisdictions like the UK and US.
11 On the transnational principle of law see www.trans-lex.org/966000/_/distribution-of-burden-of-proof/

References

Ardia, David S. 2010. Reputation in a networked world: Revisiting the social foundations of defamation law. *Harvard Civil Rights-Civil Liberties Law Review 45*(2): 261–328.

Auda, Ali. 2016. A proposed solution to the problem of libel tourism. *Journal of Private International Law 12*(1): 106–131.

Barnett Lidsky, Lyrissa and Andersen Jones, RonNell. 2016. Of reasonable readers and unreasonable speakers: Libel law in a networked world. *The Virginia Journal of Social Policy and the Law 23*(2): 155–178.

Du Bois, John W. 2007. The stance triangle. In Englebretson, Robert (ed.), *Stancetaking in Discourse: Subjectivity, Evaluation, Interaction* (pp. 139–182). Amsterdam/Philadelphia: John Benjamins.

Epstein, Richard A. 1986. Was New York Times v. Sullivan wrong? *University of Chicago Law Review 53*(3): 782–818.

Hartley, Trevor. 2010. 'Libel tourism' and conflict of laws. *International and Comparative Law Quarterly 59*(1): 25–38.

Johnson, Vincent R. 2016. Comparative defamation law: England and the United States. *University of Miami International and Comparative Law Review 24*(1): 1–98.

Jones, Rodney H. 2005. Sites of engagement as sites of attention: Time, space and culture in electronic discourse. In Norris, Sigrid and Jones, Rodney H. (eds), *Discourse in Action: Introducing Mediated Discourse Analysis* (pp. 141–154). London and New York: Routledge.

Jones, Rodney H. and Norris, Sigrid. 2005. Introducing mediational means/cultural tools. In Norris, Sigrid and Jones, Rodney H. (eds), *Discourse in Action: Introducing Mediated Discourse Analysis* (pp. 49–51). London and New York: Routledge.

Keenan, Denis. 2007. *Smith & Keenan's English Law: Text and Cases*, 15th edn. Harlow, UK: Pearson Longman.

Louw, Bill 1993. Irony in the text or insincerity in the writer? In Baker, Mona, Francis, Gill and Tognini Bonelli, Elena (eds), *Text and Technology. In Honour of John Sinclair* (pp. 157–176). Amsterdam: Benjamins.

Neuenschwander, John A. 2014. *A Guide to Oral History and the Law*, 2nd edn. Oxford: Oxford University Press.

Pan, Yuling. 2014. Nexus Analysis. In Norris, Sigrid and Maier, Carmen Daniela (eds), *Texts, Images, and Interactions: A Reader in Multimodality* (pp. 53–62). Boston/Berlin: De Gruyter Mouton.

Scollon, Ronald. 2001. *Mediated Discourse: The Nexus of Practice*. London and New York: Routledge.

Scollon, Ronald and Scollon, Suzie Wong. 2004. *Nexus Analysis: Discourse and the Emerging Internet*. London and New York: Routledge.

Scollon, Suzie Wong and de Saint-Georges, Ingrid. 2012. Mediated discourse analysis. In Gee, James Paul and Handford, Michael (eds), *The Routledge Handbook of Discourse Analysis* (pp. 66–78). New York: Routledge.

Shuy, Roger W. 2010. *The Language of Defamation Cases.* Oxford: Oxford University Press.

Swales John and Burke, Amy. 2003. It's really fascinating work: Differences in evaluative adjectives across academic registers. In Leistyna, Pepi and Meyer, Charles (eds), *Corpus Analysis: Language Structure and Language Use* (pp. 1–18). Amsterdam: Rodopi.

Tiersma, Peter M. 1987. The language of defamation. *Texas Law Review* 66(2): 303–350.

Tiersma, Peter M. 1999. *Legal Language.* Chicago and London: The University of Chicago Press.

Tiersma, Peter M. 2015. Defamatory language and the act of accusing. In Solan, Lawrence, Ainsworth, Janet and Shuy, Roger (eds), *Speaking of Language and Law: Conversations on the Work of Peter Tiersma* (pp. 159–167). Oxford: Oxford University Press.

Vamialis, Anna. 2013. Online defamation: Confronting anonymity. *International Journal of Law and Information Technology* 21(1): 31–65.

Section 3 - Challenges and way forward

13 The toxic proliferation of lies and fake news in the world of social media

Is it time for the law to "unfriend" Facebook?

Janet Ainsworth

Social media as a cultural phenomenon of modern life has often been valorized as a benign vehicle for interpersonal communication and interchange. Facebook is conceptualized as a virtual community, and Twitter as a virtual town square. What this characterization overlooks is the extraordinary, unprecedented power that corporate entities like Facebook, Google, and Twitter wield. Consider these facts about Facebook: Facebook's net worth in 2019 was over half a trillion dollars. If Facebook were a country, by net worth it would make it the world's twenty fourth largest economy – similar to Austria or Thailand. If its active users – those who log on at least once a month – were the population of a country, Facebookland would be as big as China and India combined. Ironically, this is true despite the fact that China bans Facebook and other US-based social media companies from operating in China. If Chinese citizens could access Facebook, the Facebookland "population" would no doubt be considerably higher.

One feature of social media platforms is their provision of purported news items for individual consumption by users and the tools for easy sharing of those items with others. Particularly notorious or shocking items can be shared so widely and so quickly that a term has been coined to describe that phenomenon – "going viral." Like biological viruses, viral social media items can cause harm to their consumers, as well as to those falsely accused of outrageous or wrongful behavior, and, by extension, to the body politic at large. Social media are not merely places for sharing of private information; they have become for many a major source for news and information about the world. In a 2018 poll undertaken by the Pew Research Group (Matsa and Shearer, 2018), more than two thirds of American adults reported that social media served them as a significant source of news, with 20% calling social media their primary source of news. Not surprisingly, the younger the respondents, the greater their dependence on social media for news; those under 50 were twice as likely to rely on Facebook for news than were those over 50. Overall, however, nearly half of all respondents reported getting news specifically from Facebook, by far the main source of social media-mediated news exposure. When asked in the survey why they utilized social media for news and information, the most frequent answer was "convenience."

Certainly, the pervasiveness of smartphone and computer use in everyday life do make it convenient to absorb social media messaging about current events along with the rest of the tidal wave of information transmitted through our ever-present technological devices. Unfortunately, however, an increasing proportion of news items shared via social media turn out to be misleading, distorted, or even outright lies. What is being consumed often isn't reliable news, but instead "fake news" – items that look like legitimate news stories but that instead are misleading, distorted, or in many cases, complete fabrications.

Fake news in the 2016 American presidential election and the UK Brexit referendum

A good example of the harm that social media-driven "fake news" can cause occurred during the final weeks of the Clinton-Trump presidential election campaign, when a white supremacist propagated a story on his blog that Hillary Clinton, in cahoots with one of her political supporters, was running a child-sex slavery ring out of the basement of a Washington pizza parlor (Seidenberg, 2017b). The allegation went viral, first on other extreme right-wing websites, then on more mainstream pro-Trump social media. The charge was repeated by a number of influential alt-right activists, and picked up by Infowars' Alex Jones, who featured the conspiracy-theory daily on his nationally-syndicated radio program. The story – dubbed Pizzagate by its proponents – was widely shared on social media – in fact, the Twitter hashtag #Pizzagate featured in well over a million tweets and retweets within two weeks of the first appearance of the allegation. Over the next few weeks, the story became even more elaborate – that the pizza parlor was a center of Satanic ritual torture as well as child sex slavery; that many prominent Democrats were involved, that both the local police and the FBI had confirmed the truth of the story but due to the powerful Democrats running the sex slavery ring, law enforcement had been forced to drop their investigations.

Despite the extraordinary implausibility of the claim, coupled with the un-deniable fact that the pizza parlor in question didn't even *have* a basement, this story was apparently widely believed by consumers of social media. For example, some weeks after the election, the magazine *The Economist* commissioned a poll of American voters on whether they believed that Hillary Clinton was involved in a child sex trafficking ring operating out of a pizza parlor (Rampell 2016). 46% of surveyed Trump voters responded that they believed the story. Even more shocking, 17% of surveyed Clinton voters believed that the sex abuse ring existed. Just after the election, an armed vigilante stormed into the pizza parlor in question and sprayed it with several rounds from a military-style assault rifle, intending to rescue the non-existent children said to be shackled in the non-existent basement. Fortunately, no one was hurt in the shooting.

While the ending of the Pizzagate story fortuitously turned out to be only tragicomic, fake news items propagated via social media like the Pizzagate story nevertheless do have consequences. Clinton, running for president, was politi-cally damaged by the story. As the *Economist* polling demonstrated, many voters apparently believed the story was at least partly true. Nor did the harm caused by the allegation stop there. The innocent restaurant owner lost employees who quit, fearing for their safety after receiving hundreds of death threats, and the restaurant lost customers who either believed the story or were worried about being caught in cross-fire with those who did. The propagation of the Pizzagate allegations thus had serious real-world effects. While many of those spreading the story were simply gullible individuals disinclined to question its truth, many of the key propagators cynically disseminated the story as broadly as possible in an attempt to smear Clinton and the Democrats and sway the election to Trump – and they kept the story front and center in the public imagination by daily re-velations of supposed newly discovered details of the conspiracy.

Fabricated news items like this increase a community's political polarization. People are significantly more likely to believe news items when those news items are ideologically congruent with their pre-existing beliefs (Allcott and Gentzkow, 2017: 213). Those who agree with the slant of fake news items become even more convinced of the evil of the target of the fake news story, and those who disagree are outraged by the dishonesty and craziness of those who believed, or pretended to believe, the fake news story and passed it on. This ongoing, systemic harm to the body politic of a society is corrosive, un-dermining the shared consensus about reality that is necessary for a healthy democracy to function.

While no one was killed or hurt as a result of the Pizzagate fake news story, unfortunately not all fake news cases end without tragedy. A New York Times investigation (Mozur, 2018) showed that the military government of Myanmar masterminded a Facebook campaign of incendiary fake news designed to target the Muslim minority Rohingya population. The Times's investigation docu-mented the inflammatory hate items posted on Facebook by members of the military regime, which incited the rapes and murder of many Rohingya and fa-cilitated what the Times called "the largest forced human migration in recent history." Postings designed to inflame passions, can be quickly transmitted by social media as propaganda to recruit others to extremism. Videos of terroristic mass shootings by white supremacists in New Zealand and the United States were uploaded to social media platforms by the perpetrators and their sym-pathizers just as earlier ISIS jihadists uploaded the beheadings of supposed in-fidels. White supremacist groups have apparently learned from the social media success of jihadist groups that social media is the ideal platform from which to spread their ideology and to encourage new attacks by their followers.

There has always been "fake news," of course. In the nineteenth century, American newspapers often published stories that were entirely fabricated in order to sell more papers and promote political positions that the editors supported – practices inconsistent with modern journalistic standards mandating that reporting be factually accurate. (Seidenberg, 2017a). Hoaxes and conspiracy theories long predate social media. However, the speed of transmission and the breadth of dissemination of fake news is what makes today's social media fake news a kind of weaponized fake news, rendering society vulnerable to politically moti-vated persons or groups who want to manipulate public opinion. In some cases, pernicious fake news is spread by persons who are indifferent to its content but who just want to make money by spreading outrageous lies likely to draw viewers. For instance, during the 2016 US presidential election, a group of teenagers in the Balkan state of Macedonia created literally thousands of fake right-wing news items – not because they wanted to promote right wing ideology in the United States but simply to provoke social media users into clicking on their websites so that the teenagers would make money through online ads on their sites (Allcott and Gentzkow, 2017: 217).

Even though fake news may only be a small fraction of available online news, it has outsized influence. For example, Buzzfeed (Silverman, 2016) tracked the most liked, shared, and commented-on news items in the last few months of the 2016 US presidential campaign; it found that the top 20 *false* news items on Facebook far outstripped in influence the top 20 *legitimate* news items from mainstream journalism. They were "liked" more, believed more, shared with others more often, and more likely to be remembered later. Heavy users of social media had the most pronounced tendency to believe false news items with which they perceived an ideological alignment. (Allcott and Gentzkow 2017: 230). Perhaps even more troubling, heavy consumers of social media were also more inclined to express doubt about the reliability of objectively verifiable facts. This suggests that efforts to debunk fake news by showing factual evidence of its falsity may be ineffective in countering the effect of fake news. This self-reinforcing process of exposure to fake news that is congruent with one's ideology, sharing it with other like-minded individuals, and resisting information that would contradict the item has created a social media world in which networks become increasingly ideologically segregated echo chambers. (Flaxman et al., 2016; Allcott and Gentzkow, 2017: 221).

Echo chambers, however, function to increase the profitability of social media platforms, since they encourage users to share and re-share items that confirm their world view, whether true or false. Clicks and eyeballs are the metrics by which social media corporations gauge their success, in that reading and sharing material translates directly into greater advertisement revenue. Disruption of the blossoming of echo chambers would obviously undercut the business model of social media companies like Facebook. Because eyeballs and clicks are the metric that determines the value of any social media platform, these platforms are designed to maximize user engagement by supplying users with more of what they have shown the media platform that they already want to see. Click a few times on any subject, and your social media platform will supply you with an endless stream of similar content. That may be reasonably harmless if what you are clicking on is cat videos or makeup tutorials; the worst-case scenario is probably a waste of your time. But suppose the clicks are on extremist material such as white nationalism or jihadist sites – YouTube will continue to suggest similar extremist materials until they may come to seem normalized (O'Callaghan et al., 2015). In one study (Berger, 2013), Twitter users who followed a single Al Qaeda affiliate were besieged with other violent extremist Twitter accounts to follow. This process is beyond the creation of mere echo chambers; it is the creation of virtual alternative realities, complete with suggested actions to take in support of the now-normalized extremist positions articulated in the social media postings.

However, in 2018, events unfolded that forced Facebook to begin to reckon with the corrupting impact of the deliberate use of fake news to create echo chambers. In early spring of 2018, the New York Times began reporting on its investigation concerning actions of the data analytic firm Cambridge Analytica during the 2016 US presidential election. (Confessore, 2018). Cambridge Analytica, owned by a large donor to far-right organizations, apparently sought to play a major role in assuring the election of Donald Trump. To that end, they surreptitiously obtained personal data from Facebook to develop profiles on tens of millions of potential American voters in order to selectively target them with misleading pro-Trump and anti-Clinton ads. Cambridge Analytica harvested not only the results of psychological surveys that Facebook users had taken, but also information on anyone linked as "friends" to the leaked Facebook accounts, vastly expanding the range of victims of the leak.

At first, Facebook's corporate leadership was silent in the face of the developing Cambridge Analytica scandal. Eventually, Facebook's chief technology officer conceded that accounts of as many as 87 million Facebook users had been compromised by Cambridge Analytica. On the heels of that concession, in early April of 2018, Facebook's chief information security officer, Alex Stamos, announced his resignation from Facebook over disagreements with top Facebook leaders concerning his recommendation that Facebook disclose to the public the degree to which its platform had been used by Russian operatives to interfere with the 2016 US election. Mark Zuckerberg, CEO of Facebook, was subpoenaed in April of 2018 to appear before both branches of the US Congress, and, after initially playing down the impact of the Cambridge Analytica breach of Facebook users' accounts, Zuckerberg conceded under hostile questioning that Facebook's security had not been adequate to protect the personal data of its users, and to prevent Cambridge Analytica from skirting election laws.

Meanwhile, Cambridge Analytica became embroiled in a second Facebook-associated scandal; this time involving harvesting of data from Facebook users in Britain, with the aim of targeting disinformation to susceptible voters in the Brexit referendum. Its principal officer, Alexander Nix, was suspended from the firm after a video was leaked of him boasting about using seduction and bribery to influence foreign elections. In testimony before Parliament, a former Cambridge Analytica employee acknowledged that the company had helped pro-Brexit groups in the lead-up to the referendum. It was no longer possible for the executives of social media platforms to deny that the unregulated "Wild West" of social media could do serious damage to civic society and its institutions. Mark Zuckerberg's naïve Facebook corporate slogan, "Move fast and break things" appeared to be all too accurate; Facebook had moved at blinding speed in the growth of its reach and power, and the evidence was mounting that among the things that were at risk of being broken in the process was democracy itself.

Fake news and market manipulation

Manipulation of the political process is not the only form of surreptitious manipulation that can be achieved though fake online postings. Online corporations collect vast realms of data about everyone who uses the Internet – our medical information, our political and religious beliefs, what we buy and what we are even thinking about buying. That data is then commodified and sold to anyone who wants to target us – whether for financial gain or political manipulation. For example, Facebook has been implicated (Dwoskin and Timberg, 2018) in the provision of fake reviews on e-commerce sites such as Amazon.com. Facebook hosts hundreds of groups who organize paid review-writing campaigns designed to move a particular product up the Amazon charts. In Dwoskin and Timberg's investigative study, they found the example of a hitherto-unknown brand of Chinese headphones that had garnered only a handful of reviews on the Amazon site, until, in one five-day stretch, the headphones received 300 new 5-star reviews. Within two months, these headphones had nearly a thousand reviews, and had become the top-rated headphones, supplanting famous headphone brands. As it turns out, fake news can infest the marketplace as perniciously as the political arena.

Legal responses to fake news in social media: the United States

Given the serious harm that social media-driven fake news can cause to society, what can the law do to deal with false information propagated through social media? The traditional legal remedy for damaging lies has been through the law of libel, which provides money damages to compensate victims of lies for the harm caused to their reputations and livelihood. Large damage awards in libel actions might drive some purveyors of false information out of business. Even the mere possibility of a ruinous libel judgment might cause purveyors of fake news to think twice about recklessly spreading falsehoods.

However, libel law in the United States turns out to be especially ill-equipped to stem the flow of fake news shared via social media, or even to provide redress after the fact for those harmed by it. American constitutional law, through its First Amendment jurisprudence, presumes that the appropriate cure for "bad speech" or even "false speech" is to counter it with "good" and "true" speech. This sanguine hope that truth will inevitably triumph over falsity seems hopelessly naïve. Well over a century ago, it was said "A lie can be halfway around the world while the truth is still putting its boots on." Even earlier, in the eighteenth century, Jonathan Swift wrote, "Falsehood flies, but the truth comes limping slowly after it." So, it has long been recognized that, as a practical matter, truth cannot easily displace lies in the public discourse. This is even truer today in light of the instantaneous transmissibility of viral social media posts.

There are many legal stumbling blocks for those who would attempt to sue fake news creators for libel in the United States. In order to sue someone that has authored a damaging lie and propagated it online, the victim must know the identity of that person. However, many fake news items are posted anonymously or under pseudonyms, and the injured party has no way of finding out the identity of the person who authored the harmful item. Even if the injured party can successfully identify the person or entity that lied about them, it is not enough to win an American libel action to show that someone disseminated false and damaging information that harmed one's reputation. In order to win a libel action concerning a public figure or an issue of public interest, the victim must prove that the libeling party knew that the statement was false or probably false (New York Times v. Sullivan 1964). It isn't enough to show that a reasonable person would have known that the statement in question was untrue. Proving what someone actually knew in this context is often impossible. This is why the majority of US libel actions are actually dismissed before trial.

Assuming that the libel victim knows who has posted the lie and can prove that the posting person knew that the information was untrue, the libel victim has an additional hurdle often standing in the way of vindication in court. Bringing a libel action is not cheap. Only victims with substantial financial assets can afford to go to court and litigate a libel action. Further, if the defendant in question has limited assets, the victim will probably never recoup their litigation costs even if they win the case. So, while libel as a cause of action may be technically available to victims of fake news, as a practical matter libel law seldom works to redress the harm caused to the libeled party.

Could a victim of false information online successfully sue the platform that hosted the libelous item? After all Facebook, YouTube, and Twitter are fantastically wealthy companies, and thus have the net worth to be well worth suing. Libel law generally does allow injured parties to sue those who repeat a libel, even if they did not originate the lie themselves. Since companies like Facebook clearly have the financial wherewithal to pay large judgments against them, one might ask why people harmed by lies propagated on social media don't sue Facebook and other social media entities. The answer to that question is buried in what was a small subsection of the omnibus Communications Decency Act passed by the US Congress in 1996. The thrust of the act was to create legal regulations for the expanding Internet, especially with respect to sexually explicit content that children surfing the Web might stumble upon in cyberspace. The Communications Decency Act provided a complex regulatory framework designed to prevent minors from accessing indecent or sexually explicit materials online. However, one small section of the law, Section 230, contained a provision stating that online service providers and platforms that are not themselves the content authors are absolutely immune from all legal liability for the things they disseminate. This blanket immunity would hold true even when the provider is given specific notice that content being hosted is malicious, untrue, or out-and-out unlawful (*Jones v. Dirty World Entertainment Recordings LLC*, 2014).

In 1997, shortly after passage of the Communications Decency Act, the American Civil Liberties Union sued to have the law declared unconstitutional in *Reno v. ACLU*. The Supreme Court agreed with almost every argument advanced by the ACLU, including the argument that terms like "indecent" and "patently offensive" to describe the content that would have to be blocked for children were indeed too vague in their denoted scope to satisfy due process. Virtually the entire Communications Decency Act was overturned, except for one small provision: Section 230. In the end, the parts of the law that gave the law its name were invalidated, but the section of the law giving absolute immunity to online platforms from legal liability in all contexts survived.

Lower courts agreed that Congress, whether wisely or not, had granted complete immunity for Internet platforms that were not themselves the author of harmful content hosted by the platform. For example, a number of lawsuits were filed against the website Backpages, which published online personal ads soliciting sexual services. Some of those lawsuits were filed on behalf of minors who had been sex trafficked through Backpages hosted ads, and, in some cases, violently assaulted and even killed in the course of that trafficking. In one of these actions, *Doe v. Backpages.com LLC* (2016), the court held that, even in the face of crimes as serious as sex trafficking of minors, the plain language of Section 230 conferred absolute immunity for online platforms regarding harms caused by content hosted on the platform. A federal court in New York (*Cohen v. Facebook*, 2017) likewise ruled that Facebook was immune from legal liability for knowingly allowing a terrorist organization to post content on Facebook inciting and encouraging terrorist violence. In a case brought against Google in 2010, the reviewing court held that even endorsement, sponsorship, or encouragement by online platforms of illegal conduct by content providers did not defeat Section 230's absolute immunity from liability for the online platforms (*Black v. Google*, 2010).

Courts interpreting Section 230 as constituting absolute immunity from all legal liability often justify this position by analogy to situations where a mere transmitter of information ought not be legally liable for harm caused by that information. For example, someone who happened to deliver a newspaper to a house should not be liable for defamatory content within the newspaper simply because they had caused the offending paper to be deposited on someone's doorstep. Internet platforms, say these courts, are doing nothing more than allowing content created by others to land on our metaphorical doorsteps. A second line of argument, particularly in the earliest cases decided under Section 230, emphasized the nascent, vulnerable quality of internet businesses; requiring online platforms to screen out unlawful content would stifle these vulnerable businesses and interfere with the full development of the internet.

Legal responses to fake news in social media: the world outside the United States

If American law has shown no real ability to police the social media world, is the European Union better positioned to check social media abuses? In theory, most EU member states have libel and fraud laws that are friendlier to victims of smears and lies than is the case in the US. For example, in most EU countries, the libel victim only needs to prove that a reasonable person would have appreciated that the libel was false, as opposed to the US requirement that the libeling party knew that the libel was false. But, though the legal rules are more favorable to victims of fake news in the EU, EU libel victims still face the same practical considerations that make libel cases an unrealistic way to address the harm of fake news in the US – that is, the cost and time-consuming nature of libel actions make them impractical as a meaningful remedy for being lied about. In addition, many harmful "fake news" stories propagated on social media are not directly defamatory of a particular individual, such that no one would have standing to sue for libel in any event.

Some European countries are considering other legal tools to hold social media providers responsible for hosting fake news. In the wake of the Cambridge Analytica scandal in connection with the Brexit referendum, the UK has opened a parliamentary investigation into the threat to democratic institutions posed by the proliferation of fake news and on what legal action could be taken to combat it. Germany has proposed a stringent law that would impose hefty corporate fines of up to 50 million euros when social media providers fail to promptly block and delete fake news from their services. Corporate officials themselves would be personally liable for up to five million euros per episode.

Other countries concerned about the corrosive impact of social media-propagated fake news have also begun to take action. Singapore, for example, passed the Protection from Online Falsehoods and Manipulation Bill in early 2019 in order to combat fake news – a bill which has been criticized as providing a potential vehicle for government censorship of dissent. Since the bill is very recent, it is not clear whether those fears of government misuse of the law will come to pass. However, as a multi-ethnic society, Singapore is particularly vulnerable to online extremist propaganda designed to sow racial tensions. In the face of worldwide use of inflammatory social media postings to support extremist ideologies, government inaction would be unwise if not irresponsible. Even if the Singaporean law is ultimately used exclusively in those kinds of cases and not to stifle legitimate voices of dissent, however, it is difficult to see how Singapore can enforce this law against US-based companies in a meaningful way. The maximum fine permitted against Internet platforms such as Facebook is one million Singaporean dollars, or a bit less than 750,000 US dollars.

Financial punishments like those contemplated in the German and Singapore statutes are not remotely high enough to deter social media corporations from continuing to profit from disseminating fake news. In 2019, Facebook was hit with a five-billion-dollar fine from the US Federal Trade Commission for violating an earlier consent decree regarding failure to protection personal user information (New York Times Editorial Board, 2019). This fine was by far the largest fine ever levied by the Federal Trade Commission. The next day, Facebook's stock actually went up in value. The market recognized that, for a corporation as wealthy as Facebook, even a five-billion-dollar fine is trivial to their profitability. Even if the fines assessed were more substantial, social media companies are simply too big and too wealthy to be impacted by the actions of the individual nation-states whose cohesion and civic societies are threatened by divisive fake news propagated by social media. Social media corporations appear to have little to fear from piecemeal legal regulation on a national level.

Self-regulation by social media corporations to respond to fake news on their platforms

In the mid-1990s, when the Communications Decency Act was passed by the US Congress, online platforms successfully argued that it would be unfair to impose liability on them when they had no technologically practical way of assessing their postings for pernicious content. The volume of postings, they argued, was simply too high to be adequately screened. If they were required to pre-screen postings for malicious or false content, they claimed, the Internet would choke on the bottleneck created. A healthy and vibrant online world could only be achieved at the price of allowing a certain amount of harmful postings along with all the valuable content.

If this were ever true, it is not the case today. The use of machine learning iterative algorithms in assessing collections of data make it possible to analyze enormous quantities of raw data for content. Indeed, if this weren't the case, the kind of user-identified data-scraping that Facebook and other social media sites do for purposes of targeted advertising would be of little value to them. We know that Facebook, for example, analyzes staggering quantities of consumer data using algorithms in order to enhance its revenue stream. In fact, during the hearing in which Mark Zuckerberg, Facebook's CEO, testified before Congress, Zuckerberg conceded that Facebook had the capacity to analyze bulk user content. The scale of what Facebook can do in this regard was revealed indirectly in that hearing when Zuckerberg was asked about the invisible pixels that Facebook imbeds into non-Facebook websites – a practice that permits Facebook to collect and analyze data from users of those websites even if those users do not have Facebook accounts themselves. When asked from how many such websites Facebook scrapes data, Zuckerberg said, "I'll have to get back to you on that." When the follow-up question was asked, "Could it be as many as 100 million websites?" Zuckerberg did not deny that that number could be correct. Add to the users of those hundreds of millions of websites the online data created by the 2.2 billion people with active Facebook accounts, and it becomes clear that social media corporations do currently have the capability to monitor vast quantities of content-data when it is to their financial benefit to do so. In fact, they already do so.

Despite the technological ability of social media corporations to detect and deal with misuse of their platforms, to date they have been remarkably slow to respond to the issue of misuse of their platforms. Take the example of a Twitter account owned by the Russian intelligence operation Internet Research Agency that masqueraded as the Twitter feed for the Republican party of the state of Tennessee (Ebert, 2017). The fake Russian Twitter account ended up with ten times the followers of the actual Twitter account of the Tennessee Republican Party. The fake Russian Twitter account was quoted dozens of times by conservative news outlets and blogs during the final months of the 2016 election cycle. And, when the governor and the Republican Party of Tennessee complained to Twitter about the bogus account in their name, Twitter did nothing. They lodged three separate complaints to Twitter in the final weeks of 2016 and Twitter ignored them. Not until the recent Congressional hearings on Russian use of social media in election interference did Twitter quietly suspend that particular fake Russian account.

In the wake of public outcry over the use of social media in manipulating the democratic process with fake news stories, governments are stirring themselves to act, even contemplating government regulation of social media. In response, Facebook and other social media are finally conceding that they must develop forms of self-regulation, perhaps hoping to avoid government-imposed rules that might do economic harm to their business models. While self-regulation may sound like allowing the fox to guard the henhouse – and there is no question that the self-interest of social media corporations in pre-empting government regulation plays a huge role in their new-found enthusiasm for developing ways to make social media less toxic – it must be said that government regulation is generally slow and reactive rather than proactive. If Facebook's motto was "Move fast and break things," government regulation often lives by the motto, "Go slow and maybe things will get better on their own."

Facebook and other social media platforms have assured the public that government action is not necessary, since they have promised that they will self-regulate to prevent their services from being used in harmful ways. Unfortunately, though, there are good reasons to think that voluntary self-regulation is not up to the task of reining in those aspects of social media corporations that are most worrisome to Western democracies. Russian trolls and bots provided false and misleading news to more than half of the American electorate during the 2016 presidential election; and the British populace apparently was similarly affected during the run-up to the Brexit vote. Yet, despite the great concern expressed by the American Congress and the British Parliament about the potential for foreign interference in their electoral processes, social media corporations have still not developed adequate internal safeguards to prevent future activities of this sort.

Facing increasing public criticism and the potential for government action, social media corporations have begun to take steps to police the flow of harmful content on their platforms. Facebook, for example, has hired 50 fact-checking firms to try to weed out fake news from their platforms (Lu, 2019). The British non-profit fact-checking organization Full Fact issued a report on Facebook's efforts in this regard. It concluded that Facebook has taken the first steps towards developing a partially automated fact checking system, but that the company has not publicly released enough information about their processes to allow external assessment of whether, and by how much, fake news items are being spotted and removed from circulation. Greater transparency is needed before we can be confident that social media mega-corporations like Facebook will voluntarily develop mechanisms to purge destructive and divisive material from their platforms. This is particularly so when their advertising-based business model still depends on maximizing user clicks and eyeballs on their sites.

A coordinated approach in law and policy to de-weaponizing fake news in social media

Social media corporations do have vastly greater technological resources than government agencies have to police new and growing threats to society from those bent on using social media to destabilize democratic institutions and undermine social cohesion. For that reason, governmental regulation, while essential, cannot itself solve problem of the misuse of social media. Despite the sanguine assurances of social media executives, neither can self-regulation by social media corporations be society's sole form of defense against harmful social media postings. However, corporate responsibility principles demand that social media take responsibility to protect society from pernicious use of their platforms. In that regard, self-regulation by social media platforms, backed by government sanctions for failure to adequately screen content posted, needs to be part of a comprehensive approach to de-weaponizing social media.

As this chapter has described, piecemeal regulatory schemes on a national level are doomed to irrelevance given the ability of these mega-corporations to absorb fines for the harm caused on their platforms. It would take an internationally-coordinated effort to develop enforceable international conventions capable of holding companies like Facebook accountable for failing to prevent harm caused by their platforms. Unfortunately, it is hard to imagine the United States currently joining this kind of international convention. Since the United States Supreme Court has ruled that corporations have the right to spend unlimited money in the electoral process (*Citizens United v. Federal Election Commission*, 2010), a company like Facebook that can shrug off a five billion dollar fine would no doubt be willing to spend a great deal more than that to ensure its immunity from liability will continue to be enshrined in US law.

There may be alternative legal theories that could successfully pressure social media corporations to take effective action to prevent harmful use of their platforms. One avenue of potential legal regulation would be via data privacy laws such as the European Union's General Data Protection Regulation (see generally Abate 2018). The German competition regulatory agency Bundeskartellamt in 2017 investigated whether Facebook was violating the GDPR in failing to get informed consent from users for its data collection and dissemination practices, and it issued a report finding that Facebook's practices were not in compliance with the GDPR. The investigation was not empowered to sanction Facebook, however. Similar investigations are underway in Italy, Belgium, France, the Netherlands, and Spain. If European regulators determine that the GDPR has been violated, the sanctions available include fines of up to 20 million euros or 4% of the company's annual global revenue. Fines of that latter amount ought to get the attention of social media corporations. It is unclear, however, whether requiring Facebook and other social media platforms to obtain more explicit consent from users to their data collection practices will result in changes to how platforms propagate false information. After all, propagation of fake news is not itself a violation of the GDPR.

A more immediate tool to get the attention of social media corporations could be through the use of antitrust law. Antitrust law exists to prevent consolidation within an industry that would permit monopolistic practices to be adopted that harm consumers. Classically, the harm that antitrust law was designed to prevent was monopoly pricing. A number of antitrust scholars (Srinivasan, 2018; Deeks, 2019; Katz, 2019) have suggested that the harms caused by social media consolidation, although not the price-gouging regulated by classical antitrust law, could and should give rise to antitrust remedies.

Among the sanctions that can be imposed for antitrust violations is the forced break-up of the monopolistic enterprise. Given the draconian potential remedy of the break-up of social media conglomerates, this legal tool ought to be exceptionally effective in pressuring social media platforms to prioritize preventing their platforms from being used to harm democratic societies. Of course, it is the very draconian nature of the forced dismemberment of these companies that makes it certain that they would fight antitrust regulation with every weapon they could bring to bear. In the end, these mega-corporations are simply too big, too wealthy, too pervasive, and too powerful to expect political and legal institutions to be able to rein them in without an epic legal fight. Still, the threat of this "mother of all legal battles" might well cause companies like Facebook to consider whether preventing this kind of high-stakes litigation would be preferable to risking a break-up by fighting it. Keeping the antitrust option on the table would likely be further encouragement to Facebook to take seriously its corporate responsibility to ensure that it is not harboring content that undermines the fabric of the societies in which they operate.

Digital literacy as a resource in the fight against fake news

While both legal regulation and corporate self-regulation have a role to play in banishing fake news from social media, there is an additional resource that could be deployed to de-weaponize fake news: public education. One reason why the public is so susceptible to the siren song of fake news is that citizens lack education in how to make critical judgments concerning what is promulgated online. The Canadian government has recently begun requiring secondary schools to teach young people about media literacy – how to assess the credibility and reliability about what they see online. That kind of digital literacy education would be a step in the right direction to fight the socially corrosive effects of false news through education in critical assessment of information received online. If basic education is designed to equip people with the knowledge and skills needed for decision-making in everyday life, then digital literacy and critical thinking about digitally-acquired information should be within the core mission of any educational system in the present day (Petrucco and Ferranti, 2017). Libraries, traditionally the public custodians of knowledge, could play a vital role in this mission as well (Cooke, 2017). In fact, even in the absence of specific training in digital literacy, general education incorporating critical thinking skills has been correlated with greater skepticism regarding the reliability of online news and more accurate discernment of the reliability of individual online news items (Allcott and Gentzkow, 2017: 228–229).

It has been suggested that social media platforms do not yet have the information assessment algorithms needed to accurately categorize reliable news as opposed to fake news. At this time, that is probably true. However, current machine-learning algorithms are able to flag items as likely or potentially fake news, even when they cannot discriminate those categories with precision. Warning labels on potentially false news items could alert consumers to their unreliability. European journalistic organizations have developed a collaborative fact-checking network to help label questionable "news" as untrustworthy – a network that so far extends to 37 news and media groups – including the BBC, *le Monde*, Bloomberg, the *International Business Times*, and Reuters. *Le Monde* has gone a step further – developing Chrome and Firefox plug-ins that provide automatic pop-up warnings when online users view dubious stories. Such signals would warn consumers to be especially careful in assessing the accuracy and reliability of online information that might otherwise be believed.

Conclusion

Law is unlikely on its own to have the power to take the steps needed to "unfriend" Facebook, Twitter, YouTube, and Google. Nor is legal regulation likely to successfully keep purveyors of fake news and proponents of violent extremism from attempting to undermine democratic institutions and sow deep and dangerous divisions within democratic societies. Legal regulation clearly has a role to play in blunting the bite of fake news, as does self-regulation by social media platforms in the shadow of potential legal liability. In addition, education in digital literacy and critical thinking can help to inoculate the public against being fooled by fake news or radicalized by extremists. Perhaps the ultimate question is not so much should the law "unfriend" Facebook, but rather, shouldn't we all?

References

Abate, Serafino. 2018. Antitrust and consumer enforcement in data markets – Are new theories of harm based on privacy degradation hitting the mark? http://hdl.handle.net/10419/184924.

Allcott, Hunt and Gentzkow, Matthew. 2017. Social media and fake news in the 2016 election. *Journal of Economic Perspectives 3*, 211–236.

Berger, J. M. 2013. Zero degrees of al Qaeda. *Foreign Policy*, 14 August.

Black v. Google. 2010. WL 3222147 (N.D. Cal. 2010).

Citizens United v. Federal Election Commission. 2010. 558 US 310.

Cohen v. Facebook. 2017. U.S. Dist. LEXIS 76701. E.D. N.Y.

Confessore, Nicholas. 2018. Cambridge Analytica and Facebook: The scandal and the fallout so far. www.nytimes.com/2018/04/04/us/politics/cambridge-analytica-scandal-fallout.html.

Cooke, Nicole A. 2017. Post-truth, truthiness, and alternative facts: Information behavior and critical information consumption for a new age. *The Library Quarterly 87*, 211–221.

Deeks, Ashley. 2019. Facebook unbound? *Virginia Law Review 105*, 1–17.

Doe v. Backpages.com LLC. 2016. 817 F.3d 12. 1st. Cir.

Dwoskin, Elizabeth and Timberg, Craig. 2018. How merchants use Facebook to flood Amazon with fake reviews. www.washingtonpost.com/business/economy/how-merchants-secretly-use-facebook-to-flood-amazon-with-fake-reviews/2018/04/23/5dad1e30-4392-11e8-8569-26fda6b404c7_story.html.

Ebert, Joel. 2017. Twitter suspends fake Tennessee GOP account later linked to Russian "troll farm." www.tennessean.com/story/news/politics/2017/10/18/twitter-suspends-fake-tennessee-gop-account-later-linked-russian-troll-farm/776937001/.

Flaxman, Seth, Goel, Sharad and Rao, Justin M. 2016. Filter bubbles, echo chambers, and online news consumption. *Public Opinion Quarterly 80*, S1, 298–320.

Jones v. Dirty World Entertainment Recordings LLC. 2014. 755 F.3d 398. 6th Cir.

Katz, Michael L. 2019. Multi-sided platforms, big data, and a little antitrust policy. *Review of Industrial Organization 54*, 695–716.

Lu, Donna. 2019. The facts about Facebook's fact-checking. *New Scientist*, August 3, p. 9.

Matsa, Katerina Eva and Shearer, Elisa. 2018. News use across social media platforms in 2018. www.journalism.org/2018/09/10/news-use-across-social-media-platforms-2018/.

Mozur, Paul. 2018. A genocide incited by Facebook, with posts from Myanmar's Military. www.nytimes.com/2018/10/15/technology/myanmar-facebook-genocide.html

New York Times v. Sullivan. 1964. 376 U.S. 254.

New York Times Editorial Board. 2019. A $5 billion fine for Facebook won't fix privacy. www.nytimes.com/2019/07/25/opinion/facebook-fine-5-billion.html.

O'Callaghan, Derek, Greene, Derek, Conway, Maura, Carthy, Joe and Cunningham, Padraig. (2015). Down the (white) rabbit hole: The extreme right and online recommender systems. *Social Science Computer Review 33*, 459–478.

Petrucco, Corrado and Ferranti, Cinzia. 2017. Developing critical thinking in online search. *Journal of the E-learning and Knowledge Society 13*, 35–45.

Rampell, Katherine. 2016. Americans – especially but not exclusively Trump voters – believe crazy, wrong things. www.washingtonpost.com/news/rampage/wp/2016/12/28/americans-especially-but-not-exclusively-trump-voters-believe-crazy-wrong-things/.

Reno v. American Civil Liberties Union. 1997. 521 U.S. 844.

Seidenberg, Steven. 2017a. Yesterday's fake news. *American Bar Association Journal 103*, 24–27.

Seidenberg, Steven. 2017b. Lies and libel. *American Bar Association Journal 103*, 27–28.

Silverman, Craig. 2016. This analysis shows how fake election news stories outperformed real news on Facebook. *BuzzFeedNews*, November 16.

Srinivasan, Dina. 2018. The antitrust case against Facebook: A monopolist's journey toward pervasive surveillance in spite of consumers' preference for privacy. *Berkeley Business Law Journal 16*, 39–98.

14 "Fake news" as interdiscursive illusion

A challenge to law, social media, and free speech

Vijay K. Bhatia

Overview

Fake news is not a recent phenomenon, as is often believed. Posetti and Matthews (2018) claim that mobilising and manipulating information was a feature of history long before modern journalism established standards that define news as a genre based on particular rules of integrity. They point out that an early record dates back to ancient Rome, when Antony met Cleopatra and his political enemy Octavian launched a smear campaign against him with "short, sharp slogans written upon coins in the style of archaic Tweets, which painted Anthony as a womaniser and a drunk, implying he had become Cleopatra's puppet, having been corrupted by his affair with her" (Kaminska, 2017).[1] The perpetrator became Augustus, the first Roman Emperor and "fake news had allowed Octavian to hack the republican system once and for all." However, they further point out that the weaponization of information on an unprecedented scale has taken effect only in recent years primarily due to the new technology, especially social networks that are often exploited by anti-democratic governments, populist politicians and dishonest corporate entities.

Fake news is now seen as one of the greatest threats to democracy, free debate and the Western order. It was also named as word of the year in 2017, raising tensions between nations, and is very much likely to lead to regulation of social media. A Google search of "fake news" listed more than 1.4 billion results on the 30 October 2019, which include all sorts of variations in alternative news, such as misinformation, spin, conspiracy theories, reporting mistakes, satire, parodies, propaganda, and reporting that people just don't like, etc. which makes the term "fake news" confusing and sometimes meaningless. In order to gain credibility, fake news is often spread through the use of appropriated news websites, which often impersonate well-known news sources.

Fake news: modern incarnation

During the 2016 US Presidential campaign, fake news became President Donald Trump's most favourite epithet to express his grudge against the news media. He took up the phrase in January 2017 when in response to a question, he said "you are fake news" to CNN reporter Jim Acosta. Around the same time, he started repeating the phrase on Twitter, which Trump supporters widely accepted and made their own. Jeff Hemsley, a Syracuse University professor in social media claims that Trump started using this term for any news that was not favourable to him or which he simply disliked. Alcott and Gentzkow (2017) claim that fake news was both widely shared on Facebook and heavily tilted in favour of Donald Trump. They found that 115 pro-Trump fake stories were shared 30 million times, whereas 41 pro-Clinton fake stories were shared 7.6 million times. During this US presidential campaign, so many social media posts with competing (dis) information and accusations about Trump and Hillary Clinton became viral that it became almost impossible to distinguish fake from the real. Most social media platforms encourage and make it possible for users to see what they want to see or believe in rather than what is real or factual.

As briefly mentioned earlier, fake news is meant to mislead, disinform, mostly by fictitious or fabricated content with an intention to undermine a person's character, integrity, belief system, or status. Most often the purpose of initiating or propagating fake news is to take political advantage, or profit from advertising on fake news websites. Jestin Coler (2016), a self-proclaimed godfather of fake news, who started one of the first companies responsible for fake news *Disinfomedia*, claimed that one could earn thousands of dollars a month from advertisements alone when people read fake news in social media, particularly Facebook.

It is also interesting to observe that most fake news stories are disguised as factual news, often in social media, sometimes with serious, most often negative, social consequences. For instance, on 1 April 2018, social media in India projected misleading claims against the Central Government that they were undermining the interests of the Dalits, which led to nation-wide protests, often violent all-over the country resulting in several deaths and injuries. Similarly, Polonski (2016) claims that, "a large-scale analysis of social media in the lead up to Brexit showed that not only were there twice as many Leave Brexit supporters on Instagram, but they were also five times more active than Remain activists."[2] Similar patterns emerged on Twitter. Foreign accounts were reported to have sent "hundreds of thousands of pro-leave tweets on polling day" (Posetti and Matthews, 2018). Similarly, Dewey (2016) of the *Washington Post*, based on her interview of Paul Horner, who is a prolific fake-news creator, claimed that he believed that Trump was in the White House because of him. "His followers don't fact-check anything – they'll post everything, believe anything." He continued,

Honestly, people are definitely dumber. They just keep passing stuff around. Nobody fact-checks anything anymore – I mean, that's how Trump got elected. He just said whatever he wanted, and people believed everything, and when the things he said turned out not to be true, people didn't care because they'd already accepted it. It's real scary. I've never seen anything like it.

The phenomenon has thus gained so much notoriety in recent years that most Americans, as revealed in a recent Pew Research Center study, rate it as a larger problem than racism, climate change, or terrorism (Mitchell et al., 2019). The most important and yet scary fact about fake news is its use of social media, which is no less than a cyborg[3] with unlimited reach to millions of readers in no time as compared to conventional news media. Technology seems to have given a strong potential for its misuse as a threat to social order.

Demystifying alternative news

Discussing the complexity and variations in and around fake news, Sharma et al. (2018: 3–4). claim that most definitions of fake news as factually false or incorrect and designed to deceive the reader into believing it is true are narrow and restricted either by the type of information or the intent of deception. They claim the definition should capture and differentiate "fabricated content (completely false), misleading content (misleading use of information to frame an issue), imposter content (genuine sources impersonated with false sources), manipulated content (genuine information manipulated to deceive) … and false context (genuine content shared with false contextual information)." Savvas et al. (2018) also point out different types of fake news identified by their motive or intent, such as "malicious intent (to hurt or disrepute), profit (for financial gain by increasing views), influence (to manipulate public opinion), sow discord (to create disorder and confusion), passion (to promote ideological biases), amusement (individual entertainment)."

Similarly, Wardle (2017) categorizes seven types of mis- and disinformation;

1   Satire or parody, with no intention to cause harm to others;
2   False connection, when headlines, visuals or captions don't support the content;
3   Misleading content to frame an issue or individual;
4   False context, when genuine content is shared with false contextual information;
5   Imposter content, when genuine sources are impersonated with made-up sources;
6   Manipulated content, when genuine information is manipulated to deceive;
7   Fabricated content, when new content is false, and designed to deceive and harm.

As one can see from these studies, fake news is a term that has been used as a catch-all term to refer to a wide range of complex appropriations of conventional news, especially in the context of the present-day (dis)information explosion through the electronically mediated social media, which can reach millions of readers within no time. Social media, such as YouTube, WhatsApp, Facebook, Instagram, and many other such media applications have the capability to make any news viral and buzzworthy, a facility which one could never imagine through print media. Figure 14.1 below illustrates some of the factors that make fake news popular and, at the same time, dangerous considering our unprecedented dependence on social media.

It's hardly surprising that many of these electronically mediated sites often boast of many times more visitors than conventional authentic news websites. More often than not, a news item becomes visible to us only when it is electronically shared, forwarded, or re-posted with or without any comments. Whichever way one may define or view these complex variations of fake news, there are at the very least two characteristics that are common to all of them: they all are what Bhatia (2017) calls "interdiscursive appropriations" of conventional factually verifiable news reports, and at the same time, they are what Bhatia (2015) refers to as "discursive illusions." In order to understand more about these two aspects of fake news, let me first give a brief account of these two concepts, i.e., "Interdiscursivity in Critical Genre Analysis" (Bhatia, 2017) and "Discourse of Illusion" (Bhatia, 2015).

Interdiscursivity in critical genre analysis

The concept of interdiscursivity, which is sometimes subsumed under intertextuality, is not entirely new and can be traced back to the works of Foucault (1981), Bakhtin (1986), Kristeva (1980), Fairclough (1995), Candlin and Maley (1997), Bhatia (2004) and a number of other scholars. However, these two concepts have not been fully explored and sufficiently developed to investigate some of the complexities we often encounter in discursive and professional practices in genre analysis. To make an initial distinction between these two related concepts, Bhatia (2010) argues that intertextuality refers to the appropriation of prior texts transforming the past into the present in relatively

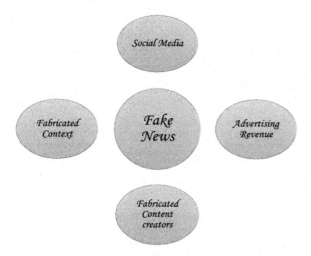

Figure 14.1 Contextual configuration of fake news

conventionalized and often standardized contexts. One of most distinctive aspects of intertextuality is that such text-internal appropriations are visible in the two texts, one that is appropriated from, and the other it is used in. Generally, these appropriations are explicitly referred to or adequately signalled in the present text.

Interdiscursivity, on the other hand, refers to more innovative attempts to create various forms of hybrid (such as mixing, embedding or bending of generic norms) and other relatively novel constructs by appropriating or exploiting text-external discursive resources, primarily shared conventions typically associated with other genres, professional practices, and disciplinary cultures, as indicated in Figure 14.2.

Interdiscursivity thus accounts for a variety of discursive as well as professional practices interdiscursively appropriated across genres and professional practices. More generally, interdiscursivity can thus be regarded as the appropriation of primarily text-external semiotic resources (which may include generic, professional and more generally socio-pragmatic) across any two or more genres, professional practices and/or professional culture. Appropriations across texts thus give rise to intertextual relations, whereas appropriations across conventions of specific genres, practices and cultures constitute interdiscursive relations. It is important to remember that although these two rhetorical resources are conceptually distinctive, they may often be co-present in the same generic construct.

In order to develop a comprehensive and evidence-based awareness of the motives and intentions of such disciplinary and professional practices, we need to look closely at the multiple discourses, actions and voices that play a significant role in the formation of specific discursive practices within or even across relevant institutional and organizational frameworks used to fulfil professional objectives of specific disciplinary or discourse communities. Such discursive interactions invariably take place and are accountable within the framework of interdiscursivity.

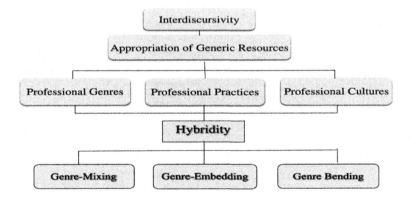

Figure 14.2 Interdiscursive appropriation across genres

Source: Bhatia, 2017: 37.

Interdiscursive appropriation in alternative news

The conventional news report as a genre has been well-established for a long time with its unique and typical communicative purpose of objectively reporting everyday happenings in the world. News reports have always been regarded as factual in their content as well as context, and they often reflect their typical conventions, some of which include, reporting content based on the events of the day objectively without any bias in the context that is real and authentic, often attributing information to reliable and established sources, invariably using the principle of recenticity. Most of these conventions are meant to validate the reliability of reporting, although it is not always true that conventional news reports are entirely factual, true or objectively reported. Sometimes news reporters can and do make mistakes, and may misinform, or have a slant on the factual content encouraging a specific interpretation they would like their readers to favour, but they rarely attempt to disinform or mislead readers. In today's practice however, we often find a variety of alternative news, which largely appropriate news reporting conventions mentioned here. One of the common variations is what is popularly known as parodies or satires for humour or entertainment, which may be called infotainment, a special form of alternative news. Its primary motivation is pure entertainment. It often makes use of current news as pegs to appropriate both content and context, and also conventions of news reporting to entertain live audiences on television. One of the prime examples of such infotainment was the famous British television comedy "Not the Nine O'clock News" on BBC2 (1979–1982), which was a comic alternative to the popular "Nine O'clock News" on BBC1. It featured satirical sketches on current news stories and popular culture featuring Rowan Atkinson and Mel Smith. The idea perhaps came from the 1978 faux publication of *Not The New York Times,* a spoof of the famous newspaper (Dwyer, 2008) which was not published for more than two months at the time because of a general strike in New York City, thus leaving it without papers. Parodies or satires thus used for entertainment can be viewed as a form of appropriation of conventional news, which appropriate factual content for humour often in cleverly managed fictional context.

Yet another subtle variation on factual news emerged from an ideological and political bias in news reporting when opinions were presented as factual news. This alternative form of news is what I would like to view as "discursive illusions" (Bhatia, 2015), where one is inclined to interpret content that suits the reporter's ideological bias or political beliefs. It is interesting to note that such subjective interpretations of objective or factual presentations of events is becoming increasing popular in today's ideologically compelling world. Another factor that has encouraged this trend is the commercialization of media houses where powerful entities, especially ruling parties, find it easier to manipulate news media through favours in the form of advertising revenue.

Fake news reports, on the other hand, invariably appropriate most of these conventions for the sake of giving face validity to their fabricated content in the context that may resemble the real but is often fabricated. Fake news writers also try their best to fake some of the real and well-established news sources, especially websites. They also appropriate the principle of recenticity by using a catchy and sensational headline to attract their believers and unsuspecting readers. When they refer to real events or developments, they do not hesitate to cross the limits of favoured interpretation by re-contextualising content often in fabricating contexts. Sometimes the selection and recontextualization of content is managed through an ideological lens, favouring a specific inter-pretation appropriate for what Bhatia (2017) calls "private intentions" of the reporter in the socially shared context.

As discussed here, both fake news and parodies are different forms of in-terdiscursive appropriation of conventions typically associated with factual news reporting. In the case of fake news, both the content as well as the context are fabricated or manipulated to mislead, misinform, or disinform audiences for negative purposes, whereas in the case of satires and parodies, content and contexts are manipulated for humour. However, the common denominator in all these various appropriated forms of conventional news is the nature and function of what Bhatia (2017) calls interdiscursive appropriation of content, context, and above all, conventions for various objectives. So, in order to ac-count for the process of constructing most forms of fake news we need not only a good understanding of interdiscursivity as appropriation of text-external re-sources, including conventions of factual news reporting, but also to combine it with Discourse of Illusion (Bhatia, 2015), and consider various incarnations of fake news as interdiscursive illusions, which seems to offer a valid explanation to various forms of discursive constructions of news reporting, the conven-tional and the fake news. As a matter of principle, both can be accounted for by the rhetorical effects of appropriation. Let me give more substance to this line of argument.

Fake news as interdiscursive illusion

Defining Discourse of Illusion, Bhatia (2015) observes that we inhabit two realities: the subjective reality that we know and construct through our thinking, and the objective, physical reality of what is really out-there. She further points out that we cannot access this objective reality directly, although our conceptual systems do enable us to create a reconceptualization of it. Our minds, she points out, construct (or more appropriately subjectively re-conceptualize) the reality we confront, which is invariably influenced by our past experiences, cultural and socio-political ideologies, beliefs, and under-standings, all within a wider socio-pragmatic space, as indicated in Figure 14.3 (adapted from Bhatia, 2017).

Discursive illusions thus originate from our subjective reconceptualization of our perceptions of objective realities and are created only when we mistake this subjectivity for the actual objective reality, and act on these subjective re-constructions without any consideration of an alternate reality. She views the

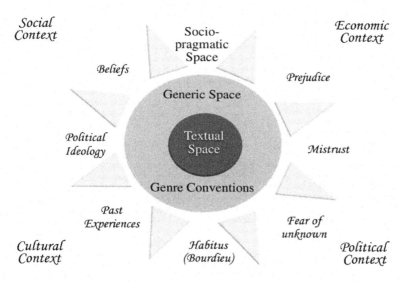

Figure 14.3 Socio-pragmatics of discursive illusion
Source: Bhatia, 2017.

Discourse of Illusion as an attempt by writers or speakers to convince their audiences that their conceptualization of reality is the objective one. Illusions are invariably created through discourse when writers and speakers, through various modalities (such as speeches, press releases, newspaper reports, etc.), seek legitimization of their arguments and beliefs. The discourse thus becomes the modality, the means to transform audiences' perceptions of the world (Bhatia, 2015). Discursive illusions thus tend to create an overarching narrative which defines or frames an issue or event in a subjective or ideological manner to which a particular discourse clan adheres. In other words, different discourse clans generate different narratives representing an issue or event based on their subjective conceptualizations of reality, and it is the emergence of various narratives, each fighting to become the dominant narrative, that gives rise to multiple discursive illusions.

Combining interdiscursive appropriation with the intention on the part of the news reporters gives expression to their individual interpretations or ma-nipulations of everyday events in the world as discursive illusions, often as alternative news, rather than reporting them factually. This is often achieved by manipulating or fabricating content and/or context for disinformation to con-struct and disseminate content and amounts to nothing less than discursive illusion. It is generally achieved through appropriation of content, context, and conventions of conventional news reporting to make it seem real. Thus, most forms of fake news discussed in the preceding sections can be considered interdiscursively ap-propriated illusions. The following diagram thus summarizes different forms of news, including conventional as well as some of the variations in alternative news.

Figure 14.4 Interdiscursive appropriation of conventional news

Socio-legal remedies to control fake news

A recent Pew Research Center Survey (2016) points out that people have grown distrustful of institutional media and hence have turned to alternative sources, especially digital forms of news reporting, including social media applications, such as WhatsApp, YouTube, Instagram, Twitter, and thousands of other (fake) news websites. Referring to the above survey, Katy Steinmetz reports in *Time* (9 August 2018) that

> only 18 percent of people have a lot of trust in national news organizations; nearly 75 percent said news organizations are biased.... Many users of social media do not look for serious reads or information, but for attractive catchy and sensational headings and, when they spot one, their natural instinct is to share it.

She further points out that

> the problem is not just malicious bots or chaos-loving trolls or Macedonian teenagers pushing phony stories for profit. The problem is also us, the susceptible readers. The better we understand the way we think in the digital world, the better chance we have to be part of the solution.

There have been innumerable instances across the globe where indiscriminate spread of different forms of fake news has triggered negative and undesirable consequences often resulting in serious disruptions in everyday life. Nugent (2018), referring to WhatsApp in *Time* reported that

> [o]n the evening of June 8, a 29-year-old sound engineer and a 30-year-old businessman were on their way to a picnic spot in India's Assam state when they stopped at a village to ask for directions. The villagers had been told, in a video circulating on the messaging app WhatsApp that child kidnappers were roaming the country. Believing these strangers were the ones they'd been warned about, the villagers formed a large mob, and, before the men could convince them otherwise, beat them to death.

> The video they had seen was actually an instructional safety video made in Pakistan but was shared with some text warning about kidnappers in the local area, causing fear and anger among the community.

Instances like these prompted the Indian Government into action, and the technology ministry said in a statement on 19 July that

> [T]he company would face legal action if it remained a "mute spectator" to the violent consequences of false stories circulating. "When rumours and fake news get propagated," it said, "the medium used for such propagation cannot evade responsibility."

These instances are not uncommon in the rest of the world, especially in Southeast Asia. One may legitimately ask, what could be the likely solution? One could think of two possible remedies, introducing laws to curb disinformation by various governments, and public awareness and education to distinguish fake news from genuine news.

Legal remedies and free speech

One of the most potent deterrents to introduce law against fake news is that any constraint on the spread of fake news is viewed as an infringement of free speech: one man's fake news is another man's free speech. This was first claimed by John Milton in 1644 when he specified freedom of speech as a multi-dimensional right that included the right to seek, receive, and disseminate information and ideas. Free speech is also guaranteed under Article 19 of the Universal Declaration of Human Rights adopted by the United Nations in 1948, which says:

Everyone has the right

- to freedom of opinion and expression; this right includes freedom
- to hold opinions without interference and
- to seek, receive and impart information and ideas through any media.

It is also recognized in various international laws, such as,

- International Covenant on Civil and Political Rights,
- European Convention on Human Rights,
- American Convention on Human Rights.

The only alternative is media literacy to encourage readers to become more media literate by checking what they read against other reliable sources.

Let us look at some of the measures undertaken in various jurisdictions, beginning with the USA.

United States of America

The First Amendment protects Americans' rights to freely exchange ideas – even false or controversial ones. If the government passed laws outlawing fake news, it would be seen as censorship that would have a chilling effect on real news that people disagree with. Freedom of the press in the United States is also protected by the First Amendment to the US Constitution, which prevents the government from interfering with the distribution of information and opinions; however, freedom of the press is subject to limitations in defamation law, such as the requirement to prove that the news outlet acted with actual malice and reckless disregard for the truth or otherwise.

United Kingdom

In the UK, legal action may be possible where posts are defamatory, give rise to an invasion of privacy, or incite violence, hatred or terrorism. The Office of Communications (OFCOM) in the UK regulates broadcast media rather than news on the internet; and the UK press regulators, such as the Independent Press Standards Organization (IPSO) and the Independent Monitor for the Press (IMPRESS) will only regulate those newspapers (traditional and online) that sign up to their terms and conditions, which are very few in number. In any event, neither IPSO nor IMPRESS are known to have taken any significant regulatory action to date.

A UK parliamentary committee has commenced an enquiry into some of the problems related to fake news, such as the following:

- What is "fake news"; and when does legitimate commentary become fake news?
- The impact of fake news on public understanding and the response to traditional journalism.
- The difference in the way people of different ages, social backgrounds and genders use and respond to fake news.
- Whether advertising has encouraged the growth of fake news.

- What responsibilities the social media platforms should have in tackling the issue.

The Final Report of The UK House of Commons Digital, Culture, Media and Sport Committee (2019) on *Disinformation and "fake news"*[4] points out that there has always been propaganda and politically-aligned bias which purports to be news, but this activity has taken on new forms and has been hugely magnified by information technology and social media. People are able to accept and give credence to information that reinforces their views, no matter how distorted or inaccurate, while dismissing content with which they do not agree as fake news. When these factors are brought to bear directly in election campaigns then the very fabric of our democracy is threatened. In a democracy, although we need to experience a plurality of voices, we also need to have the critical skills, experience and knowledge to gauge the veracity of those voices. It rightly points out that while the Internet has brought many freedoms across the world and an unprecedented ability to communicate, it also carries the insidious ability to distort, to mislead and to produce hatred and instability. It functions on a scale and at a speed that is unprecedented in human history. The current use of technology tends to hijack our minds and society. This situation, it concludes, is unlikely to change.

France

France already has a repressive law banning the publication or broadcasting of disinformation in bad faith. Under Article 27 of the Press Law of 1881, dissemination of false information "by whatever means" is punishable by a hefty fine. The Press Law applies only to information that has "disturbed the public peace," which can be very difficult to define, let alone prove. President Emmanuel Macron has proposed a new law to prevent the spread of disinformation online. His challenge is to introduce legislation for the digital age. But even if France's restrictions work as intended, fake news is a global problem, and it will require a global solution.[5]

Germany

Germany's parliament recently passed the Network Enforcement Act, "NetzDG" for short, which requires social networks such as Facebook, Twitter, and YouTube to remove all illegal content posted by users – which includes hate speech, in addition to disinformation – within 24 hours, or face a fine of up to €50 million. The law is the most ambitious effort by a Western democracy to control what appears on social media. It will enforce online Germany's tough curbs on hate speech, including pro-Nazi ideology, by giving sites a 24-hour deadline to remove banned content or face fines of up to 50 million euros. Since it was adopted, German officials have said too much online content was being blocked and are weighing changes.

The Republic of India

The freedom of press in India has acquired the status of a fundamental right by judicial interpretation. Recently, the Information and Broadcasting Ministry of India issued Guidelines for Accreditation of Journalists Amended to Regulate Fake News, considering it a global menace. The circular had generated a huge controversy as a number of people took to social media to criticize what they termed as an attempt to curb free speech and press freedom. Opponents of the move attacked the government, terming it an attempt to muzzle the media. The Prime Minister stepped in and had the notice withdrawn, entrusting the responsibility to clamp down on fake news on the Press Council of India.

Since late June, WhatsApp has been responding with a series of unprecedented interventions to curb sharing on the app. It added a setting that would allow only administrators to send messages in a group, and also reduced the number of people a message can be forwarded to from 100 to five in India (and to 20 in the rest of the world). It also removed the "quick forward" button that appears next to messages containing photos, video or audio. It also introduced a "suspicious link" label which will appear alongside links where WhatsApp detects an obvious problem, such as a strange combination of characters. The company took out newspaper ads in nine states warning people to "question information that upsets you."[6]

Malaysia

Malaysia's ousted former government was among the first to adopt a law against fake news, which critics say was used to curb free speech ahead of last year's general elections, which it lost. The measure was seen as a tool to fend off criticism over graft and mismanagement of funds by then prime minister Najib Razak, who now faces charges linked to a multibillion-dollar scandal at state fund 1Malaysia Development Berhad.[7] The new government's bid to deliver on an election promise to repeal the law was blocked by the opposition-led Senate, however.

Singapore

Legislation against fake news is regarded by some as a further attempt to curb the free flow of information, so that only the "real news," as dictated by the government, gets disseminated to the public. A state-run website in Singapore, "Factually," has been set up by the Ministry of Communications and Information to present the government's version of news, purportedly to represent "facts" and counter "falsehoods," especially on issues of public interest such as environment, housing and transport.[8]

More recently, Singapore government proposed its anti-fake news law in parliament. The BBC (4 April 2019) reported "Concern over Singapore's anti-fake news law."[9] It points out that the government says the law is necessary to protect Singaporeans from fake news and educate them about potential damage it can cause – in particular inciting racial and religious disharmony. But critics say this new law puts too much power in the hands of the Singapore government, potentially threatening civil liberties.

Russia

Recently, President Vladimir Putin signed into law tough new fines for Russians who spread what the authorities regard as fake news or who show "blatant disrespect" for the state online. Critics have warned the law could aid state censorship, but lawmakers say it is needed to combat false news and abusive online comment.

Response from the social media

Social media sites, such as Facebook and Google have been widely criticized for facilitating the spread of fake news. So far as the social media is concerned, most social media sites and search engines, such as Facebook and Google received criticism for facilitating the spread of fake news. Although Mark Zuckerberg, CEO of Facebook, initially declined to accept the role of Facebook in the spread of false news, he has promised to introduce measures to stop its platform being used to distribute false information. However, more concerted and rigorous action is needed.

Google, in order to control the devaluation of original news by inspired reports, has recently changed its algorithm to privilege original reporting to ensure that readers interested in the latest news can find the story that started it all (Marc, 2019).

Concluding remarks

In this chapter, I have made an attempt, first, to demystify what we commonly associate with fake news, particularly discussing fake news as a specific development as a form of interdiscursive illusion, which is being practised primarily through social media with the specific aim of misleading, disinforming and misguiding ideologically committed and gullible readership. It is often disguised as coming from fake news websites that make use of credible media houses, often using fake content embedded in imaginary contexts. It is effectively used to sway political events, such as electoral processes and to adversely influence in favour of a specific candidate or form of ideology. Sometimes, it is also used to defame political adversaries or media celebrities. Of course, one of the motivations can also be to earn advertising dollars. One thing that most institutions and responsible entities agree on is that because of its rapid explosion through social media, fake news is a potential danger for democratic processes and societies at large. In spite of imminent dangers that most countries regularly face, it is almost impossible to contain the spread of fake news because of the constraints such protective actions might impose on the idea of free speech, which is unequivocally preserved in most democratic contexts. Any strict measure to curb its spread is firmly resisted by most media houses as an infringement of their right to free dissemination of information. Managing legal remedies without conflict with free speech is one of the most difficult and almost impossible tasks facing western democracies today.

Constraints on free speech thus leave the other option to encourage self-control by institutions responsible for fake news, which again conflicts with the commercial interests of the social media providers, though some of them have publicly made statements to take effective measures to control the spread of fake news. The jury is still out, and it is difficult to predict if these intentions will be translated into effective actions in the coming years.

The final option that is open to readers themselves is to develop media literacy in audiences to identify and monitor fake news by going to the original sources of information to assess the extent to which particular sources are credible, which once again requires some training in the evaluation of news sources, and encouraging readers to refrain from recirculating any information that has dubious origin. Again, the success of this effort will largely depend on the extent to which individual readers resist the temptation to be swayed by sensational news or ideologically committed views.

Finally, this chapter makes a theoretical claim that the twin concepts of interdiscursive appropriation of information, contexts, genre conventions and ideologies within and across socio-pragmatic space and the theory of discursive illusion can offer a valid and useful framework for analysing various forms of alternative news, which may include parodies, satires, ideologically appropriated factual reports and fake news, all interdiscursively appropriated from conventional news reports.

Notes

1 www.icfj.org/sites/default/files/2018-07/A%20Short%20Guide%20to%20History%20of%20Fake%20News%20and%20Disinformation_ICFJ%20Final.pdf.
2 www.referendumanalysis.eu/eu-referendum-analysis-2016/section-7-social-media/impact-of-social-media-on-the-outcome-of-the-eu-referendum/.
3 English Oxford dictionary defines *cyborg* as "a fictional or a hypothetical person whose physical abilities are extended beyond normal human limitations by mechanical elements built into the body." Social media, similarly has acquire unlimited capacity to reach innumerable audiences across the globe in no time.
4 www.parliament.uk/business/committees/committees-a-z/commons-select/digital-culture-media-and-sport-committee/news/fake-news-report-published-17-19/.
5 www.project-syndicate.org/commentary/macron-french-fake-news-law-by-rapha-l-hadas-lebel-2018-01.
6 https://time.com/5352516/india-whatsapp-fake-news/.
7 www.reuters.com/article/us-malaysia-politics-1mdb-goldman/malaysia-goldman-discuss-smaller-penalty-over-1mdb-scandal-bloomberg-idUSKBN1X208L.
8 www.straitstimes.com/singapore/factually-website-clarifies-widespread-falsehoods.
9 www.bbc.com/news/business-47782470.

References

Allcott, Hunt and Gentzkow, Matthew. 2017. Social media and fake news in the 2016 election. *Journal of Economic Perspectives 31*, 2, 211–236.

Bakhtin, Mikhail M. 1986. *Speech Genres and Other Late Essays*. Austin: University of Texas Press.

Bhatia, Aditi. 2015. *Discursive Illusions in Public Discourse: Theory and Practice*. New York: Routledge.

Bhatia, Vijay K. 2004. *Worlds of Written Discourse: A Genre-Based View*. London: Continuum International.

Bhatia, Vijay K. 2008. Towards critical genre analysis. In Bhatia, Vijay K., Flowerdew, John and Jones, Rodney (eds), *Advances in Discourse Studies*. London: Routledge.

Bhatia, Vijay K. 2010. Interdiscursivity in professional communication. *Discourse and Communication 21*, 32–50.

Bhatia, Vijay K. 2017. *Critical Genre Analysis: Investigating Interdiscursive Performance in Professional Practice*. London & New York: Routledge.

Candlin, Christopher N. and Maley, Yon. 1997. Intertextuality and interdiscursivity in the discourse of alternative dispute resolution. In Gunnarsson, Britt-Louise, Linnel, Per and Nordberg, Bengt (eds), *The Construction of Professional Discourse*. London: Longman, (201–222).

Coler, Jestin. 2016. We tracked down a fake-news creator in the suburbs: Here's what we learned. Interview by Laura Sydell published in *NPR*, November 23. www.npr.org/sections/alltechconsidered/2016/11/23/503146770/npr-finds-the-head-of-a-covert-fake-news-operation-in-the-suburbs [accessed 31 October 2019].

Dewey, Caitlin. 2016. Facebook fake-news writer: "I think Donald Trump is in the White House because of me." *Washington Post*, November 17. www.washingtonpost.com/news/the-intersect/wp/2016/11/17/facebook-fake-news-writer-i-think-donald-trump-is-in-the-white-house-because-of-e/?utm_term=.973d97ab98d0 [accessed 16 July 2019].

Dwyer, Jim. 2008. In 1978, a faux paper was real genius. www.nytimes.com/2008/11/15/nyregion/15about.html [accessed 31 October 2019].

Fairclough, Norman. 1995. *Critical Discourse Analysis: The Critical Study of Language*. London: Longman.

Foucault, Michel. 1981. *The Archaeology of Knowledge*. New York: Pantheon Books.

Hemsley, Jeff. 2017. Social media and misinformation: An interview with Jeff Hemsley. Interview by Kayla Del Biondo in *INFOSPACE – The Official Blog of the Syracuse University iSchool*, November 29. https://ischool.syr.edu/infospace/2017/11/29/social-media-misinformation-interview-jeff-hemsley [accessed 31 October 2019].

Kaminska, Izabella. 2017. A lesson in fake news from the info-wars of ancient Rome. *Financial Times*. www.ft.com/content/aaf2bb08-dca2-11e6-86ac-f253db7791c6 [accessed 31 October 2019].

Kristeva, Julia. 1980. Word, dialogue and novel. In Kristeva, J. (ed.) *Desire in Language*. Oxford: Blackwell (64–91).

Mitchell, Amy, Gottfried, Jeffrey, Barthel, Michael and Nami, Sumida. 2018. Distinguishing between factual and opinion statements in the news. Pew Research Center. www.journalism.org/2018/06/18/distinguishing-between-factual-and-opinion-statements-in-the-news/ [accessed 8 July 2019].

Mitchell, Amy, Gottfried, Jeffrey, Stocking, Galen, Walker, Mason and Fedeli, Sophia. 2019. Many Americans say made-up news is a critical problem that needs to be fixed. Pew Research Center. www.journalism.org/2019/06/05/many-americans-say-made-up-news-is-a-critical-problem-that-needs-to-be-fixed/ [accessed 31 October 2019].

Nugent, Ciara. 2018. WhatsApp's fake news problem has turned deadly in India. Here's how to stop it. *Time*, August 1. https://time.com/5352516/india-whatsapp-fake-news/ [accessed on 30 July 2019].

Pew Research Center Survey. 2016. How Americans are talking about Trump's election in 6 charts. www.pewresearch.org/fact-tank/2016/12/22/how-americans-are-talking-about-trumps-election-in-6-charts/ [accessed 31 October 2019].

Polonski, Vyacheslav. 2016. Impact of social media on the outcome of the EU referendum, EU Referendum Analysis 2016. www.referendumanalysis.eu/eu-referendum-analysis-2016/section-7-social-media/impact-of-social-media-on-the-outcome-of-the-eu-referendum/ [accessed 3 August 2019].

Posetti, Julie and Matthews, Alice. 2018. A short guide to the history of "fake news" and disinformation: A new ICFJ learning module. www.icfj.org/news/short-guide-history-fake-news-and-disinformation-new-icfj-learning-module [accessed 8 July 2019].

Sharma, Karishma, Qian, Feng, Jiang, He, Ruchansky, Natali, Zhang, Ming and Liu, Yan. 2018. Combating fake news: A survey on identification and mitigation techniques. *ACM Trans. Intell. Syst. Technol. 37*, 4, Article 111. https://doi.org/10.1145/1122445.1122456 [accessed 31 October 2019].

Steinmetz, Katy. 2018. How your brain tricks you into believing fake news. *Time*, 9 August. https://time.com/5362183/the-real-fake-news-crisis/ [accessed 31 October 2019].

Tracy, Marc. 2019. Google says a change in its algorithm will highlight "original reporting." www.nytimes.com/2019/09/12/business/media/google-algorithm-original-reporting.html?searchResultPosition=1 [accessed 31 October 2019].

Wardle, Claire. 2017. Fake news. It's complicated. *firstdraftnews.org.* https://firstdraftnews.org/fake-news-complicated/ [accessed on 26 July 2019].

Zannettou, Savvas, Sirivianos, Michael, Blackburn, Jeremy and Kourtellis, Nicolas. 2018. The web of false information: Rumors, fake news, hoaxes, clickbait, and various other shenanigans. *arXiv*, preprint arXiv:1804.03461.

15 Information and communication technology in alternative dispute resolution

Is it facilitative or disruptive?

Rajesh Sharma[1]

Introduction

The Supreme Court of India recently directed the Indian government to draw up guidelines to deal with fake news, on social media.[2] Countries like Singapore, Australia, Malaysia, as well as the EU have already formulated laws to control the spread of fake news, which attract heavy fine and jail sentences.[3] On the other hand, information available on the web and social media is being used in courts as evidence and judges are sometimes relying on or rejecting such evidence. There is no denial that technology like Artificial Intelligence (AI) could offer useful tools for courts, and such technology has already been used successfully in court proceedings.[4] There is a big push to use technology in the alternative dispute resolution space as well, and many technology companies have already established ADR platforms for online dispute resolution. The UNCITRAL has even drafted guidelines for such online dispute resolution providers.[5]

Whilst technology is helpful and is being used in courts and ADR, it still begs the question as to whether these technologies can substitute judges or arbitrators. Would these technologies be able to apply the concept of fairness and discretion used by decision makers? My simple response to both these questions is NO.

During the onset of the millennium, when worldwide web and ICT were on peak demand and all sectors of services and industries were computerized, there was fear that the computer would substitute humans. However, the fear soon proved to be unfounded; on the contrary computers increased the use of humans and created more jobs for them. Similarly, online sales, e-commerce, and dot-coms were once considered a threat to human jobs, but were soon found to be helpful in job creation. Many economies like India registered phenomenal growth and were instrumental in creating demand for humans with computer skills. Service economies started contributing to the GDP in a big way. In the field of e-commerce, the new Model Law on E-Commerce was considered ground-breaking, and was once considered as likely to replace old concepts of black letter law; however, in the last 20 years we have realized that long established concepts of law still hold good.[6] A recent example could be seen as the development of intrusion law in the USA, which is based on trespass to land; by using that old concept of law, the government is trying to protect cyber space and enforcing cyber security.[7] It is expected that a similar development is more than likely to take effect in the use of ICT in courts and ADR processes. ICT will be a good, reliable tool for decision makers like judges and arbitrators, though it can never replace humans because a machine cannot exercise discretion and deliver fairness and justice in the same way human judges or arbitrators can. This is a very pertinent factor in the treatment of illegally obtained and unverified evidence in the prediction of outcomes of likely decisions by courts and tribunals. It is necessary to keep in mind that the laws or rules related to evidence are drafted in such a way that only human judges or arbitrators are expected to interpret and apply, especially by the use of discretionary power to decide to admit or not to admit such evidence. In conclusion, I will try to argue as to how technology and humans can be combined to deliver speedy, low cost, fair and just decisions.

Illegally obtained and unverified evidence: courts' and tribunals' approach

Evidence, which serves the purpose of assisting tribunals in determining the truth to solve disputes, is an important and crucial aspect in international arbitration proceedings. In the arbitral process, parties present relevant documents or other forms of evidence to prove their case. However, it is worth mentioning that "applications to admit illegally or improperly obtained evidence (including evidence obtained by hacking) are on the rise in commercial disputes between private parties."[8]

The issue of admissibility of illegally or unlawfully obtained evidence has been widely discussed in recent years, especially after the release of the WikiLeaks diplomatic cables. Being the largest set of confidential documents ever to be released into the public space, WikiLeaks describes the release of 251,287 leaked cables from 274 embassies,[9] which provides more opportunities for parties seeking to introduce those cables as evidence, particularly, in investment arbitrations. Besides, there are also plenty of cases where parties intend to provide illegally obtained evidence. This raises a fundamental question: is illegally obtained evidence admissible in international arbitration? Should the tribunal allow such evidence to be admitted? How much weight should such evidence be given? Is there any specific and uniform standard or rule to determine the admissibility of illegally obtained evidence? Let us consider how courts and tribunals have dealt with this issue.

The *Corfu Channel* case is one of the earliest cases which involved the issue of admissibility of unlawfully obtained evidence and the International Court of Justice had to make a decision. The dispute arose between the United Kingdom and Albania. When passing through the North Corfu Strait, two British destroyers were severely damaged after hitting hidden mines in Albanian waters. The Albanian government replied that foreign vessels did not have the right of passage through Albanian waters without permission. The United Kingdom, however, decided to proceed to sweep the Corfu Strait without permission of the Albanian government, thus violating sovereignty of Albania. Nevertheless, the United Kingdom retrieved 22 mines, which were submitted to the International Court of Justice as evidence of Albania's culpability in the destruction of its two destroyers.[10] Furthermore, the United Kingdom argued that the minesweeping was a "self-help" in response to Albania's hostility.[11] The Court held that "the action of the British Navy constituted a violation of Albanian sovereignty" but refused to apply any serious sanction against the UK. It declared that the unlawfulness of the United Kingdom's act is "in itself appropriate satisfaction."[12] It is to be noted that the ICJ in this case admitted the mines as evidence, which was obtained illegally.

In the defence of the ICJ, Jessica O. Ireton opined that the Corfu Channel case "was decided prior to the international regime for protection of diplomatic communications established by the Vienna Conventions on Diplomatic and Consular Relations."[13] Whether the decision of the ICJ would have been different had the Convention come into effect is doubtful. As Professor Reisman has pointed out, the phenomenon of a judgement that affirms a norm, while allowing illegal fruits of its violation to be enjoyed by the violator, is not unusual and some violations will be tolerated.[14] This case indeed showed a possibility that illegally obtained evidence could be admitted, even though the method of obtaining that evidence is prohibited in practice. Perhaps this is acceptable in the delivery of a fair and just decision by courts and tribunals. However, one has to be careful about the extent to which such violations may be tolerated by courts and tribunals.

In the *Iranian Hostage Case*,[15] the Court faced a similar situation when Iran tried to present evidence which it had obtained during the hostage crisis to argue its case. In 1979, the US Embassy in Tehran was taken over by militants and all personnel, documents and archives were seized while the Iranian government took no measures to protect such diplomatic information, thus violating Vienna Conventions on the Diplomatic and Consular Relations. In this case, the Iranian government argued that its action was a response to oppression and crimes against the Iranian people committed by the US. To prove this, the only way to acquire the evidence was to take unlawful appropriation of these documents as evidence before that evidence could be destroyed. The Court did not allow the evidence to be admitted in the proceeding and ordered that all documents should be returned to the US government. Unlike the *Corfu Channel* case, the Court rejected this argument by Iran, which is similar to the self-help argument made by the United Kingdom. The Court opined that those unlawful activities would disrupt relations between US and Iran and even disturb the entire world order.

It is clear on the face of the decision that the ICJ made different decisions under similar circumstances. This time the ICJ was more concerned with relations between countries and the wider peaceful order of the international community. To an extent, the ICJ decision was also affected by some aggravating factors including the seizure of personnel of a diplomatic mission and keeping them under hostage, which brought US and Iran close to war and disturbed not only peace in the Middle East but across the entire world. However, the decision of the ICJ in a way restricted the extent of "violation" which could be "tolerated" by courts and tribunals in dealing with illegally obtained evidence. Thus, self-help arguments of governments with regards to illegally obtained evidence require careful consideration based on the circumstances of the case and its impact on the community.

Perhaps the first time an arbitration tribunal faced a situation of admissibility of illegally obtained evidence was in the *Methanex* case. In this case the tribunal evaluated the admissibility of illegally or unlawfully obtained evidence. In 1999, Methanex brought a claim against the United States for 970 million USD for compensation caused by losses incurred after California banned the gasoline additive "MTBE."[16] Later, Methanex proceeded to acquire the personal business documents of the head of an organization by trespassing into the head's office.[17] The tribunal therefore was asked to admit these documents, which had been "obtained by successive and multiple acts of trespass committed by Methanex over five and a half months in order to obtain an unfair advantage over the USA as a Disputing Party to these pending arbitration proceedings."[18] The tribunal held that "it would be wrong to allow Methanex to introduce this documentation into these proceedings in violation of its general duty of good faith." Moreover, Methanex's conduct, committed during these arbitration proceedings, offended the basic principles of justice and fairness required of all parties in every international arbitration.[19]

It is clear that the decision of this tribunal was based on the "duty of good faith in international arbitration." It is to note that the tribunal did not totally focus on the fact that the evidence was "obtained unlawfully" but rather relied on the "good faith" principle. Therefore, this case failed to establish a specific standard relating to the admissibility of illegally obtained evidence. Another noteworthy aspect of the case is that a party to the dispute was itself involved in obtaining illegal evidence so one may question, according to the good faith theory, is it true that even if the evidence was obtained illegally, it can still be admitted if it does not "impinge upon a party's right to due process"[20] (such as when the party did not act illegally itself)?

In the *Libananco v Republic of Turkey* case, Libananco filed for ICSID arbitration in 2006, claiming that Turkey expropriated its investment, which resulted in losses of 10 billion USD. It then argued that the Turkish government conducted surveillance and intercepted the company's privileged and confidential business e-mails in violation of the ICSID Convention Rules and also requested Turkey's exclusion from that particular phase of arbitration. In contrast, Turkey argued that its action was to stop the criminal act of the money laundering operation of Libananco.[21] While the tribunal did not exclude Turkey from arbitration, it held that all evidence obtained through Turkish government surveillance should be excluded considering the importance of protecting the confidential information of Libananco. Rather than focusing on upholding the Turkish sovereign right to act against a criminal money laundering operation, the Tribunal tended to put more emphasis on the need to protect the privileged and confidential information of one of the parties. At least, the tribunal showed reluctance in admitting illegally obtained evidence even if it was collected by the government in the pretext of its policing power. However, there was no sanction imposed on the Turkish government. Moreover, the tribunal used protection of "privileged and confidential information" as a ground to reject the evidence. In a similar vein, the tribunal did not use "self-help" or "good faith" arguments but rather introduced a new ground to decide on admissibility of illegally obtained evidence.

From 2006 when WikiLeaks documents started to appear on the internet, it added a twist to the rules of admissibility of evidence obtained from WikiLeaks. Though one may argue that documents appearing on WikiLeaks are illegally obtained it is also a fact that parties to a case are not involved in those leaks. So, can these WikiLeaks documents be used as evidence in a court case or a tribunal, as it does not involve "self-help," or "violation of good faith"? These documents are publicly available and therefore, on the face of it, cannot be considered "privileged and confidential."

The arbitration tribunal in *ConocoPhillips v Venezuela* perhaps for the first time dealt with admissibility of evidence obtained from WikiLeaks. This case is about a long-term dispute between ConocoPhillips and the Republic of Venezuela over the expropriation of oil and gas assets of ConcoPhillips under the Chavez regime.[22] In this case, ConocoPhillips alleged that Venezuela illegally forced it to cede its majority holding in the gas projects and was unwilling to negotiate fair compensation for the government's action of expropriation.[23] The tribunal made a decision that Venezuela "breached its obligation to negotiate in good faith," which was challenged later by Venezuela. To argue that Venezuela did not violate the principal of good faith, counsel for Venezuela submitted an open letter to the Tribunal. Venezuela relied on diplomatic cables from WikiLeaks, which contained confidential communications between ConocoPhillips' counsel and representatives from the United States Embassy.[24] Venezuela then argued that the tribunal had the authority to decide on any procedural question including whether to re-evaluate their previous decision according to Article 44 of the ICSID Convention and Article 38(2) ICSID Arbitration Rule. The tribunal in its majority decision held that it did not have the power to reconsider its decision. Unfortunately, the tribunal did not make any evaluation of the diplomatic cables from WikiLeaks and their admissibility as evidence. However, Georges Abi-Saab, the only arbitrator who was willing to consider the admissibility of WikiLeaks cables, held that the evidence should be admitted and opined that the important information in WikiLeaks cables pointed to the tribunal's mistake and thus required reconsideration.

In this case the tribunal had the opportunity to rule upon the admissibility of evidence obtained from WikiLeaks; however, the majority decision chose to be silent on the admissibility of such diplomatic cables as evidence in international arbitration. Thus, it did not nip in the bud WikiLeaks cables as evidence and thus failed to provide a general standard for future tribunals and courts to be guided with regard to admission of such evidence. On the contrary, Georges Abi-Saab definitely considered the WikiLeaks cables as valid evidence and asserted that it should be admitted. The reason for his argument being that this evidence was of a "high degree of credibility" and met the necessary "level of detail." It is submitted that George Abo-Saab's view about WikiLeaks evidence having a high degree of credibility is questionable. In the absence of government affirmation about the content of those cables the veracity of the content cannot be ascertained. If his view is followed, then even fake information spreading on some social media or internet may be admitted as evidence, if that evidence has a considerable level of detail. In the decision-making process, the content of evidence has to be corroborated and the veracity of WikiLeaks cables cannot be ascertained unless the writer affirms it before the court or tribunal.

Courts have also faced the issue of admission of WikiLeaks documents as evidence. In *R. (on the application of Bancoult) v. Secretary of State for Foreign and Commonwealth Affairs ("Bancoult I")* the Court had to consider a leaked cable between two governments which was produced by a party. In this case, the United Kingdom and the United States entered into an agreement under which one area would be used for a US naval base. The United Kingdom then made an order for removal of the population from the islands. The plaintiffs claimed that taking that area as a Marine Protected Area was unlawful and excluding the population there should not be allowed. The plaintiff also provided evidence pertaining to conversations between the US and UK governments obtained from a leaked cable. The Secretary of State for Foreign and Commonwealth Affairs submitted that it would be wrong to order cross examination on the basis of documents that had been unlawfully obtained by WikiLeaks.[25] The judge in this case acknowledged that "these documents must have been obtained unlawfully,"[26] however "they were indeed published widely"[27] and "appeared to be a detailed record, which could fairly be the basis of cross examination." In addition, the Judge believed that the present claim could not "be fairly or justly determined without resolving the allegation made by the Claimant based on the WikiLeaks documents."[28]

However, at the High Court (in *Bancoult II*), the court first considered that "extensive prior disclosure of the document and of the information contained in it means that the further disclosure effected by its use in these proceedings is not damaging."[29] The High Court made a conclusion that the 1961 Vienna Convention requires exclusion of "illicitly obtained diplomatic documents and correspondence from judicial proceedings"[30] and accordingly consider the document to be inadmissible as evidence in the proceedings. Therefore, in *Bancoult II*, the court used the Vienna Convention to exclude WikiLeaks documents as evidence. However, it is arguable as to how the court reached the decision that cables on WikiLeaks are illegally obtained. At least there should be some judicial pronouncement to that effect.

The Court of Appeal in the same case (*Bancoult III*) reconsidered the Secretary of State's objection that admitting the diplomatic cables would violate provisions of the Vienna Convention on Diplomatic Relations. It held that the "inviolability" under the Vienna Convention did not "encompass the passive use of already disclosed documents as evidence." Rather, if "a relevant document has found its way into the hands of a third party, even in consequence of a breach of inviolability, it is *prima facie* admissible in evidence."[31] However, the Court eventually held that the diplomatic cable had no effect on the proceedings and declined to allow the appeal on the merits to go forward for that reason.[32] In the Bancoult cases, the courts took a number of factors into consideration and finally made decisions after balancing all of them. Although the courts did consider the issue of the admissibility of the diplomatic cables, it is still difficult to summarize a logical and specific standard for ascertaining the admissibility and reliability of evidence obtained through illegal means.

The last case related to WikiLeaks evidence for our discussion is *Caratube International Oil Company and Mr Devincci Saleh Hourani v Kazakhstan*, where the claimant applied to admit into evidence leaked emails published on a WikiLeaks-type website, following a hacking attack against the Kazakh government's computer network. Whilst the tribunal appreciated the need to protect against computer and cybercrime, and the potential unfairness of allowing confidential evidence obtained through hacking to be admitted, it also referred to the need for the tribunal to have access to information that is in the public domain, allegedly relevant and material to the dispute. The tribunal held that, of the 11 documents to which the application related, any non-privileged leaked documents should be admitted first. With regards to the issue of authenticity and weight attached to the leaked documents, this should be resolved after they had been admitted in the proceedings.

In fact, when the case involves the issue of admissibility of illegally obtained evidence, there are usually two different directions for tribunals. On the one hand, the tribunal may choose to ignore or refuse involvement in this issue consciously (see *ConocoPhillips v Venezuela*). On the other hand, if issue of admissibility of illegally obtained evidence is to be evaluated, tribunals will usually take a number of different factors into consideration, such as the relationship between countries, order of the international community, confidentiality and privilege concerns. In addition, research has found that "tribunals in international arbitration proceedings appear more willing to routinely admit into evidence documents leaked online."[33]

From this brief survey of cases, it can be seen that there is no specific or uniform standard approach to determine whether the tribunal should admit evidence obtained through illegal or unlawful means. The above case analysis actually points out that the decision of the tribunal or the outcome of the whole case varies widely from case to case and judges and tribunals have wide discretion to apply. Such discretion is impossible to apply by machine or AI. It requires a human judge and arbitrator to consider relevant circumstances and impact on the public or public policy which cannot be ascertained as a mathematical formula or algorithm.

Response from rules related to evidence and illegally obtained evidence

The issue of admissibility of evidence has also been reflected in many international arbitral rules. However, these rules fail to address the question of privileged evidence expressly.[34] Nevertheless, we may find some inspiration from these rules for this issue.

The International Bar Association issued the IBA Rules on the Taking of Evidence in International Arbitration as a resource to parties and to arbitrators to provide an efficient, economical and fair process for the taking of evidence in international arbitration, which reflects a compromise between different legal systems and has gained wide acceptance within the international arbitral community.[35] For our concern here, Article 9 IBA Rules is highly relevant.

The Title of Article 9 is "Admissibility and Assessment of Evidence." Article 9 (1) provides that:

> The Arbitral Tribunal shall determine the admissibility, relevance, materiality and weight of evidence.[36]

This provision grants arbitral tribunals broad authority to determine the admissibility, relevance, materiality and weight of evidence. In practice, while parties generally are free to provide evidence that they consider useful, it is the arbitral tribunal that has the final discretion to decide on its admissibility, relevance, materiality and weight of evidence. In other words, evaluation of the evidence is "entirely within the discretion of the tribunal."[37]

Article 9(2) further elaborates that:

> The Arbitral Tribunal shall, at the request of a party or on its own motion, exclude from evidence or production any document, statement, oral testimony or inspection for any of the following reasons:
>
> [...]
>
> (b) legal impediment or privilege;
>
> [...]
>
> (f) grounds of special political or institutional sensitivity (including evidence that has been classified as secret by a government or a public international institution).[38]

In this Article, the word "shall" instead of "may" reflects that the IBA Rules actually "require a tribunal to weigh the value of privileged evidence and take into account materials of a secret or sensitive nature, such as those pertaining to government officials."[39]

It is also helpful to raise the *William* case to further understand this section, during the course of which Article 9(2) (f) has been interpreted. In this case, the tribunal of the North American Free Trade Agreement depicted that:

> [I]n view of an evolving jurisprudence constante by prior NAFTA tribunals, [...] any refusal to produce documents based on their political or institutional sensitivity requires a balancing process, weighing, on the one hand,

the compelling nature of the requested party's asserted sensitivities and, on the other, the extent to which disclosure would advance the requesting party's case.[40]

However, J. H. Boykin also stated that "despite the availability of tool like Article 9(2)(f) of the IBA Rules, one finds very few examples of their application in arbitrations in which the WikiLeaks cables were introduced as evidence."[41]

Article 9(3) of the IBA Guidelines on the Taking of Evidence addresses some factors that may be taken into account. It provides that:

> In considering issues of legal impediment or privilege under Article 9.2(b) [...] the Arbitral Tribunal may take into account: (a) any need to protect the confidentiality of a Document created or statement or oral communication made in connection with and for the purpose of providing or obtaining legal advice; (b) any need to protect the confidentiality of a Document created or statement or oral communication made in connection with and for the purpose of settlement negotiations; (c) the expectations of the Parties and their advisors at the time the legal impediment or privilege is said to have arisen; (d) any possible waiver of any applicable legal impediment or privilege by virtue of consent, earlier disclosure, affirmative use of the Document, statement, oral communication or advice contained therein, or otherwise; and (e) the need to maintain fairness and equality as between the Parties, particularly if they are subject to different legal or ethical rules.

This provision does not mandate to apply the above consideration. However, it indeed provides some guidelines when determining the admissibility of evidence which was obtained illegally. For instance, sometimes the tribunal should balance the conflicts between different interests, such as the need to protect the confidentiality of a document and the need to maintain fairness and equality.

Clean hands doctrine and other theories to be used for illegally obtained evidences

Clean hands doctrine

Among those cases in practice, the important question is whether the party seeking to introduce unlawfully obtained evidence into arbitral proceedings has played any part in procuring that evidence. Nikki O'Sullivan has pointed out that

> tribunals in investment treaty arbitrations have tended to take the approach that, if a party seeking to introduce the evidence participated in the unlawful

activity that led to its disclosure, the evidence is inadmissible on the basis that a party should not be permitted to profit from its own misconduct (the 'clean hands' doctrine).[42]

The application of "clean hands doctrine" has been reflected in the two cases. In the *Libananco* case Turkey intercepted the Claimant's confidential emails through "government surveillance" and sought to introduce them as evidence. The arbitral tribunal finally did not admit that evidence to "protect a party's privileged and confidential information." Similarly, in the *Methanex* case, as described above, the tribunal refused to admit the document as evidence submitted by Methanex which was obtained through "successive and multiple acts of trespass committed by Methanex" itself, on the ground that allowing that evidence into the proceedings would be "a violation of its general duty of good faith and offend against the basic principles of justice and fairness required of all parties in every international arbitration." However, it is also important to note that this doctrine is not absolute and tribunals in international arbitration do not have to follow it. One famous exception is the *Corfu Channel* case, during the course of which the unlawfully obtained evidence (the mines) was admitted while the method of obtaining it was held to be a violation of Albanian sovereignty by the UK.

A three-step test theory

As James H. Boykin and Malik Havalic observed, it is difficult to discern from the cases surveyed any clear standard for analysing the admissibility of evidence obtained by hacking or through other similarly unlawful methods. However, there would appear to be one common thread running through the cases.[43] They suggest a three-step test to decide whether unlawfully obtained evidence should be admitted in international arbitration:

1   Did the party seeking to introduce the evidence participate in unlawful activity that led to its disclosure? If no, proceed to the next step. If yes, then the evidence is presumptively inadmissible.
2   Is the evidence material to an issue in the case which the tribunal is required to decide? If the answer to that question is no, then the evidence should not be admitted.
3   Was the evidence unlawfully obtained from the files of a party to the arbitration, although at no fault of the party seeking to introduce the evidence? If no, the evidence should be admissible. If yes, the evidence should be presumptively inadmissible unless it is the only evidence available and absolutely necessary to the party to prove its case.[44]

The above theory is reasonable and logical to some extent, for it has a theoretical basis and also takes into account specific and comprehensive case analysis. It is hoped that tribunals and courts will use these steps in deciding admissibility of illegally obtained documents which are available on the Internet e.g., WikiLeaks.

A two-step admissibility test

Similarly, Cherie Blair QC has proposed a two-step admissibility test that takes account of:[45]

1   whether the wrongdoing was by the party seeking to benefit from the evidence;
2   whereby documents subject to privilege should always be inadmissible (considering public interest).

This test requires the tribunal to first find out whether the party who would benefit from the evidence did wrong things or had "dirty hands." On the other hand, the tribunal should also balance public interest to decide the admissibility of the illegally obtained evidence.

Concluding remarks

One might discern from the above cases and theories that there are three essential factors when determining the admissibility of illegally obtained evidence. The first being the question of whether the party has "clean hands," the second being the materiality of that evidence and how much it will count for the outcome of the case, and thirdly, what would happen to the public order after admitting that evidence. However, it is also worthwhile noticing that with the rapid development of science and technology, the increase of high-tech crime is almost inevitable and "tribunals in international arbitration proceedings appear more willing to routinely admit into evidence documents leaked online."[46] Obviously, a uniform and specific approach to determine the admissibility of illegally obtained evidence has not been articulated or elaborated in the international community and the outcome of the case varies widely from case to case. However, it is certain that a standard test would increase the certainty and efficiency of the proceedings of the case in question, and the currently available theories will provide guidance as well. Hopefully, future tribunals which are given the opportunity to decide this issue will face it directly and provide detailed analysis about how they balance the conflicts between different interests. From a quick survey of cases, it can be seen that there is no specific and uniform standard approach to determine whether the tribunal should admit evidence which was obtained through illegal or unlawful means and is available on the Internet or social media. The above case analysis actually points out that the decision of the tribunal or the outcome of the whole case varies widely from case to case and judges and tribunals have wide discretion to apply. Such discretion is impossible to apply by machine or AI. It requires a human judge and arbitrator to consider all the circumstances and impacts on the public or public policy, which cannot be ascertained as a mathematical formula or algorithm.

Notes

1 The author would like to thank Ms. Chen Yazheng for her excellent research done in the preparation of this paper.
2 See "How the world regulates fake news and misinformation on social media," *Times of India*, 26 September 2019 available at https://timesofindia.indiatimes.com/world/how-the-world-regulates-fake-news-misinformation-on-social-media/articleshow/71304908.cms.
3 Ibid.
4 See Tania Sourdin, "Judge v robot? Artificial intelligence and judicial decision making" [2018] UNSWLaw JI 38, available at www.austlii.edu.au/au/journals/UNSWLJ/2018/38.html.
5 See "UNCITRAL Technical Notes on Online Dispute Resolution" available at https://uncitral.un.org/sites/uncitral.un.org/files/media documents/uncitral/en/v1700382_english_technical_notes_on_odr.pdf.
6 See "UNCITRAL Model Law on Electronic Commerce," available at https://uncitral.un.org/sites/uncitral.un.org/files/media-documents/uncitral/en/19-04970_ebook.pdf.
7 Restatement of the Law, Second, Torts, § 652 available at https://cyber.harvard.edu/privacy/Privacy_R2d_Torts_Sections.htm.
8 Nikki O'Sullivan, "Lagging behind: Is there a clear set of rules for the treatment of illegally obtained evidence in international arbitrations?" available at http://arbitrationblog.practicallaw.com/lagging-behind-is-there-a-clear-set-of-rules-for-the-treatment-of-illegally-obtained-evidence-in-international-arbitrations/.
9 Secret US Embassy Cables, WikiLeaks, https://wikileaks.org/cablegate.html.
10 *Corfu Channel Case (UK v Albania)* (Merits) [1949] ICJ Rep 4, 6, 16, 27, 51.
11 Ibid., 67.
12 Ibid., 35.
13 Jessica O. Ireton, "The admissibility of evidence in ICSID arbitration: Considering the validity of WikiLeaks cables as evidence," *ICSID Review - Foreign Investment Law Journal*, Volume 30, Issue 1 (Winter 2015), pp. 231–242, at p. 234. https://doi.org/10.1093/icsidreview/siu029.
14 W. Michael Reisman and Eric E. Freedman, "The plaintiff's dilemma: Illegally obtained evidence and admissibility in international adjudication," *The American Journal of International Law*, Volume 76, Issue 4 (Oct., 1982), pp. 737–753, at p. 747.
15 United States Diplomatic and Consular Staff in Tehran (United States of America v. Iran), www.icj-cij.org/en/case/64.
16 *Methanex Corporation v United States of America*, UNCITRAL, Final Award of the Tribunal on Jurisdiction and Merits (3 August 2005), www.italaw.com/cases/683, Preface, Para 1.
17 Ibid., Pt II, ch. I, para 55.
18 Ibid., Pt II, ch. I, para 54.
19 Ibid., Pt II, ch. I, para 59.
20 Ireton, "The admissibility of evidence," p. 236.
21 *Libananco Holdings Co v Republic of Turkey*, ICSID Case No. ARB/06/09, Decision on Preliminary Issues (23 June 2008), www.italaw.com/cases/626 para 43–47.
22 See *ConocoPhillips Petrozuata BV, ConocoPhillips Hamaca BV and ConocoPhillips Gulf of Paria BV v Bolivarian Republic of Venezuela*, ICSID Case No ARB/07/30, Decision on Jurisdiction and the Merits (3 September 2013).
23 Ibid., para 212.
24 Kyriaki Karadelis, 'Venezuela requests new hearing in Conoco Case,' *Latin*

Lawyer (20 September 2013), http://latinlawyer.com/news/article/45561/venezuela-requests-new-hearing-conoco-case.

25 *R. (on the application of Bancoult) v. Secretary of State for Foreign and Commonwealth Affairs) ("Bancoult I")*, [2012] EWHC 2115 (Admin), para 3, 6.

26 Ibid. para 15.

27 Ibid. para 16.

28 Ibid. para 17.

29 *R. (on the application of Bancoult) v. Secretary of State for Foreign and Commonwealth Affairs ("Bancoult II")*, [2013] EWHC 1502 (Admin) para 36.

30 Ibid. para 51.

31 *R. (on the application of Bancoult) v. Secretary of State for Foreign and Commonwealth Affairs) ("Bancoult III")*, [2014] EWCA Civ. 708, para 58.

32 Ibid. para 93.

33 O'Sullivan, "Lagging behind," p. 1.

34 Privilege in International Arbitration' Practical Law (2013) http://us.practicallaw.com/resource/5-381-7464.

35 IBA Rules on the Taking of Evidence in International Arbitration, Adopted by a resolution of the IBA Council 29 May 2010 International Bar Association, Forewords, p. 2.

36 IBA Rules on the Taking of Evidence in International Arbitration (29 May 2010) art. 9(1).

37 Robert Pietrowski, Evidence in International Arbitration, *Arbitration International*, Vol. 22, No. 3, p. 374.

38 IBA Rules on the Taking of Evidence in International Arbitration (29 May 2010) art. 9(2).

39 Ireton, "The admissibility of evidence," p. 235.

40 William Ralph Clayton, William Richard Clayton, Douglas Clayton, Daniel Clayton and Bilcon Delaware Inc. v. Government of Canada, PCA Case No. 2009–04, Procedural Order No. 13, 11 July 2012, 22.

41 J.H. Boykin and M. Havalic, "Fruits of the poisonous tree: The admissibility of unlawfully obtained evidence in international arbitration," *TDM* (2014), p. 37 available at www.law.columbia.edu/sites/default/files/microsites/clwa/CIAA/panel_2_evidence.pdf.

42 O'Sullivan, "Lagging behind," p. 1.

43 Boykin and Havalic, "Fruits of the poisonous tree," p. 32, available at www.law.columbia.edu/sites/default/files/microsites/clwa/CIAA/panel_2_evidence.pdf.

44 Ibid., p. 33.

45 "Cherie Blair QC proposed a two-step admissibility test." Available at https://globalarbitrationreview.com/article/1140718/blair's-two-step-test-for-illegally-obtained-evidence.

46 O'Sullivan, "Lagging behind," p. 2.

Index

Note: **Bold** page numbers refer to tables; *Italic* page numbers refer to figures and page numbers followed by 'n' denote notes.